Please return/renew this item by the last date shown on this label, or on your self-service receipt.

To renew this item, visit **www.librarieswest.org.uk** or contact your library

Your borrower number and PIN are required.

D0260698

Churchill's Confidant

Churchill's Confidant

ENEMY TO LIFELONG FRIEND

RICHARD STEYN

ROBINSON

ROBINSON

First published in South Africa in 2017 by Jonathan Ball Publishers
First published in Great Britain in 2018 by Robinson

13 5 7 9 10 8 6 4 2

A CIP catalogue record for this book
is available from the British Library.

ISBN: 978-1-47214-076-0

Typeset in Adobe Garamond Pro by Triple M Design, Johannesburg
Printed and bound in Great Britain by Clays Ltd, St Ives plc

Papers used by Robinson are from well-managed forests
and other responsible sources.

MIX
Paper from
responsible sources
FSC® C104740

Robinson
An imprint of
Little, Brown Book Group
Carmelite House
50 Victoria Embankment
London EC4Y 0DZ

An Hachette UK Company
www.hachette.co.uk

www.littlebrown.co.uk

To Jonathan,
who inspired this book

NOTE ON TERMINOLOGY

Modern South Africa is a terminological minefield. In Smuts's time, the law and custom distinguished between Europeans (or Whites), Coloureds (mixed race), Asiatics (or Indians) and Natives (Africans). The term 'native' – as in the South African Native National Congress – did not have the pejorative meaning it has acquired today. In this book, I have used the racial descriptions applicable at the time: so the words 'native', 'black' and 'African', for instance, are used interchangeably.

Contents

Prologue

If a picture is worth a thousand words, the photograph of Jan Smuts displayed prominently on Winston Churchill's old writing desk at his country estate, Chartwell, in Kent, is the most striking expression of the close relationship between these two grand old men of Empire. Almost every other photo on the desk is of a member of the Churchill family.

The friendship between Churchill and Smuts was unbroken for almost half a century. Distance meant that it was never the kind of intimate relationship that Churchill enjoyed with the likes of Lords Birkenhead, Beaverbrook, or Bracken. However, it was a companionship based upon mutual regard and a respect for the values and interests they shared, foremost among them a belief in the civilising mission of the British Empire.

As biographers of the most famous Englishman of the twentieth century remind us, South Africa was the place where much of the early Churchillian legend was born. It was the young Winston's capture during the Anglo-Boer War and subsequent escape from the Boers' clutches that brought him worldwide fame and, through his written accounts of it, provided him with the income he needed to embark on a political career.

One way or another, Winston Churchill was concerned with matters South African for most of his political life – from his support for the Afrikaner cause after the Anglo-Boer War, to his appointment as Under-Secretary for the Colonies at the time of the Union of South Africa, through World War I – when he developed a high regard for Louis Botha – to his close alliance with Smuts during World War II. It was only after Smuts's death in 1950, and the advent of apartheid, that Churchill lost much of his interest in South Africa's affairs.

There have been few men in history whose lives have been more minutely chronicled, careers so closely examined, and about whom so many stories have been told and retold, as Winston Churchill. The reason, as a book reviewer wrote shortly after his death, is that 'this giant of a man had faults as memorable as his triumphs were historic'.[1] Despite, or perhaps because of, these faults, the Churchillian fable continues to grow, notwithstanding sporadic attempts by modern historians to debunk it. His personality and memory, as John Keegan reminds us, have now been subsumed into something much larger: the popular memory of World War II, which has been transformed into a national saga.[2]

Jan Smuts's reputation has not been as enduring. Nevertheless, though his impact on the history of his times cannot be compared with Churchill's, he was also among the most remarkable men of the twentieth century. His role as Churchill's closest confidant in World War II has been largely overlooked, and in South Africa almost deliberately forgotten. For those who don't know of him, Smuts was a man of exceptional talents and achievements – a Cambridge-educated lawyer, guerrilla fighter, soldier, philosopher, scientist and political leader, a member of Britain's War Cabinet in two world wars and the only person to have been present at the ceremonies at the end of both of those wars. He played a leading role in the founding of the League of Nations in the aftermath of World War I, and helped draft the Charter of the United Nations Organization after World War II.

Esteemed by American presidents from Woodrow Wilson to Harry Truman, Smuts was regarded with particular admiration by George V and Lloyd George – Britain's king and prime minister, respectively, during World War I – and in World War II by George VI and numerous British military leaders, notably Field Marshal Lord Alanbrooke and Lord Tedder, who both extolled his strategic vision and soundness of judgement.

Churchill came to regard Smuts with an affection and respect bordering on awe. Besides Franklin D Roosevelt, there was no other Allied leader in World War II with whom he corresponded so frequently. Between them, the pair

Churchill's writing desk at his country estate, Chartwell, Kent.
The photo of Smuts is towards the right.

PAUL POPPER/POPPERFOTO/GETTY IMAGES

had to grapple with some of the twentieth century's most intractable issues, most notably how to square the imperatives of Empire with the advance of liberalism, non-racialism and democracy, and how to restore peace and prosperity to Europe after two of mankind's bloodiest wars. In so doing, they ran up against another of history's most complex and intriguing figures, in the form of India's Mahatma Gandhi. Although this book is primarily an account of how the lives of Churchill and Smuts intersected, one of its sub-themes is their complex relationship with India's enigmatic sage.*

Today's world is one that Churchill, Smuts and Gandhi helped to guide and shape, even though it conflicted with their Victorian upbringing and ideals. The three believed that the enlightenment and timeless principles of Western civilisation had to be preserved; that there were higher values than materialism; and that bravery and courage were the ultimate measures of human character, whether in men of war or apostles of non-violence.[3] They

---

* In 2015 a statue of Gandhi was added to those of Churchill and Smuts in London's Parliament Square.

also supposed that destiny had endowed them with a special purpose in life.

When Smuts died in 1950, the warmest and most eloquent tributes to him came from Winston Churchill, who had treasured their long-lasting relationship and never forgot it. With his almost mystical sense of history and tradition, one might assume that Britain's 'Man of the Century' would have wanted to be reminded of some eminent Briton – the Duke of Wellington or Horatio Nelson perhaps – or a distinguished American, such as Franklin Roosevelt or George C Marshall, to keep before him on the desk in his private study.

Instead, he chose to remember his enduring friendship with Jan Smuts – for reasons this book will endeavour to explain.

CHAPTER I

A study in contrasts

After all, a man's Life must be nailed to a cross either of
Thought or Action. Without work there is no play.
— THE YOUNG CHURCHILL[1]

Not Law, but the Person is the highest reality.
— THE YOUNG SMUTS[2]

The almost half-century-long comradeship between Winston Churchill and Jan Smuts provides a rich study in contrasts. In background, upbringing and personality, the pair could hardly have been more different. They were born only four years apart, but in starkly dissimilar circumstances.

Winston Leonard Spencer-Churchill first drew breath on 30 November 1874 at Blenheim Palace, Woodstock, in Oxfordshire, the largest private home in Britain. The magnificent estate had been given by Queen Anne to his ancestor, John Spencer-Churchill, the first Duke of Marlborough, as a reward for defeating the French at Blenheim, in Bavaria, during the War of the Spanish Succession. Surrounded by some 3 000 acres of luxuriant parkland, the mansion boasted some 320 rooms, reception areas, marble halls and galleries. It was almost unequalled in size and splendour by any other country house in Victorian Britain. Winston, who grew up in various childhood homes, described it as 'an Italian palace in an English park' and used to spend school holidays there. He once said, 'At Blenheim, I took two important decisions: to be born and to marry.'[3]

His father, Lord Randolph Churchill, twenty-five when Winston was born, hugely talented but emotionally unstable, was to become one of Britain's best-known and controversial politicians; his mother, Jennie Jerome, an American-born social butterfly, was among the most admired beauties of her time. As parents, Lord and Lady Randolph Churchill were aptly described as being 'remote and tantalisingly glamorous'.[4] Neither thought it necessary to spend much time with their two sons, born six years apart. Randolph, a future Chancellor of the Exchequer and Leader of the House under Tory Prime Minister Lord Salisbury, was much too busy politicking and travelling to worry about his eldest son, and the easily distracted Jennie was not going to let motherhood divert her from the pursuit of men and pleasure. As a result, little Winston was brought up and nurtured by Woom, the nickname of the widowed Elizabeth Everest, the family's devoted nanny.

Shunted from one preparatory boarding school to another and scarcely visited by his parents, Winston grew up, not surprisingly, into a difficult and troublemaking child. Rebellious by nature, he did not like school and never adapted willingly to discipline. A fellow pupil at his Ascot school recalled an instance of his naughtiness. 'He had been flogged for taking sugar from the pantry, and so far from being penitent, had taken the headmaster's sacred straw hat from where it hung over the door and kicked it to pieces. His sojourn at the school had been one long feud with authority.'[5]

An exasperated Randolph, who by then had fallen seriously ill with a brain tumour[6] (and was described as 'dying by inches in public'[7]), sent his son to secondary school at Harrow, where the boy went from stroppiness to loneliness, 'shunned by his classmates and ignored by his parents'.[8] With his mother, upon whom he doted, absent most of the time and his father gradually losing his mind, Winston was a 'volatile bundle of verbal aggression and suppressed anger'.[9]

While Winston was at Harrow, the ailing Randolph, having fallen steeply from grace politically, sought to supplement his finances by going to far-off South Africa in search of investments in gold. He also made an arrangement with the *Daily Graphic* to send back letters for publication during his three-month visit there. Despite being treated like royalty, he was scathing in his denunciation of the British authorities at the Cape and the Boers of the Transvaal, whom he described as 'dirty, lazy and barbarous'.[10] He aroused resentment across the political spectrum; almost the only person to be impressed by his effusions was young Winston.[11]

The most sensible decision Lord Randolph made before he died was to allow his eldest son to embark on a military career after leaving school. As a little boy, Winston had been fascinated by warfare and would spend much of his spare time devising battle formations for his 1 500 toy soldiers. This interest in military matters was to remain with him throughout his long life. After enraging his father by twice failing the entrance exam to the Royal Military College at Sandhurst, the training ground for the sons of Britain's upper classes, Winston succeeded at his third attempt, coming 92nd out of 102 applicant cadets. Writing to Lord Randolph, he promised 'to modify your opinion of me by my work and conduct at Sandhurst'.[12] True to his word, he did well at the military college, excelling at horsemanship and fencing, and passing out 20th in his class of 130.

*

Jan Christian Smuts was born four years earlier than Churchill, on 24 May 1870, on an isolated farm at Riebeek West in the wheat- and wine-growing region of the Cape Colony. His provenance was far humbler, but more secure. Like Churchill, he was a lonely boy, whose father did not hold out high hopes for him. His deeply Calvinist parents were of Dutch origin, his father a farmer and member of the colonial Parliament, his mother a woman unusually well educated for her times. After spending his early years tending sheep and cattle on the family farm, Jan was sent to school for the first time at the age of twelve, only after the death of his elder brother, who had been destined for a ministry in the Dutch Reformed Church. His father thought his physically frail and introverted younger son 'a queer fellow without much intelligence'.[13]

At school in Riebeek West, where he encountered the English language for the first time, Jan quickly overtook his fellow pupils. In 1896 he was sent to Stellenbosch to matriculate before going on to study science and literature at Victoria College in the picturesque Western Cape town. Proving to be a brilliant scholar, with a wide range of intellectual interests, the young Smuts won the Ebden scholarship to Cambridge University, where his distinguished tutor described him as the brightest student he had ever taught. To his fellow students at Cambridge, he was a rather remote figure, far happier studying than socialising with his peers – partly because he lacked the money to do so.

Both Churchill and Smuts were born in what is commonly referred to as 'the golden afternoon'[14] of Queen Victoria's empire, the greatest and most splendid the world had seen. The United Kingdom of Great Britain and Ireland was the industrial workshop of the world, and London Europe's financial capital and largest city. Britain's overseas colonial 'possessions' – guarded and protected by the mighty Royal Navy – stretched right across the globe, from the Middle East to Asia and Africa to the Caribbean. It was said that the sun never set upon the Union Jack and that at any given moment, wherever dawn was breaking, Britain's colours would ripple up some far-off flagpole.[15]

Two events not long after Smuts and Churchill's births epitomised the extent of Britain's imperial power and reach: its acquisition of the controlling interest in Egypt's Suez Canal in 1875 and the proclamation of Queen Victoria as Empress of India in 1877. Britannia's empire was not only the most extensive on earth, but also the most cohesive: people across the world, thousands of kilometres apart – either voluntarily or by coercion – pledged allegiance and loyalty to Britain and her long-reigning Queen.[16]

Churchill, who had sailed with the Prince of Wales and mother Jennie aboard the royal yacht,[17] grew up at the epicentre of the empire; Smuts, at the foot of Africa, on its outer periphery. The Smuts forebears were descended from officials of the Dutch East India Company, which had founded a European settlement and refreshment station on the sea route to India in 1652. Since 1806, however, the Cape – the administrative centre of a huge area, covering most of southern Africa – had been under Britain's imperial rule.

The Cape's economic potential had first been recognised during the Napoleonic Wars, when Cape Town became a trading post for meat, hides, ivory and wines, and the Cape Colony a destination for Britain's surplus population and her unemployed. It took the discovery of diamonds (in 1867) and gold (in 1886) beyond the colonial borders in the north to transform a colonial backwater into a region suddenly offering immense economic opportunity – and the promise of quick profits. From around the world, fortune-seekers thronged to the diamond fields around Kimberley and the goldfields of the Transvaal, stoking tensions among the indigenous African population as well as between Boers and migrants from around the empire and beyond.

*

Wordsworth's aphorism 'the child is father to the man' expresses the truism that character traits formed at an early age endure throughout one's life. This was certainly true of Churchill and Smuts. For all the Englishman's eventual fame as a politician, journalist, historian and orator, he was first and foremost a soldier and warrior. The Afrikaner Smuts was much more philosophically and spiritually inclined, fascinated by the splendour of nature, determined to understand the nature of the universe and man's place in it.

Both were individuals of exceptional intelligence,* strongly ambitious, with an inner sense that they were destined to leave a mark on the history of their times. Each grew up to be a man of action – bold, decisive, courageous and unafraid of physical risk. Neither was much interested in accumulating wealth for its own sake, but rather by a desire to be at the very centre of events. Churchill was brought up to believe in the benevolent, civilising mission of the British Empire. Smuts was at first an admirer, then a bitter opponent, and finally a convert to the imperial cause.

One of the defining characteristics of the Victorians was their belief in the superiority of the British nation over all others, as well as the virtues of the empire, which Lord Curzon described as 'the greatest force for good the world has ever seen'.[18] The author Charles Kingsley wrote of 'the glorious work which God seems to have laid on the English race, to replenish the earth and subdue it'.[19] If the French and Germans, not to mention the Spanish, Italians and Russians – fellow Christians – could not quite measure up to British standards, then heaven help the Indians, Africans and Australian aborigines, who were in most need of Britannia's beneficence to bring them into the modern world.

Britons were ordained not only to rule over inferior races, but to lead them into a better and more prosperous future, or so the Victorians believed. As Joseph Chamberlain, a predecessor of Churchill in the Colonial Office, declared in 1895, 'I believe in this race, the greatest governing race this world has ever

---

* Like Smuts, Churchill had a photographic memory. At Harrow, where he languished in the lower forms because of his lack of interest in Latin, Greek and mathematics, he won the Headmaster's Prize for reciting to him the 1 200 lines of Macaulay's narrative poems *Lays of Ancient Rome* without making a single mistake. See Winston Churchill, *My Early Life, 1874–1904*. Scribner, 1996, p 26.

seen ... so proud, tenacious, self-confident and determined, this race which neither climate nor change can degenerate, which will infallibly be the predominant force of future history and universal civilisation.'[20] This triumphalist stuff and nonsense was given scientific legitimacy by the social Darwinist theories of Herbert Spencer, who coined the term 'the survival of the fittest', an appropriate maxim for the combative and competitive spirit of the age.

Neither Churchill nor Smuts would have endorsed these jingoistic tenets, but they were both believers in the supremacy of the European races over all others – and the responsibilities and duty of trusteeship that this superiority imposed. Churchill was able to view the aspirations of colonised people from a comfortable distance, constantly reminding British audiences that applying liberal democratic principles to the empire required great caution.[21] One of imperialism's prime objectives, he would assert, was to protect its subjects from one another and preserve civil peace.[22] He was never to waver from his belief that premature independence would be a disaster for the people of India.

For the empiricist Smuts, on the other hand, survival was the key question. Political principles should be based, he believed, not on idealistic dogma but upon a pragmatic appraisal of a situation created by history, and the needs that arose from it.[23] As for the two white races in South Africa, their dilemma was 'unique': they had to be both guardians of their own security as well as trustees of the African multitudes in whose midst they found themselves.

*

In personality, the two men were polar opposites. Churchill's silver spoon gave him a taste for the finer things of life – food, liquor, cigars, personal valets, luxurious surroundings, lengthy vacations and first-class travel. As his close friend FE Smith (Lord Birkenhead) said of him, 'Winston is a man of simple tastes. He is always prepared to put up with the best of everything.'[24] The historian Richard Holmes wrote that 'to the end of his days Winston retained the characteristics not of a deprived child, but of one excessively indulged; among these characteristics was a stubborn determination to have

The young Lieutenant Churchill.   *Jan Smuts as a student.*

his own way, which, coupled with boyish enthusiasm, unfeigned kindness and an impish sense of humour, enabled him to ride out storms that would have sunk a less self-confident man.'[25]

Smuts, by comparison, was ascetic, a non-smoker, drank little, lived in spartan conditions, rose early, walked long distances, climbed mountains and always kept himself physically fit. When feeling sorry for himself, he would sometimes say in public speeches that he was born poor and knew what poverty meant: 'I am a poor man; I shall die a poor man' – a prediction that turned out to be far from true.[26]

Both were extraordinarily hard-working and resilient, able to absorb political setbacks, put defeat behind them and focus their attention on the immediate task at hand. Each was a committee of one, confident of his own judgement, apt to act impulsively and disinclined to trust the opinion of peers, but nonetheless deeply respectful of the other's views.

During their political lives, they had to endure lengthy spells in the political wilderness, when their wider interests and hobbies uplifted and sustained them. In Churchill's case, he hunted, travelled and painted. Smuts, by contrast, immersed himself in philosophy and developed an intense interest in botany. Neither man was humble nor had much capacity for small talk. As Churchill, with his characteristic wit, once said, 'I am not usually accused, even by my friends, of being of a modest or retiring disposition.'[27]

They both enjoyed extraordinarily long political careers, extending for the better part of half a century, and were unexpectedly voted out of office after World War II while at the height of their fame. In old age, believing they were indispensable to country and party, they refused to step off the political stage and soldiered on for much longer than they should have (and for longer than their admirers wished them to). When both were out of office and in their seventies, Churchill described his relationship with Smuts as 'one of two old love-birds moulting together on a perch, but still able to peck'.[28]

*

Viewed through a wider lens, the friendship between Churchill and Smuts mirrored the relationship between Great Britain and South Africa throughout the first half of the twentieth century. Having been initially deeply hostile to the British during and after the Anglo-Boer War, Smuts was so impressed by the magnanimity of Churchill's leader, Prime Minister Campbell-Bannerman, and by the universality and idealism of the British Empire, that he and Prime Minister Louis Botha courted unpopularity by aligning their young country behind Britain in World War I, at the League of Nations, and again in World War II, in which South African forces made a notable contribution to the Allied cause.

The regard in which Churchill held his wartime colleague was primarily responsible for Smuts's popularity in the UK until his death in 1950. After that, and perhaps because he felt uncomfortable with apartheid, Churchill lost much of his interest in South Africa and stopped routinely listing the country – after Canada, but before Australia and New Zealand – as among his most favoured English-speaking nations. At a reception during the coronation of Queen Elizabeth in 1953, he barred the playing of South Africa's national anthem, 'Die Stem', saying, 'I will not have this Boer hymn.'[29] In

1961, however, he expressed his regret at South Africa's enforced departure from the Commonwealth.

Although it took four decades after Smuts's death before his Afrikaner-Nationalist successors turned their backs on apartheid and consented to black majority rule, Nelson Mandela's 'new' South Africa was the ultimate beneficiary of the international system that Smuts had helped create and Churchill in particular had fought so heroically to preserve. As president, Mandela bought wholeheartedly into Smuts's internationalist vision, immediately reversing four decades of National Party isolationism to take South Africa back into the United Nations and the Commonwealth, and to redevelop cultural, trade and social links, which had been allowed to fall into disrepair.[30]

But that's another story, for another time …

CHAPTER 2

The young thruster

Courage is rightly esteemed the first of human qualities because …
it is the quality which guarantees all others.
— CHURCHILL[1]

'Englishman, twenty-five years old, about five foot eight inches high, indifferent build, walks with a bend forward, pale appearance, red-brownish hair, small moustache hardly perceptible, talks through his nose, cannot pronounce the letter "S" properly, cannot speak Dutch, during long conversations occasionally makes a rattling noise in his throat, was last seen in a brown suit of clothes.'[2]

Such was the description of Winston Churchill in the warrant of arrest issued under the name of Jan Smuts in mid-December 1899, after the former's escape from Boer custody in Pretoria. Smuts, at the time, was the young State Attorney of the Transvaal Republic, and Churchill an even younger but already celebrated war reporter from Britain's *Morning Post*. The two men had actually encountered each other a little earlier during fighting between Boer and British forces in the vicinity of Ladysmith in Natal, but neither thought the incident worthy of mention in his written account of the war.

Churchill's career as a soldier and military correspondent had begun after he left Sandhurst in 1895. With the help of his mother's influential social connections, he secured a commission as a second lieutenant in the exclusive, upper-class cavalry regiment, the 4th (Queen's Own) Hussars. As David Cannadine explains, the leisured class in Britain was also the fighting class, duty bound and historically conditioned to protect civil society from invasion and disruption. Among the desired attributes of an officer and a gentleman in Queen Victoria's army were gallantry and loyalty, courage and chivalry, leadership and good horsemanship.[3] The 4th Hussars' new recruit possessed every one of those qualities, as well as being imbued with a keen sense of his family's and country's history.

Before Churchill had enlisted in the Hussars, his ailing father died. In his will, Lord Randolph had made no special provision for his children, leaving it to his high-living eldest son to fend for himself financially. Never one to spare expense, to the dismay of his spendthrift and ever hard-up mother, her son signed up with the grandest and richest of cavalry regiments rather than enlist in the less expensive infantry.

At Sandhurst, Churchill had worried constantly about his physical inadequacies. His childhood had been plagued by health problems (he nearly died of pneumonia in 1886), which so frustrated him that he wrote to his mother complaining of being 'cursed with so feeble a body'.[4] He was only five feet six and a half inches tall (about 1.7 metres), and his chest measurement needed expanding if he were to qualify for commission as an officer.[5] Horse riding was his favourite form of exercise.

The Sandhurst regimen of parade-ground drill and plenty of physical training was beneficial for Churchill's health: he graduated from the Royal Military College and joined his new regiment as a fit young man, with a fine cadet record, eager to go into action.[6] To him, it was a matter for regret that the British army 'had not fired on white troops' since the Crimean War of 1853–56, and that the world was growing 'so sensible and pacific – and so democratic too'.[7] He believed the road to promotion and advancement, the 'glittering gateway to distinction', lay in active service. 'It cast a glamour upon the fortunate possessor in the eyes of elderly gentlemen and young ladies.'[8]

The 4th Hussars, who were about to be sent on overseas duty to India in 1896 for no less than twelve to fourteen years, allowed their officers to take two and a half months' leave before their departure, during which they could do as they pleased. After months on the training ground, and short of money, as always, the restless Lieutenant Churchill looked around for a conflict that would offer him excitement – and the opportunity of being noticed. He found one in far-off Cuba, where the colonial power, the Spanish, were trying to put down a rebel insurrection. Exploiting his family's aristocratic network once more, he inveigled an invitation from the Spaniards to visit the island and managed also to pick up a paid assignment from a London newspaper to send back dispatches from the war zone. Travelling to Cuba via the US, he heard, on his twenty-first birthday, for the first time, 'shots fired in anger ... and bullets strike flesh or whistle through the air'.[9]

Churchill spent three weeks in Cuba, sending the *Graphic* newspaper five 'Letters from the Front', which revealed his skills as a reporter and early understanding of military strategy. He also impressed his Spanish hosts with his insouciance under enemy fire.

Back in England, the unappealing prospect of service in India lay before him. It was 1896, shortly before Victoria's diamond jubilee, and while London society celebrated the 'season' in energetic style, the restless young Hussar made the rounds of newspaper offices in Fleet Street, seeking any well-paid assignment – in the Sudan, South Africa or Rhodesia. On learning of this, the Secretary of State for War, Lord Lansdowne, wrote to Churchill's mother to say her son was risking harm to his reputation: he should rather do his duty and stay with his regiment. Putting his journalistic ambitions temporarily on hold, a reluctant Churchill set sail with his fellow officers for Bombay, where they arrived in early October* before proceeding to the regimental base at Bangalore, on the high plateau of southern India.

Regimental duties in peaceful Bangalore took no more than a few hours each day, so Lt Churchill used his free time in the long, hot afternoons to educate himself by reading Plato and the other Greek philosophers as well as eight volumes of Gibbon, twelve of Macaulay and a daunting number of other literary and historical classics sent out by his devoted mother – all the while improving his skills at polo. As John Keegan writes, 'The Young Churchill, in his leap to self-education, must have been the most unusual subaltern in any European army.'[10] Churchill wrote that 'from November to May I read for four to five hours every day ... I approached it with an empty, hungry mind, and with fairly strong jaws; and what I got I bit.'[11]

During his nineteen months in India, he was allowed to return home twice to enjoy the pleasures of London in mid-summer and on the first visit made

---

* Clambering from a small boat on to the dock in Bombay Harbour as the swell surged and fell, Churchill clutched at an iron ring and sustained a shoulder injury that was to plague him for the rest of his life. He scrambled up, 'made a few remarks of a general character, mostly beginning with the earlier letters of the alphabet', hugged his shoulder and tried to forget about the pain. (See Winston Churchill, *My Early Life, 1874–1904*. Scribner, 1996, pp 107–108.)

his first foray into politics by delivering an address in Bath in support of the Conservatives, his father's old party.

On hearing of a Muslim Pathan uprising on India's North-West Frontier in July 1897, however, Lt Churchill hastened back to India and once again exploited his connections to wangle leave from his regiment and join General Sir Bindon Blood's field force as a part combatant, part war correspondent. For six weeks, he risked life and limb along what is today the border between Afghanistan and Pakistan, fighting the warlike tribesmen who inhabited the mountainous region and were strenuously resisting Britain's attempts to rule their lives. He received a mention in dispatches for 'making himself useful at a critical moment' of the fighting.[12]

Churchill's experiences on the North-West Frontier made him keener than ever for recognition. To his mother, he wrote, 'I rode my grey pony all along the skirmish line where everyone else was lying down in cover. Foolish perhaps, but I play for high stakes and given an audience there is no act too daring or too noble. Without the gallery, things are different.' He hoped to win a campaign medal, he said, or perhaps 'a couple of clasps', and to come back 'and wear my medals at some big dinner or some other function'.[13] 'It is a pushing age,' he told his mother, 'and we must shove with the best.'[14]

The young subaltern's reports from the frontier and his subsequent book, *The Story of the Malakand Field Force: An Episode of Frontier War*, attracted much critical attention – not all of it favourable. Some of his fellow officers thought it unbecoming and 'ungentlemanly' for anyone to write for newspapers while wearing a military uniform. One wrote in his memoirs that 'Churchill was regarded in the Army as super-precocious, indeed by some as insufferably bumptious'.[15] Insufferable or not, his involvement in Malakand was, in the opinion of many modern historians, a pivotal event in a career destined from the outset to be out of the ordinary. He was, by this time, all of twenty-three years old.

Always ready to take risks in order to give his newspaper good copy (and attract more attention to himself), Churchill looked upon the emerging conflict in the Sudan, where Sir Herbert Kitchener was seeking to re-establish British authority on the upper Nile, as the next promising opportunity to burnish his credentials. Fame was his constant spur[16] and the quickest way to become famous, he reasoned, was through writing. Yet political fame was even more desirable than journalistic fame, and the best preparation for politics was a high-profile military career. Shamelessly taking advantage of family friends again, he tried unsuccessfully to join the expedition of the Sirdar (the commander of the Egyptian army) to avenge the killing of General 'Chinese' Gordon at the hands of the Mahdists. His way was blocked, however, by an obdurate Kitchener, who regarded the young Hussar – not without justification – as a 'publicity-seeking' and 'medal-hunting' 'whippersnapper'.[17] It was, as Churchill wrote later, 'a case of dislike before first sight'.[18]

The introverted, taciturn Kitchener had been affronted by Churchill's *Malakand* book because he believed it was bad for discipline if junior officers were allowed to criticise their seniors. Three times he rejected applications from Churchill to be allowed to enlist as an officer and military correspondent in the Army of the Nile. It took an interview with the prime minister and friend of his father's, Lord Salisbury, followed by a written plea to the prime minister to write to Lord Cromer, the British Consul General in Egypt, before Kitchener relented and let the young thruster join the 21st Lancers as a supernumerary lieutenant, but only on condition that he paid his own way and that the army would not be held liable should he be injured or killed.

The delighted Lt Churchill didn't bother to ask the permission of the 4th Hussars to extend his leave of absence, reasoning that the regiment was too far away to stop him anyway. Before leaving for Cairo, he appeared once again on the platform at a Conservative Party meeting in Bradford, where he spoke for 55 minutes to an enthusiastic audience.

On arriving in Egypt, Churchill hurriedly made the 1 400-mile journey up the Nile to Khartoum, where Kitchener's forces had stationed themselves for a showdown with the Khalifa Abdullah, successor to the Mahdi, Muhammad Ahmad. He was just in time to lead his own mounted patrol into the brutal Battle of Omdurman, in which the Khalifa's five-mile-wide force of 40 000 spear-carrying warriors were simply mown down by British rifles, artillery shells and Maxim guns. Narrowly escaping death in an ambush by the Dervish army, the young 21st Lancer shot and killed several of the enemy himself, in what was one of history's bloodiest massacres. In the end, 'discipline and machinery' – in Churchill's words – 'triumphed over the most desperate valour'.[19]

Because Kitchener had kept the press at arm's length from Omdurman, Churchill was the only journalist able to describe at first hand the last great cavalry battle fought by the British Army. He made the most of the opportunity: his two-volume *The River War, an Account of the Re-conquest of the Sudan*, was an instant best-seller on publication in 1899. However, his admiration for the bravery of the Dervishes and criticism of the 'inhumane slaughter of the wounded' by some British soldiers infuriated high-ups in the British Army, and Kitchener in particular. One anonymous general wrote to the *Army & Navy Gazette* wondering how a young subaltern with less than four years' experience could be allowed to act as a special correspondent 'here, there and everywhere', able to freely criticise senior officers and influence public opinion.[20] Even the Prince of Wales joined in the chorus of disapproval, telling Churchill that he understood why Kitchener viewed him with such distaste.

The furore over Churchill's war reporting resulted in the War Office prohibiting soldiers from working as reporters, and vice versa. The cause of the trouble was in no way put out, cheekily describing himself as 'that hybrid combination of subaltern officer and widely followed war correspondent which was not unnaturally obnoxious to the military mind'.[21] And despite the trouble he caused, the experience he gained in the north-eastern corner of Africa was to be one more step up the ladder leading to a prominent and successful career in politics.[22]

By late 1898, Churchill had completed over four years of army service and come to the conclusion that journalism offered many more opportunities and far better pay than a military career. After journeying to India for one last time to play in a regimental polo tournament, he took his formal leave of the 4th Hussars. A prescient London *Daily Mail* journalist accompanying him on the boat home wrote that the young Churchill seemed destined for greatness. 'Platform speeches and leading articles flow from him almost against his will. At dinner he talks and talks and you can hardly tell when he leaves off quoting his one idol, Macaulay, and begins his other, Winston Churchill ...

At the rate he goes, there will hardly be room for him in Parliament at thirty or in England at forty.'[23]

On reaching Britain in April 1899, Churchill plunged once again into party politics and at the age of twenty-four was chosen to represent the Conservatives in Oldham, a working-class district in Lancashire, in the pending general election. The Tories were not expected to hold their two seats in the constituency, and indeed did not, but the neophyte Churchill 'neither distinguished nor disgraced himself'.[24] He was mollified by a message from the Conservative leader, Arthur Balfour, who wrote that he was very sorry to hear that Churchill had lost at Oldham: 'I had greatly hoped to see you speedily in the House where your father and I fought many a good battle side by side in days gone by. I hope however you will not be discouraged ... this small reverse will have no permanent ill effect upon our political fortunes.'[25]

After the election, eager as ever to put his name before the public, Churchill sought another challenging journalistic assignment and found what he was looking for in the conflict looming between the Boers and the British over the gold riches lying beneath the earth in South Africa.

CHAPTER 3

A chance encounter

When in doubt, do the courageous thing.
— SMUTS[1]

After taking his bar examinations in London, in which he came top of his class in legal history and constitutional law,* Smuts returned to Cape Town and was admitted to the Cape Bar in 1895.[2] Cecil John Rhodes was prime minister of the Cape Colony, with the support of Jan Hendrik Hofmeyr's Afrikaner Bond. In Keith Hancock's words, 'On this rock of solidity between Cape Dutch and Cape English, the future destinies of [the] Cape Colony and the whole of South Africa … appeared secure.'[3]

Interested in politics, but out of touch after four years abroad, Smuts took for granted the permanence of the Rhodes-Bond link and before long found himself – at the behest of Hofmeyr – on a public platform in Kimberley praising the policies of the Cape premier, who had brought the 'two Teutonic peoples' of South Africa together to defend and safeguard 'civilisation'. 'Unless the white race closes its ranks,' the neophyte politician told his audience, 'its position will soon become untenable in the face of the overwhelming majority of prolific barbarism.'[4]

However, the Jameson Raid – the ill-conceived, ill-fated attempt led by

---

* Smuts was one of Cambridge University's best-ever law students. In 1970, Lord Todd, a Nobel Prize winner and Master of Christ's College, said that in its 500-year history, three of the college's members had been truly outstanding – John Milton, Charles Darwin and Jan Smuts (see SB Spies and Gail Nattrass, *Jan Smuts: Memories of the Boer War*. Jonathan Ball, 1997, p 19).

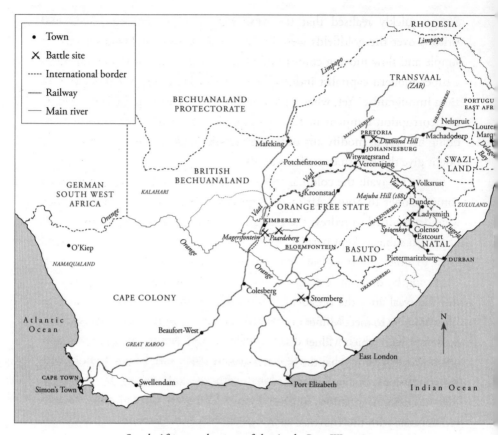

South Africa at the time of the Anglo-Boer War, 1899–1902

Rhodes's right-hand man, Leander Starr Jameson, in December 1895 to over-throw the Kruger administration in the Transvaal in order to ameliorate the lot of the British *uitlanders* – caused the scales to fall from Smuts's eyes. Declaring his loss of faith and trust in Rhodes, Smuts decided he had no political future in the Cape and moved north to the Transvaal, where there were signs that the small, weak South African Republic was being provoked into hostilities by the British. In April 1897 he returned briefly to the Cape to wed Sybella ('Isie') Krige, his Stellenbosch sweetheart, with whom he was to have a long and fulfilling marriage.

It was not long before President Kruger became aware of the exceptional abilities of the young Afrikaner lawyer in his midst. Bending the regulations, he appointed Smuts as his state attorney at the tender age of twenty-eight.

Smuts quickly realised that the simmering tensions between Boers and Britons over the goldfields were likely to end in war. As Hancock says, 'A simple and slow-moving country folk had seen suddenly arise in their midst a super-modern capitalist industry and a strident urban conglomeration of alien immigrants.'[5] Yet, when he was not trying to clean up the law-breaking and corruption rampant in Kruger's republic, the young state attorney was doing his best to modify any of the administration's policies and actions that might give the British cause for war.

But to no avail: the colonial secretary, Joseph Chamberlain, and his high commissioner in South Africa (and governor of the Cape), Alfred Milner, were determined to redress the grievances of the *uitlanders* – the 'thousands of British subjects kept permanently in the position of helots'[6] – and to find cause to annex the Transvaal by hastening an armed conflict, come what may.

Having become, in less than two years, the most important politician in the Transvaal after the president,[7] Smuts was taken by the elderly Kruger to Bloemfontein to meet Milner in a final, desperate attempt to avert war. From the contempt with which Milner dismissed Kruger's proposed franchise reforms, it was obvious to Smuts that the high commissioner was not interested in extracting concessions, but rather on finding reasons for war. After that meeting in Bloemfontein, negotiations sputtered on for some months. Both sides drew up ultimatums, with the Transvaal sending theirs on 9 October 1899. When it was formally rejected by the British Government, the Boers, to universal astonishment, went to war with the mighty British Empire.

Shortly before the war began, a document was published in England titled *A Century of Wrong*, issued by the state secretary of the South African Republic, Francis William Reitz. This was dubbed 'the official exposition of the case of the Boer against the Briton'.[8] The author of the document, who was not identified, was Smuts and the translator his wife, Isie. Rich in metaphor and classical allusion, the plainly propagandist tract set out the injustices and cruelties meted out to the Boers by the British over the previous hundred years:

> In this awful turning point in the history of South Africa, on the eve of a conflict which threatens to exterminate our people, it behoves us to speak the truth in what may be, perchance, our last message to the world. ...

As the wounded antelope awaits the coming of the lion, the jackal and the vulture, so do our poor people all over South Africa contemplate the approach of the foe.[9]

It did not take long for the identity of the writer of this purple prose to become known – and notorious – in British circles.

In the years to come, Smuts had good reason to regret one of the few instances in his life when he allowed heart to triumph over head. After he had taken the empire's side in World War I, his Afrikaner-Nationalist opponents never ceased to taunt him about his earlier bitterness towards the British, and fling back at him extracts from *A Century of Wrong*. He was never to admit his authorship of the tract and preferred not to speak of it after the Anglo-Boer War had ended.[10]

As the war with Britain began, State Attorney Smuts found himself, at the tender age of 29, running the administration in Pretoria virtually single-handedly while the Boer generals carried the fight to the enemy. Despite having no formal military training, he took it upon himself to draft an eighteen-page memorandum detailing what needed to be done to support Boer forces in the field. Restless at his forced inaction, he paid frequent visits to the war front to assess the situation at first hand.[11]

It was on one of these visits – to General Piet Joubert and the Boer forces on the outskirts of besieged Ladysmith – that Smuts encountered Winston Churchill for the first time.

*

Churchill would have imbibed his early impression of the Boers from his father, Lord Randolph. The lack of any real understanding of the situation in South Africa had not prevented him, as a young journalist, from sounding off in 1896 about the predicament in which Britain chose to find itself on the Transvaal goldfields. Writing in an unpublished paper titled 'Our Account with the Boers', he faithfully toed the party line: 'Imperial troops must curb the insolence of the

Boers', he wrote. 'There must be no half measures. Sooner or later, in a righteous cause or a picked quarrel … for the sake of our honour, for the sake of the race, we must fight the Boers.'[12] The war over the goldfields that broke out three years later caused him to temper some of these jingoistic sentiments.

In 1899, with hostilities now imminent, by playing off *The Morning Post* against a *Daily Mail* eager to secure his services as a war correspondent, Churchill was able to extract a lucrative contract from the former to report on the conflict in South Africa: a salary of one thousand pounds for four months' work, the exclusive copyright on whatever he wrote and all expenses paid. As a precaution, he notified the colonial secretary of his travel intentions. Chamberlain wired back, promising to alert the British high commissioner to the young man's arrival. The colonial secretary's actual words to Milner were: 'He has a reputation for bumptiousness; put him on the right lines.'[13]

In preparing for his assignment, *The Morning Post*'s war reporter had no intention of depriving himself of the necessities of life. Packed into his trunks were a new saddle, a telescope, field glasses, sixty bottles of Scotch whisky and French wine, and a dozen bottles of lime juice, all paid for by the newspaper. He also decided to take with him a manservant, Thomas Walden, who had accompanied Lord Randolph on an earlier visit to South Africa. By now, Churchill's exploits on the North-West Frontier and in the Sudan had made him so well known that he even got mentioned in music-hall concerts:

> You've heard of Winston Churchill
> This is all I have to say
> He's the latest and the greatest
> Correspondent of the day[14]

Every evening of the week before his departure, the young star-seeker was given a dinner party in his honour, at which there were early signs of the wit for which he became famous. On one occasion, a snooty Liberal friend of his mother's remarked that she liked neither Churchill's straggly moustache nor his politics, to which he replied, 'Madame, I see no earthly reason why you should come into contact with either.'[15]

Churchill left Southampton for Cape Town on 14 October 1899 on board the Royal Mail steamer, the *Dunottar Castle*. A huge crowd had gathered on the dockside to wave off not him, but Sir Redvers Buller, commander-in-chief of British forces in South Africa, and his entourage, who were sent on their way with rousing cheers and shouts of 'Give it to the Boers' and 'Remember Majuba'[†] ringing in their ears. During the voyage, Churchill made it his business to get to know Buller and his adjutants better. Though he liked Buller, who 'looked stolid, said little, and what he said was obscure',[16] Churchill doubted his military competence and thought he was well over the hill. He was to describe Buller, memorably, as a commander who 'plodded on from blunder to blunder and one disaster to another, without losing either the regard of his country or the trust of his troops, to whose feeding as well as his own he paid serious attention'.[17]

Buller, Churchill and company arrived in Cape Town to the grimmest of tidings: Mafeking and Kimberley had been besieged, and Major General Sir Penn Symons and 447 other men had been killed, wounded or taken prisoner in the first battle of the war, at Dundee in Natal. While Buller lingered in Cape Town awaiting the arrival of more troops, Churchill and a reporter from the *Manchester Guardian*, JB Atkins, took a train to East London and then a steamer to Durban in the hope of stealing a march on their competitors. After a nightmarish voyage, they hurried north to get as near as possible to Natal's second-largest town, Ladysmith, also now under siege by Boer forces. Managing to reach Estcourt, forty miles south of Ladysmith, they found that the railway line had been cut a little further on, at Colenso. In Estcourt, they were joined by Leo S Amery of *The Times*, whom Churchill had once pushed into the swimming pool at Harrow and who was later to become his close political colleague and 'imperialist alter ego'.[18]

Even by now it had become plain to Churchill and his fellow war correspondents that Britain had grossly underestimated the strength, resolve and fighting abilities of the Boers. Writing to his mother, he predicted a 'fierce and bloody struggle in which at least ten to twelve thousand [British] lives would be sacrificed'.[19] In another letter, to the British adjutant-general, Sir Evelyn Wood, he wrote: 'The present situation here is bad and critical. It is astonishing how we have underrated these people.'[20]

---

† The Battle of Majuba Hill was a decisive encounter in the First Boer War, 1881.

The British forces had been trained to fight set-piece battles against a conventional, visible enemy, not sporadic skirmishes against bands of mounted Boer guerrillas, who would 'attack from ambush and then disappear as silently as they had come'.[21] Moreover, the only means by which the 'khakis' could move men, equipment and supplies across vast distances in South Africa was the armoured train. The train carried an array of weaponry to be fired from gun ports along the sides of each carriage as well as a large, mounted seven-inch naval gun manned by a crew of sailors. This made it a prime target for the Boers. As Churchill wrote in *My Early Life*, 'nothing looks more formidable and impressive than an armoured train; but nothing is in fact more vulnerable and helpless. It was only necessary to blow up a bridge or culvert to leave the monster stranded, far from home and help, at the mercy of the enemy.'[22]

That is exactly what happened on 15 November 1899, when an impatient Churchill – against his better judgement and armed only with his favourite Mauser pistol – clambered aboard an armoured train under the command of his old friend Captain (later General) Aylmer Haldane, on a reconnaissance to probe Boer lines. Proceeding cautiously out of Estcourt, the train passed through Frere to Chieveley, fourteen miles to the north, where it encountered a Boer force of around 100 horsemen and was ordered by telegraph from HQ to return home.

From a nearby hilltop, Louis Botha, the Boer general in command of the area, and 500 mounted horsemen were watching as the train slowly made its way northwards. Anticipating its return, Botha ordered rocks to be strewn along the tracks around a sharp curve shortly before Frere Station on the return journey. The Boer ambush was spectacularly successful: three armoured cars were derailed and the railway line blocked. While Haldane marshalled his troops to fight off the encircling Boers with rifle fire, Churchill spent the next seventy minutes, heedless of danger, organising the clearing of the track and enabling the engine and half of the train, with the wounded aboard, to get under way and limp back to Estcourt. Haldane wrote in his official report later: 'He [Churchill] was frequently exposed to the full fire of the enemy. I cannot speak too highly of his gallant conduct.'[23] A fellow officer told the *Natal Witness* that his actions had been those 'of as brave a man as could be found'.[24]

Churchill as a prisoner of war, Pretoria, 1899.

SMUTS HOUSE MUSEUM

As the train steamed off, the remaining British troops were left without cover. Confronted by a Boer rifleman, Churchill realised he had left his Mauser on the locomotive and could not shoot back even if he'd wished to. 'I thought there was absolutely no chance of escape, if he fired he would surely hit me, so I held up my hands and surrendered myself as a prisoner of war,' he wrote afterwards.[25] Along with Haldane and 56 others, he was swiftly captured and taken into custody by the Boers.

Lining up alongside the other British prisoners, an indignant Churchill was picked out by his captors and told to stand to one side. Realising that any civilian involved in an armed conflict could be shot on sight, he managed to get rid of his two clips of 'dum-dum' cartridges (a form of expanding bullet about to be outlawed by the Hague Convention), identified himself as a war correspondent and insisted that he could not be held as a prisoner of war. 'We know who you are,' said one of Boers, adding, to the amusement of his colleagues, 'We don't catch the son of a lord every day.'[26] (Many Boers claimed afterwards to have had a part in Churchill's capture, but it is probable, though not certain, that his captor was a red-haired and bearded field cornet, one Sarel Oosthuizen, and not Louis Botha as Churchill was erroneously to assert later.)

Outside Ladysmith, Churchill was taken immediately to the tent of Commandant-General Joubert, who was away at the time. On the scene, by chance, was Jan Smuts, paying a quick visit to the war front from Pretoria. It is unlikely that the two actually exchanged words, for neither man makes mention of the other in his memoir of the war. But drawing on his phenomenal memory many years later, Smuts recalled that 'Winston was a scrubby, squat figure of a man, unshaved. He was furious, venomous, just like a viper.'[27] When Churchill protested to his adversaries that the Boers had no right to take him, a journalist, as prisoner, he was told that war correspondents did not usually take command of troops or carry arms.[‡]

Back in Estcourt, survivors of the Boer ambush who had made the journey, clinging to the engine and its tender, recounted their narrow escape to the war correspondents who had stayed behind, and spoke admiringly of the bravery of Churchill, in particular. His valet, Walden, who had been with him on the train, wrote home to Lady Randolph, 'I'm sorry to say Mr Churchill is a prisoner, but I am almost certain he is not wounded ... Every officer in Estcourt thinks Mr C and the engine-driver will get the VC [Victoria Cross].'[28]

The news of *The Morning Post*'s celebrated reporter's capture caused an immediate sensation in the popular press in Britain and beyond. All of a sudden a minor skirmish in a far-off colonial conflict had become a prominent feature on the front page of every newspaper.

The British prisoners were taken by their captors on a three-day trek around the besieged town of Ladysmith to Elandslaagte, where they were put on a train to Pretoria and incarcerated in a schoolhouse in the Boer capital. By now, Churchill's relief at not being shot as a civilian had given way to the indignant conviction that he was being held illegally by the Boers. In this, as Carlo D'Este notes wryly, Churchill was acting entirely in character: 'He still treated war as if it were an activity being conducted solely for his personal advancement.'[29]

---

‡ The two men met for the first time in 1906, when Smuts went to see Churchill in London to plead for self-government for the Transvaal. (See Eric Bolsmann, *Winston Churchill – The Making of a Hero in the South African War*. Galago, 2008, p 90.)

Churchill's anger and frustration at being held captive in a building that reminded him of his schooldays was immense. 'I certainly hated every minute of my captivity more than I have hated any other period in my whole life,'[30] he wrote later. After a week of inaction, he wrote a letter to the Transvaal Government, demanding his release 'as a non-combatant and a Press Correspondent'.[31] When that had no effect, on hearing rumours of a possible prisoner exchange, he changed tack and asked the War Office if he could be classified as a 'military officer', in the hope that he might benefit from any prisoner swap. He wrote also to his mother and the Prince of Wales, seeking their help.[32] Then, in another letter to the authorities, he undertook 'to give any parole that may be required not to serve against the Republican forces or to give any information regarding the military situation'.[33]

General Joubert, by this time, was having second thoughts. Having insisted earlier that Churchill should not be released for the duration of the war because of the damage he might do to the Boer cause, he now felt inclined to accept the parole plea of his troublesome prisoner – who was, after all, an English aristocrat and gentleman.

Before he could do so, however, Churchill had taken matters into his own hands. On the night of 12 December, he scaled the walls of his prison and got away, leaving a letter under his pillow for his captors, in which he expressed admiration for 'the chivalrous and humane character of the Republican forces' and hoped 'that when this most grievous and unhappy war shall have come to an end, a state of affairs may be created which shall preserve at once the national pride of the Boers and the security of the British, and put a final stop to the rivalry and enmity of both races'. He ended the letter cheekily: 'Regretting that circumstances have not permitted me to bid you a personal farewell, believe me, yours very sincerely, Winston S Churchill.'[34]

A few days later, Smuts telegraphed Joubert to ask, 'What truth is there in the rumour that Churchill has escaped but has been recaptured again?'[35] The frustrated Joubert replied: 'I wonder whether it would not be a good thing to make public the correspondence about the release of Churchill to show the world what a scoundrel he is.'[36]

CHAPTER 4

A reluctant peace

*Once you are so unfortunate as to be drawn into a war, no price is
too great to pay for an early and victorious peace.*
— CHURCHILL[1]

T he story of Churchill's escape from the Boers' clutches and hazardous
300-mile dash to freedom via Mozambique (then Portuguese East
Africa) has been recounted many times – most notably by the man himself
in his lively memoir, *My Early Life*. After jumping on and off the coal truck
of a freight train bound for a siding near Witbank, not far from Pretoria,
Churchill had the good fortune to find himself on the doorstep of an English
mine manager, John Howard, who hid his visitor underground for six days
before putting him on a goods train headed for Lourenço Marques (the pre-
independence name for Maputo). Two days later, Churchill cabled Howard
to say, 'Goods arrived safely', before proceeding by coastal steamer to Durban,
where the news of his escapade had already made him a household name in
the colony of Natal and around the empire.

At a time when the British public – 'reared on a rich diet of imperial heroes
and easily defeated native foes'[2] – was starved of good news from the South
African War, here was a Briton with a famous name who could be held up
as a model of bulldog determination and imperial derring-do. In Durban
Harbour, hundreds of wildly cheering people awaited Churchill's arrival by
ship and bore him triumphantly to the steps of the Town Hall, from where
he addressed an excited crowd.

The Boers, for their part, felt deeply humiliated by their inability to prevent their high-profile prisoner's escape from their custody. Notices went up across the Transvaal offering a £25 reward for the capture and delivery of 'the escaped prisoner of war Churchill, alive or dead'. Rumour ran wild that he had been abetted by accomplices in Pretoria, which caused the police to pounce on suspected British sympathisers and search homes around the capital. In London, newspapers speculated excitedly that if Churchill were found, he might conceivably be shot, since in the recent Franco-Prussian War all non-combatants found carrying arms had been summarily executed. For a short time, the Boers obsessed about the recapture of one 'very dangerous individual', whose whereabouts were the subject of intense speculation until he resurfaced into public view in Natal a fortnight later.[3]

Yet not everyone in Britain was impressed by Churchill's exploits. His earlier statement that an individual Boer was worth three to five regular soldiers had aroused deep resentment among the retired colonels and generals of what he described as the 'Buck and Dodder Club', who sent him a cable saying, 'Best friends here hope you won't go making further ass of yourself.'[4] And according to Norman Rose, when Churchill was captured in Natal, many in the clubs of London hoped that the Boers might keep him.[5]

After overnighting at the governor's residence in Pietermaritzburg, the elusive war correspondent returned to his colleagues alongside Buller's army outside Ladysmith the very next day. There he was reunited with Atkins and Amery, who found him looking exhausted after his exertions and still smarting from his capture, which he described as 'the greatest indignity of my life'.[6] He celebrated Christmas Eve with his press colleagues only a short distance away from the scene of the armoured train ambush.[7]

Buller was delighted to see him and to learn first-hand about Boer attitudes and tactics. As he wrote to a friend, 'Winston Churchill turned up here escaped from Pretoria. He really is a fine fellow and I admire him greatly. I wish he was leading irregular troops instead of writing for a rotten paper.'[8] Ignoring the War Office's ban on soldiers doubling as war correspondents, Buller responded positively to Churchill's request for a commission in the army, appointing him as a lieutenant in the South African Light Horse and granting him permission to roam as freely as he liked when not fighting.

Churchill as a war correspondent during the Anglo-Boer War, 1899.

AAI/FOTOSTOCK

He would not be allowed, however, to draw a military as well as a journalist's salary.[9]

Despite his reservations about the British commander's abilities, the now 'embedded' Churchill wrote less critically of him: 'If Sir Redvers Buller cannot relieve Ladysmith with his present force, we do not know of any other officer in the British Service who would be likely to succeed.'[10]

The *Morning Post*'s volatile reporter was still, in Roy Jenkins's words, 'as combative with words as with bullets'.[11] In many articles, he wrote admiringly of Boer determination and effectiveness in the field. 'We must face the facts. The individual Boer, mounted in suitable country, is worth three to five regular soldiers,' he said. He advocated a 'generous forgiving policy' towards the enemy. 'Peace and happiness can only come to South Africa through the fusion and concord of the Dutch and British races, who must forever live side by side under the supremacy of Britain.'* Needless to say, these supposedly 'pro-Boer' opinions did not go down well in Britain, but his reconciliatory sentiments were echoed after the war by Smuts and Louis Botha.

After resuming his obligations to *The Morning Post*, Churchill stayed on in South Africa for a further six months, taking part in Buller's bloodily unsuccessful attempt to drive the Boers off the peak of Spioenkop, where one Mohandas K Gandhi was among the stretcher-bearers. Churchill reported on the relief of Ladysmith, accompanying the officer commanding the mounted task force, the twelfth Earl of Dundonald, as British cavalry entered the liberated town.[12] There he lingered for a month, busily writing a new book, *London to Ladysmith via Pretoria*, before heading to the Orange Free State, where Buller's replacement as commander-in-chief, Lord Roberts, was spearheading a major offensive before heading north into the Transvaal.

Never able to resist the lure of battle, Churchill flung himself into a number of skirmishes with bands of Boers, narrowly escaping with his life on more than one occasion according to his own version. After accompanying Roberts's men as they triumphantly took Johannesburg and then Pretoria, he went into action for the last time at the Boers' defiant stand at Diamond Hill, in the Magaliesberg hills east of Pretoria. Here once again, he displayed 'conspicuous gallantry' under crossfire and was recommended by his commander for the Victoria Cross, the award he coveted above all others. To his disappointment, his nomination was vetoed by Roberts and Kitchener because, they said dismissively, 'he had only been a Press correspondent'.[13] As he said to friends, 'all the danger and one half percent of the glory; such is our motto and that is the reason why we expect such large salaries.'[14]

Like Roberts, Churchill mistakenly assumed that the Boers, with their

---

* Years later, Churchill wrote that the Boers were 'the most good-hearted enemy I have ever fought against in the four continents in which it has been my fortune to see Active Service'. See John Keegan (ed.), *Churchill's Generals*. Orion 1991, p 5.

capital lost and forces well beaten, would capitulate, and made preparations to return home. His journey to the Cape aboard a large troop train was interrupted by another Boer ambush on the railway line, but after firing his final shots at the enemy, the supposedly non-combatant war correspondent reached Cape Town on horseback.

In the Mother City, he had an interview with the high commissioner, Milner, and went jackal hunting with the Duke of Westminster before boarding the *Dunottar Castle* again. On the voyage home, he began working on *Ian Hamilton's March*, a collection of articles written for *The Morning Post* during his seven months in South Africa. Back in England, he wrote to Milner to suggest an early peace, and an amnesty for the Afrikaner rebels in the Cape. Recognising the younger man's growing political clout, Milner replied with a 22-page handwritten letter asking Churchill to desist. 'It is a serious matter to have suggestions of pacification coming from you, with your ability, popularity and special South African experience,' he wrote.[15]

*

The fall of Pretoria to Lord Roberts's forces in June 1900 marked the end of the first phase of the Anglo-Boer War. President Kruger had fled the capital ahead of the advancing British, putting his deputy, Schalk Burger, and Smuts in charge of the administration. After shipping the last of the South African Republic's gold along the railway line eastwards, Smuts left his wife and infant son at home and melted away to join Botha and his men at Diamond Hill, where one of the last pitched battles of the war was being fought. Though the battle ended in defeat for the Boers, their brave stand reinforced their determination to fight on against the 'khakis'. They were further emboldened by the exploits of generals Christiaan de Wet and Koos de la Rey in successfully cutting enemy supply lines in the Free State and Western Transvaal.

The Boer leaders now decided to divide the remnants of their army into three guerrilla units: Botha took command of hit-and-run operations in the Eastern Transvaal, De Wet and Hertzog in the Free State, and De la Rey accompanied by state attorney Smuts, in the Western Transvaal. On 25 October, Roberts announced Britain's formal annexation of the Transvaal and shortly afterwards departed for home, leaving his deputy, Kitchener, in charge of British forces. Kitchener intensified Roberts's tactics of herding women and children into internment camps and laying waste to Boer farms, and in doing so initiated a new and much nastier phase of the conflict.

Smuts, who had been chafing for months at his enforced exclusion from the fighting, was put in charge of a small commando operating in the Western Transvaal. More aware than his colleagues of potential Afrikaner support in the Cape, he pleaded in vain to be allowed to lead an exploratory Boer force into the colony. While waiting for permission to do so, he took lessons from his old friend and mentor, De la Rey, in how to wage guerrilla warfare against a more powerful enemy.

As Boer fortunes continued to decline at Kitchener's hands, Smuts was at last given permission to infiltrate the Cape Colony. On 1 August 1901, he led a ragged band of 340 volunteers on the first stage of an epic campaign that would last eight months, take him 2 000 miles across the Cape Colony and divert some 35 000 British troops into trying to capture him. Gathering volunteers along the route, his commando braved adverse weather and bouts of sickness to make its way south through the Stormberg mountains to Port Elizabeth, then west in the direction of Cape Town before advancing through Bushman territory to the far north of Namaqualand, near the border with friendly German South West Africa. Back in Pretoria, the British occupied Smuts's home, and shortly before their infant son, Koosie, died on 14 August 1900, sent Isie and her sister under surveillance to a small house in Pietermaritzburg.

In his much acclaimed book, *Commando* (first published in 1929), Deneys Reitz provides a first-hand account of how Smuts and his colleagues cheated death or capture on several occasions. Leading from the front, as always, the thirty-one-year-old commander displayed enormous resilience in withstanding the often extreme weather, which posed more of a threat than the pursuing 'khakis', who had put a bounty of £1 000 upon Smuts's head. In the words of historian Antony Lentin, 'Amid gruelling marches and bloody skirmishes on the open veld and high mountain ranges, [Smuts] showed himself hardy, seasoned, bold and resourceful.'[16] Whenever he had a spare moment, he would read philosophy, while in his saddle bag he carried a copy of the New Testament in Greek.

Though Smuts and his men evaded capture and caused the British forces much inconvenience and many casualties, they were unsuccessful in fomenting an Afrikaner uprising in the Cape Colony. In the north, the war continued to go badly for the Boers. When Kitchener offered peace talks in Vereeniging, Botha and his generals accepted with reluctance. Smuts – in the throes of attacking the copper-producing town of Okiep – was summoned to the negotiation and given a safe-conduct passage to the Transvaal by none other than Colonel (later Field Marshal) Douglas Haig.

At Vereeniging, he and fellow lawyer, General Hertzog, helped persuade the demoralised remnants of the Boer forces that there was nothing to be gained from holding out any longer. After negotiations with Milner and Kitchener, the Boers hesitantly accepted settlement terms and the Treaty of Vereeniging was signed on 31 May 1902. The Anglo-Boer War – to which the British had committed 450 000 soldiers to subdue between 60–70 000 Boers – was over. It had done immense damage to the prestige and self-esteem of the rulers of Empire.

*

Surrender was not, as Keith Hancock points out, all on the Boer side, however.[17] Eager by now to wind down a war that was costing a fortune and aware that the British public was losing patience with the government, Milner, Kitchener and the Colonial Office conceded to Botha and Smuts's demand that the issue of 'native' political rights should be discussed only *after* the Boers had been given self-government. The more important question of whether black people would thereafter be granted political rights by the two republics was left open. Milner had earlier advised Chamberlain that the imperial government could not deal with the so-called native question 'regardless of colonial sentiment'.[18] It would be very 'unfortunate' to insist on extending the Cape non-racial franchise[†] to the whole of South Africa, Milner warned, 'as

---

† The principle of a non-racial, qualified franchise had been entrenched since the Cape Colony was granted self-government in 1853. Any man who owned property worth £25 was entitled to vote or stand for election to the Cape's Parliament. Although no African had won a seat in Parliament, in the Eastern Cape, in particular, the African vote was politically significant. (See Martin Plaut, *Promise and Despair: The First Struggle for a Non-Racial South Africa*. Jacana, 2016, p 14.)

few Africans in the Transvaal would meet the franchise qualifications and, for the sake of a theory, it would be unwise to start a conflict with the Whites'.[19] And so, by abandoning their previous stance on the franchise, the British – at Smuts's insistence – gave way on the crucial issue that was to dominate and bedevil South African politics for the next century and beyond.

If truth be told, both sides had little alternative if there was to be a settlement. As Martin Plaut points out, the war had not been fought about 'native rights'. By extending the Cape non-racial franchise to the Boer republics, several thousand *bywoners* (tenant farmers) from the poorer and undereducated section of an Afrikaner *volk* who had trekked away from the Cape partially because of British-inspired measures to bring about greater racial equality, would have been disenfranchised. Afrikaners regarded the franchise as their God-given right and would never abandon it 'so that a small number of wealthy Africans could be given the vote'.[20]

In 1906, the new Liberal government in Britain appointed the West Ridgeway Commission to consider the most appropriate constitutions for the Transvaal and Orange Free State republics, if granted self-government. The commission confirmed that the question of the 'native franchise' should be left to the new self-governing colonies to decide, but 'it did not believe that black people could ever be placed on an equality [sic] with the white population in the matter of the franchise'.[21]

*

Churchill had arrived back in England in July 1900 to a rousing welcome, and in less than three months had been elected as Conservative MP for Oldham. The poll, which took place over six weeks in those days, was dubbed the 'Khaki Election' because the Boer War was still under way and khaki was the colour of British uniforms. Although the conflict had gradually begun to turn in Britain's favour, it was by no means over, and Lord Salisbury's Conservatives sought to increase their majority over the Liberals with slogans such as 'Every seat lost to the Government is a seat gained to [sic] the Boers' and 'Remember, to vote for a Liberal is a vote to the Boer'.[22] The Salisbury government also made capital out of General Roberts's successful capture of Pretoria, with the second and far more controversial phase of the conflict not yet having set in. As might be expected, the twenty-five-year-old, pro-war Churchill was one of the stellar attractions of the election campaign, drawing far larger crowds than most other Tory candidates. Yet his winning margin in the working-class seat of Oldham was no more than a slender 222 votes.

With the Conservatives back in power, the new House of Commons met briefly in early December to swear in new MPs and deal with matters arising from the South African War. Astonishingly, the new MP for Oldham was not to be found in the House. He had made so much money talking to audiences around Britain about his experiences in South Africa that he had departed for the US and Canada to cash in on the lecture circuit while the going was good. He found American audiences not as interested in the Boer War as the British, and his takings much less than he had hoped for, but among the Americans he met were President William McKinley, his deputy, Teddy Roosevelt, and the country's most eminent author, Mark Twain.

A few weeks later, the chamber of the lower House of Parliament was full on the evening of 18 February 1901 when the attention-seeking young MP – against the advice of older Tories – rose to deliver his maiden speech.‡ Following a virulent denunciation of the government's handling of the war by the pro-Boer Liberal, Lloyd George, a nervous Churchill asserted boldly that he did not believe the Boers would attach much importance to his opponent's strictures. 'No other people in the world received so much verbal sympathy, and so little support,' he said.[23]

Once into his stride, he had Prime Minister Balfour and Colonial Secretary Joseph Chamberlain raising their eyebrows as he declared that, in the post-war transition to democracy, the Boers should be subjected to a civilian rather than a military government: 'If I were a Boer fighting in the field … [long pause] And if I were a Boer, I hope I should be fighting in the field …'

He went on:

> I have often myself been very much ashamed to see respectable old Boer farmers – the Boer is a curious combination of the squire and the peasant

---

‡ Churchill's entire maiden speech was devoted to the subject of South Africa.

and under the rough coat of the farmer there are very often to be found the instincts of the squire … I have been ashamed to see such men ordered about peremptorily by young subaltern officers.[24]

By pleading for a generous peace for the Boers – 'it should be easy and honourable for the Boers to surrender and painful and perilous for them to continue in the field'[25] – he courted the disfavour of his own party, but was undeterred. Privately, he expressed to friends his abhorrence at Kitchener's policy of burning down farms and crops in the Orange Free State and the Transvaal, but refrained from embarrassing the Tory government by saying so in public.

Party loyalty was never an important consideration for Churchill. In William Manchester's words, while always nailing his colours firmly to the mast, it was not always the same mast.[26] As he told a Liverpool audience, 'nothing could be worse than that independent men should be snuffed out and that there should be only two opinions in England – the Government opinion and the Opposition opinion. The perpetually unanimous Cabinet disturbs me; I believe in personality.'[27]

The price he would pay for this lack of fidelity to party was to be forever distrusted.

CHAPTER 5

Reconstructing South Africa

History writes the word 'Reconciliation' over all her quarrels.
— SMUTS[1]

Churchill's dissatisfaction with his fellow Conservatives over their anti-pathy to the Boers may have been a contributing factor, but what eventually drove him out of his father's old party and into the arms of the Liberals was not South Africa, but the most divisive issue in British politics – tariff reform. Churchill disagreed strongly with Joseph Chamberlain's plan to impose taxes on foreign imports – with exemptions for goods from the empire – because it would inhibit Britain's trade with the rest of the world. As he told a friend:

> It would seem to me a fantastic policy to endeavour to shut the British Empire up in a ringed fence ... Why should we deny ourselves the good and varied merchandise which the traffic of the world offers, more especially since the more we trade with others, the more they must trade with us ...[2]

Besides his doubt about ever attaining high office in a Tory government, there were other issues, including excessive military expenditure and poverty relief, on which Churchill preferred Liberal to Conservative policies. So, having become the Tories' most effective anti-protectionist speaker, on the last day of May 1904 the Conservative member for Oldham crossed the floor of Parliament and joined the Liberal Party, which he had once colourfully accused of being 'full of prigs, prudes and faddists' and of 'hiding from public view like a toad in a hole'.[3] Some diehard Tories were never to forgive his apostasy.

For the next eighteen months, Churchill uncharacteristically kept his head down and tried to remain inconspicuous as a Liberal backbencher while he set about building a Manchester constituency in time for the next election. He also embarked on a two-volume biography of his late father, Lord Randolph, which sold well on publication.

In the aftermath of the Boer War, the political climate had changed. The electorate's disillusionment with the Tories (often referred to as the Stupid Party) over its handling of the war as well as obstructing free trade, and lurid reports of the ill-treatment of Chinese labourers on Transvaal mines brought about Balfour's resignation as prime minister in December 1905, before he could be voted out of office. The king invited the Liberal leader, Sir Henry Campbell-Bannerman, to form an interim government until the general election, due in early 1906. Offered the choice of no fewer than three posts in the new administration, the thirty-one-year-old Churchill declined the plum position of Financial Secretary to the Treasury and asked to be appointed as Under-Secretary for the Colonies to Secretary of State Lord Elgin. South Africa was among Churchill's primary responsibilities.

The new under-secretary brought to his position a belief, which he had often written and stated publicly, that once the imperial authority had been restored, peace should be made with the Boers on magnanimous terms. He wasted no time in compiling a lengthy memorandum to the Liberal Cabinet, arguing that Milner's policies had been counter-productive and that the Boers of the Transvaal and the Free State should be brought into a united South Africa on an equal footing with English-speaking settlers in the Cape and Natal. He was confident that, if justly treated, the Boers would become loyal subjects of the British Crown.[4]

Before settling into his new office, however, there was the general election of January/February 1906 to be fought. Churchill stood this time as the Liberal candidate in Manchester, a constituency with many Jewish voters who were strongly in favour of free trade. His opposition to a restrictive Aliens Bill, designed to curb Jewish immigration from Russia, gained him a reputation as being a supporter of minorities and sympathiser with Zionism, and he romped home with a comfortable majority, as did the Liberal Party.

During the election campaign, Churchill had to return to Whitehall to receive an important visitor from South Africa, General Jan Smuts, sent by Louis Botha to ascertain the new British government's attitude towards Boer independence. Smuts had written to him earlier: 'I have come from the Transvaal in the hope that I may have an opportunity to discuss with you the situation in the Transvaal and in South Africa generally.'[5]

By all accounts, the first proper meeting between the two former antagonists took place in late January 1906, in a cordial atmosphere. As was his practice, Smuts presented Churchill with a written memorandum for distribution to members of the Liberal Government, 'Points in Reference to the Transvaal Constitution'. In what Hancock describes as a 'persuasive, forceful and short' document, using language carefully designed to appeal to Liberal sentiment, Smuts wrote:

> What South Africa needs above all things after the storms and upheavals of the past is tranquillity. But that can only be secured by the removal of all just grounds of discontent and the unreserved application of Liberal principles to the government of the new Colonies, by showing a statesmanlike trust in the people of the land, of whatever race, and granting them a fair and equitable constitution under which they can work out their own salvation. There may be some danger in trusting people too soon, but there may be more danger in trusting them too late.[6]

The argument that Smuts wished Churchill and his colleagues to accept was that the time for self-government had come, but that any new dispensation had to be based on new electoral arrangements that would ensure that the liberties of the (white) people would be protected against the 'encroachment of the money power' i.e. the mining interests. On the question of voting rights for those not white, the memorandum was noticeably silent.

A somewhat sceptical Churchill asked Smuts whether he had ever known of a conquered people being allowed to govern themselves. To which Smuts replied, 'No, but we do not want to govern ourselves. We could not govern ourselves without England's assistance.'[7]

The two men warmed to each other, and afterwards Churchill wrote to Smuts: 'I will read [the memo] with attention. I shall always be glad to know your views and hope you will not hesitate to communicate them frankly.' He ended the letter by wishing his visitor 'a pleasant journey home'.[8]

Smuts then met other Liberal luminaries, but was unable to obtain any of the assurances he had hoped for. He had a sense that he was being fobbed off and, according to Hancock,[9] felt no confidence in the two ministers responsible for colonial affairs, Elgin and his deputy, Churchill. In despair at the prospect of leaving England with matters in suspense, he decided to seek another meeting, this time with Prime Minister Campbell-Bannerman himself. Their encounter was to determine the course of South African history. As Smuts wrote years afterwards,

> I put a simple case before him that night in 10 Downing Street. It was in substance: do you want friends or enemies? You can have the Boers for friends and they have proved what quality their friendship may mean. I pledge the friendship of my colleagues and myself if you wish it. You can choose to make them enemies, and possibly have another Ireland on your hands. If you do believe in liberty it is also their faith and their religion. I used no set arguments but simply spoke to him as man to man, and appealed only to the human aspect which I felt would weigh deeply with him.[10]

Smuts told his friend and biographer, Sarah Gertrude Millin: 'I could see Campbell-Bannerman was listening sympathetically. Without being brilliant, he was the sort of sane personality – large-hearted and honest – on whom people depend. He reminded me of Botha. Such men get things done. He told me there was to be a cabinet meeting next day and he said, "Smuts, you have convinced me."'

'That talk,' according to Smuts, 'settled the future of South Africa.'[11]

Campbell-Bannerman had in fact already decided that the Boers should be granted self-government under the British Crown, but his meeting with Smuts must also have dispelled any doubts he had about the loyalty of the

Boers to Britain so soon after the end of the Anglo-Boer War.[12] At his Cabinet meeting the next day, 8 February 1906, the prime minister, in a speech described by Lloyd George as the finest he had heard, persuaded his colleagues to overcome their reservations, trust their former enemies and agree to self-government for the Transvaal.

It fell to Churchill to inform Smuts of the British government's decision to grant self-government to the two former Boer republics:[13]

> You will, I dare say, also have followed the course of affairs in the House of Commons ... From all this, I trust you will have concluded that it is the desire and intention of those who now advise the Sovereign to do their best to strike a fair and just balance between the Dutch and British races in South Africa, to secure either race from danger of oppression by the other, and then, while preserving at all risks and at all costs the authority of the British Crown, to leave South Africa as much master of its own fortunes as the Australian Commonwealth or the Dominion of Canada. If we are enabled to carry this policy to its conclusion, I am not without hopes that the darkest days of South African history may have drawn to their close.[14]

*

In opting for the position of junior minister in the Colonial Office, Churchill had chosen wisely. The secretary of state, Lord Elgin, much older and far less energetic, sat in the House of Lords, which meant that Churchill had to handle colonial matters, particularly South African business, single-handedly in the House of Commons, which gave him much limelight. His Conservative opponents were outraged. Now the truth was out, they cried: the turncoat was exposed 'as a political adventurer who would do anything for his own advancement'.[15]

But Churchill was unfazed. As his son, Randolph, was to write: 'While he was a backbencher, [he] had spoken as if he were an Under-Secretary, now, as an Under-Secretary, as if a member of the Cabinet; and when he reached the Cabinet he was apt to speak as if he were Prime Minister.'[16]

In one way or another, South Africa came to dominate Churchill's first few months in office.[17] The most urgent task, as Smuts had suggested, was the drafting of a new constitution for the Transvaal and Orange River Colony, both of which had been administered after the Boer War by the authoritarian and deeply unpopular Milner. Another awkward matter was the ill-treatment of some 50 000 indentured Chinese labourers on the Witwatersrand mines, an issue that had been exploited to the full by Liberal candidates in the 1906 general election.

In defiance of his instructions by the Tory government, Milner had allowed these imported workers to be subjected to harsh treatment. They were tied in to three-year contracts without being able to see their families and flogged if any rules were broken. Campbell-Bannerman had promised that hiring Chinese workers would be discontinued after the election, but the British population in the Transvaal and the mining houses had persuaded Milner's successor, Lord Selborne, that discontinuing Chinese labour would damage the mining industry and seriously weaken the South African economy. The Liberal government decided nonetheless that the indentured labour system had to be wound down gradually. It was left to Churchill to defend the decision in the Commons but he had to distance himself from his Liberal colleagues' use of the word 'slavery' in the election. 'The Chinese labour system,' he said, was 'an evil inheritance' and had been 'a sordid experiment', but to describe it as slavery, he said, was a 'terminological inexactitude'.[18]

In Parliament, many Liberal politicians were itching to cut the now ennobled Lord Milner down to size. Eight months after returning home, the austere and self-righteous former pro-consul had made his maiden speech in the House of Lords, in which he carefully cultivated 'an aura of non-partisanship'.[19] This was too much for many MPs, one of whom introduced a motion to censure Milner in the Commons. Churchill found himself in a delicate position. Having engaged with the former high commissioner in the past as a Conservative, he now had to concur with his new Liberal colleagues, and the popular press, that Milner's actions on the Rand had been reprehensible.[20] However, as the new colonial undersecretary, it was up to him to defend the Colonial Office's conduct during the war. He told the House that he was obliged to oppose the motion to censure Milner, but used the occasion to make some derogatory comments about the generally well-respected colonial administrator.[21] The remarks that gave particular offence were these:

> Lord Milner has gone from South Africa, probably for ever. The public service knows him no more. Having exercised great authority he now exerts none. Having disposed of events which have shaped the course of history, he is now unable to deflect to the smallest degree the policy of the day. Having been for many years the arbiter of the fortunes of men who are 'rich beyond the dreams of avarice' he is today poor … After twenty years of exhausting service under the Crown he is today a retired Civil Servant, without pension or gratuity of any kind whatever. It is not worthwhile to pursue him any further … Lord Milner has ceased to be a factor in public events.[22]

This outrageously patronising 'defence' of an older and more seasoned politician (whose career of public service was actually by no means over) brought down the wrath of many upon the neophyte undersecretary's head. A distinguished academic spluttered that the speech was a pompous and impertinent effusion from a 'young jackanapes', while King Edward VII described it as 'simply scandalous. It is indeed hard on Milner to be treated in such a manner.'[23] The House of Lords passed a resolution by 170 votes to 35 thanking Milner for his service in South Africa.[24]

Churchill did much better a few months later when he managed to induce Elgin to ditch the Transvaal constitution proposed by his predecessor, Alfred Lyttelton, and by means of an eloquent plea to the Tory opposition, persuade Parliament to pass a new constitution for the Transvaal by a vote of 316 to 83.[25] Addressing the House, he declared:

> With all our majority, we can only make it the gift of a party; they can make it the gift of England. And if that were so … the first real step will be taken to withdraw South African affairs from the arena of British party politics, in which they have inflicted injury on both political parties and in which they have suffered grievous injury themselves.[26]

The issue of the 'native franchise' was not raised by a single member during the debate.

Churchill put the Cabinet's view to King Edward VII in a thirty-five-page, 4 000-word handwritten letter in August 1906: 'As I see South Africa in the years that are immediately to come, it will be racially a piebald country. Dutch and British will have to live side by side.' His Majesty, more concerned that the Boers might win an election and go to war against Britain again, replied to the letter, via his private secretary, with polite scepticism: 'The King still fears however that you are somewhat sanguine in your prognostications.'[27]

In December 1906, the Transvaal was formally granted responsible government, followed a few months later by the Orange River Colony. A joyous Smuts commented incredulously, 'They gave us back – in everything but name – our country. After four years. Has such a miracle of trust and magnanimity ever happened before? The English may make mistakes, but they're a big people.'[28]

Much of the credit, Smuts might have added, was due to the moral support and patient advocacy of Winston Churchill, whose immediate responsibilities for South Africa came to an end little over a year later when he was promoted by Prime Minister Herbert Asquith to the Cabinet as Lloyd George's successor at the Board of Trade.

*

Het Volk (The People) was the political party founded by Smuts and Louis Botha immediately after the Anglo-Boer War for the purpose of bringing Afrikaners and Englishmen together in pursuit of white unification and self-government. In the Transvaal 'independence' election of 1907, Het Volk won an absolute majority over the other parties, whereupon the more easy-going Botha became prime minister and the hard-working Smuts colonial secretary and minister of education, two posts in which he drove himself 'with colossal industry and persuasive tact'.[29] Botha, in particular, was regarded by the British as the personification of reconciliation and cooperation and accordingly invited to attend the Imperial Conference of 1907 in London.[30]

Yet it was Smuts, more than anyone else, who pushed ahead with plans to bring together and unite South Africa's four colonies into one country. In collaboration with the prime minister of the Cape, John X Merriman, he laid plans for (white) delegates from all four colonies to meet at a National Convention, which opened in Durban in 1908 and concluded its deliberations in Bloemfontein in 1909. Among many highly contentious matters debated at the convention, the thorniest was who would be entitled to the vote in the new Union. The convention resolved (or rather evaded) the matter by allowing each colony to retain its existing electoral system: the Cape could keep its limited, non-racial franchise but in the other provinces black people, Coloureds and Indians were excluded from the vote. Ignoring vehement protests, the convention decided nonetheless that a draft South Africa Bill – proposing a Union of the four colonies and supported by most white people – would be taken to London and put before the British Parliament.

Among a large contingent of the great and good who travelled by mail ship to Britain in June 1909 to shape the future of South Africa were Botha and Smuts from the Transvaal, ex-president Steyn from the Free State, Merriman from the Cape, FR Moor from Natal, as well as the chair of the National Convention, Sir Henry (later Lord) de Villiers. Leading a delegation of African and Coloured leaders opposed to the draft Union constitution was the former Cape premier, WP Schreiner, who predicted presciently that the Act of Union would in time become an act of separation between the races of South Africa.[31]

Also on the same ship, not to oppose the granting of Union but to plead the case of Indians in the Transvaal, was a slight figure who had already begun to cast his shadow over the political fortunes of both Smuts and Churchill. His reputation was growing across three continents. His name was Mohandas K Gandhi.[32]

CHAPTER 6

A troublesome saint

The price of greatness is responsibility
— CHURCHILL[1]

Gandhi was born in 1869 in the princely district of Porbandar, in India's Gujarat state, to a well-to-do and politically influential Hindu father and a deeply religious mother. He was married at the age of thirteen to Kasturba, a girl of the same age, who bore him four sons. After schooling in India – the cynosure of Queen Victoria's empire – he took himself off to England to study law for three years before being admitted to the Inner Temple as a barrister in 1891. When once asked what had tempted him to London, the heart of the British Empire and the largest city on the planet, he replied with simple honesty: 'Ambition'.[2]

During his time in London, the youthful Gandhi turned from attempting to be a faux English gentleman and dandy into becoming a serious student of various religions and a keen vegetarian. Returning to Bombay (now Mumbai), he tried, unsuccessfully, to set up a legal practice before answering a call from a prosperous businessman in South Africa to advise him in a forthcoming court case.

Gandhi arrived in Durban by steamship in 1893. By that time, the immigrant Indian population in South Africa had reached sizeable proportions. Indentured Indian labourers had been brought to the British Crown colony of Natal three decades earlier to work on the sugar plantations. Despite having to live in slave-like circumstances, the immigrants settled quickly and before

Mohandas K Gandhi as a young lawyer.

AAI/FOTOSTOCK

long outnumbered the European population of the colony, who viewed with alarm the encroachment of 'coolies' into their residential and commercial areas. Working-class white people were particularly angry at their jobs being taken by cheaper Indian labour.

The largely Hindu population in Natal was supplemented by a further influx of Muslim traders, many of whom soon left the colony for the Transvaal, where the Kruger government was struggling to accommodate the thousands of immigrants from around the world intent on making instant fortunes from the discovery of gold. The Indians were not made welcome in the Boer Republic: an 1885 law debarred them from citizenship and land ownership, and compelled them to pay a registration fee of £3 and have their fingerprints taken if they wished to trade.[3] Many put up with the humiliation because there was money to be made.

Not long after arriving in South Africa, Gandhi was subjected to racial discrimination of the crudest kind. Sent to Pretoria to prepare his court case, he was thrown out of the first-class carriage of a train en route to the Transvaal. Worse was to come when he was forced out of a stage coach in Charlestown, in Natal, and beaten by the driver, then denied a hotel room and a seat in a restaurant, and pushed into a gutter in Pretoria. As one who regarded himself as the equivalent of many whites, if not their superior, Gandhi was deeply offended. Being an educated man from an ancient civilisation, he did not deserve to be treated like an ignorant 'coolie' or a black 'native'.

His mistreatment during his trip to the Transvaal was a turning point in Gandhi's life and kindled his latent interest in social activism. In Hancock's elegant phrasing, 'His white tormentors, if only they knew it, were pushing him into politics, with consequences incalculable for the history of South Africa, of India and the world.'[4]

As Gandhi was about to return home in mid-1894, he was persuaded to stay on to fight a proposal to deny Indians a vote in Natal's Legislative Assembly. He was not to leave South Africa permanently for the next twenty years. Leading the counter-attack against the pending legislation, he busied himself drawing up petitions, making speeches and writing letters to newspapers.[5] To stiffen resistance to the legislation and to arouse popular opinion in Britain and India, in late 1894 he and others founded the Natal Indian Congress, whose membership fee ensured that it was representative of middle-class rather than working-class Indians.[6]

Gandhi's tactics were less radical than imperial, designed to stir up feelings in one part of the British Empire (India) in order to persuade London to bring pressure to bear on another part, i.e. Natal.[7] Going over the head of the Natal legislature and appealing directly to the viceroy in Delhi and the Colonial Office in London, Gandhi was unable to stop the passage of the legislation but succeeded in drawing attention in both countries to the plight of Indians in South Africa. He was also becoming a politician to be reckoned with.

On a voyage home for a brief visit in 1896 to drum up support for his cause from influential members of the Indian National Congress and collect his family, Gandhi wrote a propagandist tract, which became known as the 'Green Book'. In it he described the indignities suffered by 'respectable

Indians' in South Africa, who had to use the same public buildings and lava-tories as Africans, and were routinely insulted and spat at.[8] The pamphlet created a minor sensation in India, delighted Durban's Indians but infuriated Natal's white community.[9]

By now a well-known figure in India, Gandhi returned to South Africa in 1897, to be met on the Durban dockside by a cursing, shouting crowd deter-mined to halt further Indian immigration. He was badly beaten up and fortunate to escape with his life. News of the assault reached the ears of a concerned colonial secretary, Joseph Chamberlain, who ordered the prosecu-tion of those responsible. But Gandhi refused to lay charges: he had come to believe that non-violence was the supreme virtue of the brave and manly, and was determined to dispel the stereotype that his fellow Indians were unmanly and servile.[10] He had also resolved to re-mould his personal life according to the 'rules of chastity, poverty and menial service'.[11]

Another ten years were to go by before Gandhi was ready to apply his famous philosophy of *satyagraha* (or non-violent resistance) to the practice of politics. During this time, he took two hours out of every day to work at a hospital, educate his children, and learn about nursing and midwifery. When the Anglo-Boer War broke out in 1899, he volunteered as a stretcher-bearer. Though instinctively supportive of the Boers' fight for independence, he believed – as a loyal imperialist at that time – that Indians had a duty to support the empire. For their services, he and twenty-seven other Indian volunteers were decorated with the War Medal.[12] When Queen Victoria died in 1901, it was Gandhi who led a crowd of Indian mourners through the streets of Durban.[13]

In 1901 he sailed back to India with his family, having not yet discovered his true vocation in life. For a third time, he attempted to open a law prac-tice in Bombay, but was soon recalled to Natal by the Indian community, who wished him to represent them at a meeting with the visiting colonial secretary, Chamberlain. Failing to elicit much sympathy for his representa-tions from Chamberlain, and finding that the restrictions on Indians in the Transvaal had worsened in his absence, Gandhi resolved to stay and work in Johannesburg, hoping that British rule over the Transvaal after the Anglo-Boer War might lead to an improvement in the treatment of Indians.

He was to be deeply disappointed. Britain's colonial administrators, first Milner and then Selborne, kept the laws against Indian immigration on the statute book and enforced them 'with an efficiency which had never been known in republican times'.[14] A new law, known as the 'Black Act', closed the Transvaal to Indian immigrants, expelled existing 'illegals', enforced fingerprinting and compelled individuals to carry registration papers. The purpose of the act was to restrict any future Indian or Chinese immigration.

Hoping to forestall the need for passive resistance, Gandhi travelled to London in person to put the Indians' case before the new Liberal government, which had come to power in Britain. Many leading members of the Cabinet were known to have an interest in Indian affairs: they included the former viceroy and now colonial secretary, Lord Elgin, and his well-regarded young under-secretary, Winston Churchill.[15]

*

Liberal politicians like Elgin and Churchill were confronted by a classic dilemma: on the one hand, they wished to prevent racial oppression and enhance social justice in South Africa and elsewhere in the empire; on the other, they were respectful of the right to self-determination, especially in the case of the Boers. Also, leading Liberals such as Lloyd George had strongly opposed the Anglo-Boer War and were anxious to make amends for it. One of them was Churchill, though his experiences in South Africa had apparently persuaded him that the Boers had been fighting not so much for freedom as against a British-imposed system of justice that would 'place the native on a level with the white man'.[16] Some careful footwork would be required.

Gandhi's aim in London was to persuade the Colonial Office not to allow the passing of the Black Act. While he accepted the reality of racial prejudice and the need for immigration restrictions, he and his fellow Indians were ready to go to jail rather than be registered and fingerprinted like common criminals.[17] Uppermost in his mind was how respectable and educated citizens of the empire, like himself, could place themselves on the right side of the colour line.[18]

Accompanied by a distinguished group of titled British politicians, he was given a sympathetic hearing by Lord Elgin, who acknowledged that although the Indians had some real grievances, he understood that registration was meant to be for their own benefit. Gandhi disagreed, and expressed his hope that heavy pressure from the British government would dissuade the new Transvaal administration from enacting the ordinance.[19]

Gandhi's meeting with Churchill in 1906 – the one and only time they met – was brief, but cordial. He told the under-secretary that he understood that whites were in control in the Transvaal, but, he said: 'We do feel we are entitled to all the other rights that a British subject might enjoy.'[20] Churchill asked him what would happen if the British government were to refuse to assent to the registration ordinance and then the new Transvaal government went ahead and enacted even more restrictive legislation. Gandhi replied that no law could be worse than the present legislation, and the future could take care of itself.[21] Churchill promised to do what he could, and the two men parted 'on a friendly note'.[22]

On the way home via Madeira, Gandhi learnt with delight that Churchill had announced that the British government would withhold assent to the Black Act. But, on arrival in Johannesburg, he found the mood among Indians to be grim: they pointed out that Churchill had not said that the Crown would block a registration law passed by a *new* Transvaal legislature. And that is what happened on 21 March 1907 when the Black Act passed into law.

Gandhi was furious, and felt he had been tricked in London. But Churchill and his colleagues were in 'an indefensible position'[23] and had taken care not to commit themselves. Three weeks before their meeting with Gandhi, they had concluded that the only way out of the registration predicament was 'to disallow the old law in order to keep up imperial appearances',[24] but not to go back on their undertaking to the Transvaal government that it could make its own laws. To Gandhi, this was 'crooked thinking'; to Churchill and co., it was a sensible compromise.[25]

*

Although, strictly speaking, it was not his responsibility, as colonial secretary of the Transvaal, to implement the new restrictions on Indians (and Chinese), Smuts, as always, was given the government's trickiest problems. One of them was how to handle Gandhi. The little Indian lawyer and activist had decided after his trip to London to make *satyagraha* his 'weapon' of choice against the Transvaal government, so that he could demonstrate his movement's moral strength. Indians should refuse to register and, if arrested, go quietly and peacefully to police stations. He set up picket lines outside registration offices and urged his compatriots not to register. Even though the deadline for registration was twice extended, by the time it expired on 30 November 1907 only about 500 out of 13 000 Indians had submitted registration certificates.[26]

Smuts was uncertain how to react. From London came guidance from Under-Secretary Churchill, via the agent-general, Sir Richard Solomon: 'You have great strength, and I am sure you will use it wisely with every regard for the feelings of these unfortunate Asiatics, keeping only in view the main object of the law, that is to have the Asiatics in the Colony registered in such a way as to prevent evasions of the Immigration Act ...'[27]

Smuts was ready to follow the advice but, in the meantime, the law had to be upheld. He decided to make an example of Gandhi and other leaders, who were ordered to leave the Transvaal within fourteen days, on pain of a prison sentence. By the end of January 1908, Gandhi and more than 150 *satyagrahis* were behind bars.[28]

As prison became a real prospect rather than a theoretical possibility, however, Gandhi's followers began to desert him. A letter Gandhi wrote to Smuts on 28 January 1908 was the prelude to a first meeting between the two men, at which Gandhi promised that in return for the release of all prisoners, Indians would agree to be fingerprinted 'voluntarily', but not in obedience to the law.[29] It was not the fingerprinting itself, but the compulsion that was objectionable, he asserted. After Smuts had agreed to the proposal, Gandhi claimed that since the government had yielded, Indians could now register 'with honour'. Many of his followers were outraged.

When Gandhi led the way to the Johannesburg registration office on 10 February 1908, he was viciously assaulted by two Pathans and so badly hurt that he had to complete his registration and fingerprinting in bed. In

Durban, in March, he was assaulted again and had to be rescued by police. He declined again to prosecute his attackers, but by now his movement had collapsed and his reputation was in tatters.[30] Most Indians in the Transvaal submitted to registration.

Gandhi then claimed, unconvincingly, that Smuts had broken faith with him by not repealing the Black Act, as he had promised to do, but the two men had misunderstood each other and it had been more of a 'promise to consider' on Smuts's part than any firm undertaking. (Twenty years later, Gandhi admitted that it was quite possible that, in behaving towards the Indians in the way he did in 1908, 'General Smuts was not guilty of a deliberate breach of faith'.[31])

Yet the determined Gandhi still felt that Smuts had given him cause to renew the political battle between them. In August 1908 he organised a mass burning of registration certificates outside a Johannesburg mosque. Two months later, he went to prison again, sending out a message to supporters in an Indian newspaper: 'Keep absolutely firm to the end. Suffering is our only remedy. Victory is certain.'[32] After a third prison sentence, of three months, in 1909, a deadlock had been reached. Gandhi could make no further headway with his *satyagraha* campaign, and Smuts would not yield to moral suasion. In despair, the local British India Association decided that Gandhi should make one last personal appeal to the Colonial Office to persuade the Transvaal to amend its Asiatic legislation. In June 1909, he and a colleague were given two first-class passages on the RMS *Kenilworth Castle* to England.[33]

*

Gandhi arrived in London with little hope of success and no idea of what might happen next. Despite the support of two ex-viceroys, lords Ampthill and Curzon, he was unable to persuade the colonial secretary to bring pressure on Smuts, who was in London on an important mission – to negotiate and settle the final details of the legislation that would bring into being the Union of South Africa. As Gandhi had feared, his small voice was drowned 'in the loud roar of British and Boer lions'.[34]

On 27 July, along with the delegation led by WP Schreiner, the former

Cape prime minister (and brother of the author Olive Schreiner), Gandhi listened from the House of Commons' Strangers' Gallery as the South Africa Bill passed through the House of Lords, with only seven peers taking part in the debate.[35] In the Commons a fortnight later, the deputy colonial secretary explained that it had been impossible to find a formula to provide for a uniform franchise in all four South African colonies. If conciliation between the white races were to break down, he claimed, the effect on the indigenous races would be disastrous.[36] Prime Minister Asquith acknowledged 'the absolute unanimity of opinion in the way of regret' about the franchise and other clauses in the bill, but also asserted that white people in South Africa would deal with questions of colour more effectively if they were united rather than divided.[37]

No one mentioned the true reason for government's urgent desire to settle the future of South Africa: war with Germany was looming and the Union would be a key link in the defensive chain that protected Britain and her far-flung Empire.[38] Despite the lobbying efforts of Schreiner's delegation and the vehement protestations of a handful of Labour and Liberal MPs, the South Africa Act was passed unamended by both Houses of Parliament and granted the royal assent in September 1909.

*

By the time Gandhi boarded his ship for the voyage back to Cape Town, he had decided that his battle for Indian rights in South Africa should become part of India's own struggle for independence. 'The centre of gravity is shifting to India,' he wrote to a friend in Johannesburg.[39] With time on his hands, he composed his own personal manifesto, a highly original moral treatise, *Hind Swaraj* (Indian Self-Rule), which guided his actions for the rest of his life. In the words of an American historian, the tract marked the end of a journey that had begun on a rail platform in Natal and reached a decisive turn in his 1906 encounter with Churchill in the Colonial Office: 'In every respect, the work signalled Gandhi's point of no return.'[40] From then on, he made sure he kept in close contact with Indian nationalists, especially the moderate leader, SK Gokhale.

Back in the Transvaal, Gandhi and his much diminished band of *satyagrahis* doggedly kept up their campaign against the Asiatic law. He brought some of them together on Tolstoy Farm, outside Johannesburg, an experiment in simple communal living, which became the base for his activities in South Africa.

Smuts, by now, was becoming adept at finding ways *not* to imprison *satyagrahis* and was seeking a legislative settlement that would be acceptable to Gandhi.[41] The two men met in April 1911 and reached a vague compromise on immigration rules that either could claim was a victory.[42] In January 1912, the Union government promulgated a new bill to limit Asiatic immigration, transfer the regulation of Indian affairs from the provinces to the national government, do away with the Transvaal's Black Act, and 'rationalise and humanise' the regulation of Indians.[43]

Gandhi was still not satisfied. His white opponents were proving too strong, his movement too weak and the mass of Indians too apathetic.[44] He needed a campaign issue that would reignite Indian indignation and found it in the £3 tax imposed in Natal two decades earlier, and a refusal by a Cape court to recognise Indian marriages.[45]

Once again alleging that Smuts had broken a promise – this time to the visiting SK Gokhale to have the £3 tax repealed – Gandhi masterminded a strike by thousands of Indian mineworkers in Newcastle, Natal, many of whom were arrested and brutalised by the police. Gandhi himself was imprisoned but, as he wrote later, 'The Union Government had not the power to keep thousands of innocent men in gaol. The Viceroy would not tolerate it, and all the world was waiting to see what General Smuts would do.'[46]

On 18 December 1913, Smuts announced a commission of inquiry into Indian grievances, and Gandhi was released. He and Smuts met in Cape Town and began to feel each other out about a settlement. Smuts made it clear that he wanted a complete and permanent agreement, while Gandhi consented to call off his *satyagrahis* while the commission was deliberating. For the next two months, the two men kept in close touch with each other and at the end of June they accepted the commission's main recommendations as the basis of a settlement. The Indian Relief Act, which passed quickly through Parliament, put an end to the registration tax and recognised Indian marriages.

Over the protests of some of his followers, Gandhi announced that his settlement with Smuts had satisfied the immediate claims of his *satyagrahis*, but gave notice that there were other objectives to strive for in the future, including franchise rights. With his work in South Africa now at an end, and war clouds gathering over Europe, he set sail via England for India.

After Gandhi had departed, Smuts wrote: 'The saint has left our shores; I sincerely hope for ever.'[47] Yet his dealings with the Indian sage were by no means over, and the unlikely ties the two men had forged during Gandhi's time in South Africa were never finally severed. 'It was my fate to be the protagonist of a man for whom even then I had the highest respect,'[48] Smuts was to reflect many years later.

As Hancock writes, 'Smuts never quite learnt to take Gandhi for granted, nor to disentangle the feelings of fascination, admiration and irritation which Gandhi's words aroused in him at different times.'[49]

CHAPTER 7

Honouring an undertaking

At this moment there arrives in England from the outer marches of the Empire
a new and altogether extraordinary man ... The stormy and hazardous roads
he has travelled by would fill all the acts and scenes of a drama. He has warred
against us – well we knew it. He has quelled rebellion against our own flag with
unswerving loyalty and unfailing shrewdness. He has led raids at desperate odds
and conquered provinces by scientific strategy. His astonishing career and his
versatile achievements are only the index of a profound sagacity and a cool,
far-reaching comprehension ...[1]

– WINSTON CHURCHILL

The author of this rapturous welcome to a former foe, on 17 March 1917, was Winston Churchill the journalist, and the object of his enthusiasm General Jan Smuts, fresh from his exploits as Commander-in-Chief of Imperial Forces in East Africa. Sent by Louis Botha to represent South Africa at the first wartime conference of prime ministers from Britain and the dominions, Smuts had come to London with a sense of relief at being able to escape the acrimony of the Afrikaner Nationalist rebellion against his and Botha's support of Empire since the end of the Anglo-Boer War. Much water had flowed beneath the bridge since he and Churchill had last encountered one another almost a decade previously.

After the establishment of the Union in South Africa in May 1910, Botha and Smuts had aroused admiration in Britain by choosing to honour their international obligations in the face of bitter internal opposition and commit their new country to defending the British Empire. World War I could not have come at a more inopportune time for the two advocates of reconciliation, but Botha nonetheless wrote immediately to the British government to accept responsibility for the security of South Africa, thereby releasing the imperial garrison in the country for duty elsewhere. Smuts, as Minister of Defence, set about building a new military force from scratch.

He had the difficult task of uniting the forces of the two former British colonies and the two Boer Republics into one before the Union Defence Force (UDF), comprising a Permanent Force, an Active Citizen Force and a Naval Reserve, came into being in 1912. Its first test came only two years later, in response to an appeal from Britain for an invasion of neighbouring German South West Africa in order to deny the Germans port facilities at Lüderitzbucht and Swakopmund, and to knock out a wireless transmitter at Windhoek. To build up the UDF's strength, Smuts announced plans to recruit another four regiments of volunteers.

Both Botha and Smuts had mixed feelings about invading German South West Africa. They were well aware of the pro-German sentiments of many of their former comrades in the Boer army. Smuts, especially, had always held Germany in high regard. 'I love German thought and culture and hope it will yet do much for mankind. But a stern limit must be set to her political system, which is a menace to the world even worse than Bonapartism was,'[2] he wrote to an English friend.

Before the UDF could go properly into action, however, the Botha government was faced, in 1914, with an armed revolt of 11 500 Boer War veterans, abetted by none other than the UDF head, General Christiaan Beyers, who resigned his post in order to encourage and join the rebellion. As the responsible minister, Smuts assumed personal command of the UDF and declared martial law. During the uprising, Beyers, as well as Smuts's old wartime mentor, Koos de la Rey, accidentally lost their lives, along with 190 other rebels and 132 government troops. Smuts's reputation among diehard Afrikaners was never to recover.

In February 1915, with a flair for the dramatic that Churchill would have envied, Prime Minister General Botha himself took command of South African forces in South West Africa, mounted on a white charger.[3] Dividing the huge, arid territory of present-day Namibia into two zones, Botha assumed responsibility for the northern zone and put Smuts in charge of operations in the south. Within a few months, the battle was over. Even with the disparity in numbers – only 8 000 of the Kaiser's men against 50 000 South Africans – the campaign to drive the Germans out of their colony was nevertheless remarkable for its swiftness and effectiveness.[4] The German surrender was greeted with wild enthusiasm in sections of the British and South African press, and hailed as the first Allied victory of World War I.

Botha and Smuts returned to South Africa in July 1915 to be welcomed as heroes in the cities, but as 'turncoats' in many rural towns. They received torrents of abuse and threats to their safety from former Boer comrades, many of whom had fallen on hard times. The ensuing (whites-only) general election later that year was notable for the viciousness of the exchanges between the governing South African Party and the Afrikaner Nationalists, led by the redoubtable JBM Hertzog, himself a former Boer general. The election result gave great encouragement to the Hertzogites. Botha and Smuts were able to stay in power only with the help of the pro-British Unionist party, and a few independents. To one hostile audience on the hustings, Smuts declared: 'I would like nothing better than to be out of this hell into which I have wandered, and in which I have lived for the last two years ...'[5]

It was with some relief, therefore, that Smuts accepted an invitation from Britain in early 1916 to assume the rank of lieutenant-general and take command of a polyglot collection of 45 000 imperial troops in German East Africa – 20 000 of them South African. The territory that is Tanzania today was huge, disease-ridden and inhospitable to man and beast, but it was 'the jewel of the German empire',[6] For reasons that had partly to do with keeping UDF volunteers fully occupied, and partly in the hope that it might eventually lead to the extension of South Africa's own territorial borders, Smuts agreed to the assignment, arriving in Mombasa on 19 February 1916. His counterpart on the German side was the formidable and elusive General Paul von Lettow-Vorbeck.

German East Africa was aptly described as a tropical hell-hole. After an early tactical success soon after Smuts's arrival, when his men were able to drive the German Army out of the strategically important Taveta Gap, the gateway to East Africa via the foothills of Kilimanjaro, the imperial forces became bogged down by incessant rainfall, impassable mountain ranges, swollen rivers, trackless forests and impenetrable bush. For every man injured in battle, thirty fell victim to malaria and other diseases, and horses died in their thousands from tsetse-fly infestation. Smuts himself came down with malaria, from which he was never fully to recover for the rest of his life.

Despite these hardships, Smuts managed to keep Von Lettow-Vorbeck constantly on the run, unable to defeat or capture the wily German but successfully gaining control of large swathes of territory and seizing the key rail link between Lake Tanganyika and Dar es Salaam. Although he drove his men hard, Smuts was always in the thick of the action himself, never asking others to do what he was not prepared to do himself. The personal risks he ran and his desire always to see for himself what was holding up the advance led to criticism from some senior officers, who felt he was being unnecessarily reckless. But he rejected the charge, insisting that a commander who played for safety might as well have stayed at home.[7]

By January 1917, even though the war in East Africa had not been won, Smuts had fulfilled his mandate from the British and was looking forward to studying some of the flora and fauna of East Africa in his spare time, when out of the blue came a telegram from Louis Botha asking him to go to London to represent South Africa at the forthcoming Imperial Conference. With some reluctance, he turned over his command to his deputy, General Jaap van Deventer, and returned home to Doornkloof, his farm outside Pretoria, for a 'sort of honeymoon' with Isie. A few days later, he left for London, where he was given an unexpectedly enthusiastic reception.

*

Winston Churchill's fortunes, political and financial, had waxed and waned appreciably over the intervening years. At the Board of Trade, he had turned his attention from colonial to domestic affairs, because, the cynics suggested, social reform offered a quicker route into the Cabinet than colonial administration.[8] But there was no doubting the sincerity with which he and his fellow Liberal Lloyd George proposed legislation to make Britain a fairer and more egalitarian society. Together, the two Liberal politicians formed a formidable political alliance from which much of modern Britain stems.[9] At the age of 35, Churchill was rapidly becoming one of the government's leading lights – to the fury of his erstwhile Conservative colleagues, who accused him of being a traitor to his class.

In 1908 the most important event in Churchill's personal life occurred when he married Clementine Hozier, who was not – unlike several other young women – deterred by his extravagances or devotion to politics. To quote Geoffrey Best, 'Thus began one of the most remarkable marriages of any great man in twentieth-century political public life.'[10] A woman of discernment and common sense, Clementine was able to see her husband as others saw him and to exercise a restraining hand at critical moments. However, as the *Dictionary of National Biography* notes, 'her invariably sound advice was always cheerfully received, yet rarely taken'.[11]

In 1909, Lloyd George's so-called 'People's Budget', which laid the foundations for Britain's welfare state, provoked a constitutional crisis when it was voted down by the Conservative-dominated House of Lords. After the Liberals had narrowly won two rancorous general elections in 1910, Churchill was promoted to Home Secretary, where he took a keen interest in prison reform and policing, and in protecting the British public from any public violence resulting from class-based 'socialism'.

Less than two years later, the growing threat to British naval supremacy from German rearmament, exemplified by the Kaiser's gunboat diplomacy at the Moroccan port of Agadir, prompted Prime Minister Asquith to switch around the Home Secretary and First Lord of the Admiralty. Churchill was given the latter post with a brief to make the fusty Royal Navy – the custodian of imperial power and reach – suitably equipped and battle-ready for any hostilities with Germany. Having once argued forcefully for cutbacks in naval expenditure to fund social reforms, the new First Lord suddenly had to change his tune and become a forceful advocate of military and naval preparedness.

The ever impecunious Churchill accepted his new post with enthusiasm. He was now not only in control of the world's most powerful navy, but also had the use of the stately Admiralty House, overlooking Horse Guards Parade in London, as well as the Royal Navy's 4 000-ton yacht HMS *Enchantress*, with its crew of 196 officers and ratings. Not surprisingly, he spent eight of his thirty-three months at the Admiralty on the yacht, inspecting the fleet at sea.[12]

His appointment as First Lord did not go down well with the navy, however, who resented his past opposition to building more Dreadnought battleships and, more importantly, feared that his arrival heralded radical change. And so it did. It took Churchill just four days to form a naval war staff and not much longer to retire several elderly sea lords and admirals, whose better days were behind them. When an admiral accused the new First Lord of impugning the traditions of the Royal Navy, Churchill replied sarcastically in words he later denied: 'What are the traditions of the Navy? I shall tell you in three words. Rum, Sodomy and the lash.'[13]

Yet he invited criticism by his eagerness to concentrate all possible authority on himself, and especially for deciding to recall into service as First Sea Lord the ageing, aggressive and disruptive Sir John Fisher. Both strong characters who liked getting their own way, Fisher and Churchill together at the Admiralty were to interact like 'two scorpions in a bottle'.[14]

The outbreak of World War I in 1914 led to a lengthy game of cat and mouse at sea between the British and German navies, while on land an armed confrontation along battle lines drawn between France and Germany had begun. By the end of the year, hopes that there might be an early end to hostilities had disappeared. Always thinking ahead strategically, and searching for an alternative 'to chewing barbed wire' on the Western Front,[15] Churchill put forward a plan for a joint military and naval advance through the Dardanelles to Ottoman-held Constantinople, in Turkey. Defeating the Turks would not only remove a strategically important ally of Germany, he argued, but might also encourage Bulgaria, Romania, Greece or Italy to join the war on the Allied side.

The Dardanelles campaign was not Churchill's initiative alone: it was approved by the War Council and endorsed by experienced old hands, including lords Kitchener and Fisher. But the First Lord of the Admiralty was its most enthusiastic and forceful advocate. When the campaign began to go disastrously wrong at Gallipoli because there were too few Allied troops on the ground to counter some unexpectedly stiff resistance from the Turks, the cantankerous Fisher resigned, leaving Churchill to face the political music on his own. He had barely time to replace Fisher before Asquith decided the time had come for a coalition government to direct Britain's conduct of the war. One of conditions laid down by the Tory leader, Bonar Law, however, was that Churchill be removed from the Admiralty forthwith: he had still not been forgiven for his defection to the Liberals a decade earlier.

A devastated and deeply despairing Churchill fought, unavailingly, to stay on at the Admiralty, but was given the sinecure of Chancellor of the Duchy of Lancaster in Asquith's new wartime coalition. A newspaper cartoon depicted him as saying, 'What is a Duchy, and where is Lancaster?'[16] The pundits assumed it to be the end of his political career, but shrewder observers, such as *The Observer*'s editor JL Garvin, thought otherwise. 'He is young. He has lion-hearted courage. No number of enemies can fight down his ability and force. His hour of triumph will come,'[17] Garvin wrote presciently.

After nearly six months of relative idleness in the least important government post, during which he continued nonetheless to produce a series of thoughtful papers on military and political affairs, he resigned from the Cabinet and, as Major Churchill of the Queen's Own Oxfordshire Hussars, took up his commission in the Territorial Force (reserve army) in order to join in the fighting in France. Hoping for command of a brigade, he had to be satisfied with the rank of lieutenant colonel and was put in charge of 6th Battalion Royal Scots Fusiliers, then holding the line at Ploegsteert (known as Plug Street) in Belgium while recovering from awful losses sustained at the Battle of Loos.*

That the new commanding officer was able to escape injury at Plug Street was not because he kept away from the action, but because he was heedless of danger and put into daily practice his preaching that it was pointless to duck when one heard a passing shell or bullet, since if it hadn't already hit you it never would.[18] His constant preoccupation while at the battlefront, nonetheless, remained the conduct of the war itself. In May 1916 the 6th and 7th Battalions of the Royal Scots Fusiliers were amalgamated under a senior officer with a regular commission, and the commander of the 6th Battalion went back permanently to writing and politics.

---

* Churchill arrived to take command of the Royal Scots Fusiliers seated on a black charger. He was accompanied by his second-in-command, Archie Sinclair, a pair of mounted grooms and a large pile of luggage above regulation weight, which included a full-length bath and a boiler for heating the water.

Churchill could not realistically hope to return to the centre of British politi-cal life until an official inquiry into the failure of the Dardanelles campaign had either vindicated him personally or distributed responsibility for the debacle more fairly. By early 1917, Asquith had resigned and Lloyd George was prime minister and head of a reconstituted coalition. The new war leader would have liked to restore Churchill, by far the best-qualified politician in military mat-ters, to the Cabinet, but the Conservatives would still not hear of it. When the Dardanelles report came out, however, it found fault with Asquith and Kitchener's conduct in the campaign, and exonerated the First Lord of the Admiralty of the charge that he had acted impetuously and on his own.[19]

The way was now open for Churchill's return to high office and Lloyd George duly appointed him to the key post of Minister of Munitions in July 1917. His old newspaper, the staunchly Conservative *Morning Post*, com-mented sourly that 'although we have not yet invented the unsinkable ship, we have discovered the unsinkable politician'.[20]

Strongly supporting Churchill's appointment as Munitions minister was one of the most well-regarded members of the British War Cabinet – Jan Smuts.[21]

CHAPTER 8

In the War Cabinet

War is too serious a business to be entrusted to soldiers.

— ARISTIDE BRIAND[1]

Smuts had arrived in England in March 1917, at a time when British morale was at its lowest ebb. Many thousands of young men had lost their lives on the Western Front, food was in short supply as a result of U-boat attacks on shipping, while across the Channel the French army had fallen to pieces. In Russia, the Tsar and his family had been murdered and his demoralised troops were about to desert the Allies.

Britain was sorely in need of uplifting news and it fell to the unsuspecting visitor from Africa to provide it. Smuts was hailed on all sides as 'the hero of the hour',[2] a former foe of the Empire turned friend, a beacon in the gloom. One overexcited commentator described him as having 'a remarkable collection of talents not usually found in the same person, unless, indeed, that person belongs to the small select class of which the Caesars and Cromwells and the Napoleons are the outstanding types'.[3] Academic honours, invitations and the freedom of cities were showered upon him. Protesting that he was only 'a simple Boer', Smuts sought to escape the adulation by retreating from his suite at the Savoy Hotel into the countryside at weekends to visit old, mostly Quaker, friends.

Only three days after Smuts's arrival in London, Lloyd George introduced him to members of the Imperial War Cabinet (the empire's war coordinating body, comprising Britain's own War Cabinet plus the visiting dominion prime ministers) as 'one of the most brilliant generals in this war'[4]. The premier was later to describe Smuts in his memoirs as 'the gifted and versatile Dutchman, who could be safely trusted to examine into the intricacies of any of our multifarious problems and unravel and smooth them out'.[5] Churchill, writing for a newspaper, proposed that Smuts be taken into the British War Cabinet without delay, remarking to a friend, Lord Riddell, that he was 'the only unwounded statesman of outstanding ability in the Empire'.[6]

Lloyd George wasted little time before sending Smuts to the Western Front in France and Belgium to assess the military situation at first hand. The visitor's wide-ranging survey of the war so impressed the prime minister that he prevailed upon Smuts to remain in England after the Imperial Conference to serve as the seventh member of the British War Cabinet. As minister without portfolio, South Africa's Minister of Defence joined Britain's supreme military decision-making body 'on loan', but drew no pay from His Majesty's Government.

Smuts's role while in Britain, as Hancock points out, combined three elements: strategic decision making, war organisation and preparation for the post-war peace.[7] His work as a war organiser included the key task of combining the army and navy's separate air arms into one service – the Royal Air Force (RAF). He was also called upon to reassert government control over all industrial production in Britain. It was the hardest he had worked in his life and he felt the strain, confessing to his wife, 'I long much for you and I am really tired of this country and all its trouble. I feel like Odysseus on Calypso's island and look constantly in the direction of the far south where my heart is and is always drawn.'[8]

*

The person who had first recognised the potential of air power was not Smuts, however, but Churchill. As early as 1909, while at the Board of Trade, Churchill had foreseen that aviation would become the most significant factor in wartime and suggested to the Cabinet that 'we should place ourselves in communication with Mr [Orville] Wright and avail ourselves of his knowledge'.[9] At the Admiralty, he founded the Royal Naval Air Service to provide protection for naval harbours, oil depots and other key installations. To his family's alarm, he even took to the air himself with enthusiasm, proving too

The Imperial War Conference, London, 1917.
Smuts is seated in the front row, third from the left.

CENTRAL ARCHIVES REPOSITORY

impatient, however, to be a good pupil but often flying as many as ten times a day. As William Manchester writes, 'It is astonishing to reflect that Churchill was flying over Kent before the young RAF pilots who won the Battle of Britain [in World War II] were born.'[10]

In July 1917, the War Cabinet, worried about the damage being inflicted on south-east England by German Zeppelins, deputed the prime minister and Smuts to examine home defences against air raids and propose ways of coordinating aerial operations. Lloyd George was too busy with other matters and left the task to Smuts. Within two weeks, the newest member of the Cabinet had produced a report on Britain's alarming unreadiness to defend itself against aerial attack, and put forward proposals for the urgent restructuring of air-defence units.[11] In another report, Smuts predicted that air operations might soon become the most decisive aspect of warfare, more important even than army and naval operations. Unless Britain established a central authority to 'command and control' air services, he warned, the country faced the prospect of losing the battle in the air.[12]

The task of welding the air arms of the British Army and Navy into one would have daunted most men, but not Smuts. As chairman of the Air Organisation

Committee, he had to placate, and sometimes override, a bevy of hypersensitive, turf-conscious generals and admirals in order to create a new fighting entity. As Lloyd George was to acknowledge later in his war memoirs, Smuts, more than anyone else, had the right to be called the 'father of the RAF'[13] – a claim that might be disputed by admirers of Sir Hugh (later Viscount) Trenchard, the first Marshal of the RAF.

Impressed by his exceptional administrative abilities and capacity for hard work, the War Cabinet also called upon Smuts to chair the War Priorities Committee (WPC). As an 'outsider' to Britain, he had been struck by how a lack of coordination between the armed services and industry, as well as petty interdepartmental rivalries, were hampering the production of war materiel. He recommended to the Cabinet a series of measures to eliminate overlapping and inefficiencies. As the only Cabinet member on the WPC, he presided over a group that included, among others, the newly appointed Minister of Munitions, Winston Churchill. According to Richard Toye, Smuts gave Churchill some tactfully phrased advice about not making enemies among his colleagues: 'Now that you are well in the saddle … you must not ride too far ahead of your more slow-going friends.'[14] It was the first time the two men had worked closely together and, as Smuts's son noted, it was 'the start of a long and great friendship'.[15]

The burden of work and mental strain from having to resolve differences between heavily entrenched interests would have taxed any lesser man, but Smuts never wavered or complained. As Churchill was to record later in *The Great War*, 'On [the WPC] the Departments fought and tore for every ton of steel and freight. Never, I suspect, in all the vicissitudes of his career, has General Smuts stood more in need of those qualities of tact and adroitness for which among his many virtues he is renowned.'[16]

Churchill's own responsibilities as Minister of Munitions were immense. He had to coordinate the activities of some five million people producing the huge quantities of ammunition, bombs, torpedoes and equipment needed by Britain's military machine.[17] In an obituary many years later, *The Times* commented, 'No episode in the whole of Churchill's career is so eloquent of his exceptional capacity as a departmental head than the success with which he imposed unity and order on this vast organisation and established himself as the source and controller of its multitudinous activities.'[18]

By improvising boldly, he managed to trim an overstaffed ministry of fifty separate departments employing 12 000 people into twelve departments employing far fewer. Though chafing at not being a member of the War Cabinet himself, in his spare moments Churchill immersed himself, typically, in many aspects of the war beyond his remit and produced a series of useful memoranda for Lloyd George on how the battle could and should be fought more effectively.

As in the Boer War, Churchill's experiences in the field in France made him much more sensitive than most politicians to the hardships experienced by the soldiers in the trenches. He told MPs:

> I say to myself every day, 'What is going on while we sit here, while we go away to dinner or home to bed?' Nearly 1 000 men, Britishers – men of our own race – are knocked into bundles of bloody rags every twenty-four hours, and carried away to hasty graves or to field ambulances.[19]

*

When, on 11 November 1918, World War I came to an abrupt end, Churchill was in a much more positive frame of mind than Smuts, who feared that although the Allies might have won the war, they were about to squander the peace. Despite a serious deterioration in his personal finances as a result of having to forgo any earnings from journalism[20] (which he tried to remedy by investing in South African gold shares), Britain's Minister of Munitions had restored his political fortunes by having made a notable contribution to the victory over Germany. His relationship with Lloyd George had remained close and he could look forward to high office in the Cabinet once again.

After the fighting in Europe was over, Churchill reflected deeply on the lessons to be learnt from the conflict, lamenting the military strategy that had squandered Britain's lifeblood so needlessly in pursuit of the near fanatical idea that 'the last man standing in France would be declared the winner'.[21] It convinced him that in any future war no admirals, generals or air marshals should be trusted to run their own operations beyond the oversight and control of the Cabinet.[22]

In December 1918, immediately after the armistice, Britain held her second 'Khaki' election of the century to decide whether to keep the wartime coalition in office or revert to party rule. Churchill was a leading advocate for maintaining the coalition but found himself to be one of the few members of the government who opposed the harsh treatment of Germany.[23] As he'd done during and after the Boer War, Churchill pleaded in the election campaign for magnanimity to be shown to the defeated enemy. He told his constituents that the Germans must be 'clothed, sheltered and fed', and argued that the Allies 'ought not to be drawn into extravagances by the fullness of their victory'.[24]

This was not a message the citizens of Dundee, which had lost 6 000 men in the war, wanted to hear, but they and the rest of the electorate nonetheless put Lloyd George's coalition, and their own MP, back in power by a comfortable majority. The prime minister promptly restored the former Minister of Munitions to the Cabinet in the dual post of Secretary for War and for Air, where his primary responsibility was to demobilise the impatient, near mutinous armed forces, many of them ordinary civilians intent on being discharged immediately from military service.[25]

Within a few weeks, Churchill had orchestrated the repatriation of a million soldiers, and inside eight months had reduced Britain's military expenditure by 70 per cent.[26] Politically, he had never lost his belief in the importance of free trade but had become, by now, a natural middle-roader and supporter of coalition government. His pet aversions were still workers' strikes, which damaged the public interest, and the socialist policies of the Labour Party, which he opposed for liberal rather than any class-based reasons.[27]

*

With his customary foresight, Smuts had spent the final months of the war agonising about the difficulties of the coming peace. In January 1918, he drafted a speech for Lloyd George, in which the prime minister proclaimed, 'in the language of moral and political principle',[28] that Britain's war aims were based upon achieving justice for those who had suffered, rather than a desire for vengeance. Lloyd George's speech was echoed only days later by the US president, Woodrow Wilson, whose 'fourteen points' upon which the peace treaty should be based reflected similarly high-minded – but ultimately unrealisable – sentiments.

Deeply concerned that the fighting in Europe might spread to other continents, Smuts pleaded publicly, in a speech of his own in Glasgow shortly before the war ended, for a 'decent' peace: 'I don't think an out-and out victory is possible for any group of nations in this war because it will mean an interminable campaign. It will mean that decimated nations will be called upon to wage war for many years to come and what would the results be?' he asked rhetorically.[29] He continued:

> When this great nation made its great choice in August 1914, it went into the war as a war of defence, of defence of the liberties of mankind, of the rights of small nations … that is what we are out for. That is our idea of victory … We are not out to smash any country or Government. We are not making this war drag on endlessly in order to attain some impossible victory. We have a limited object …[30]

In December 1918, Smuts put a state paper before the Imperial War Cabinet, which Lloyd George described as one of the most 'able' he had ever read.[31] Published later as 'The League of Nations, a practical suggestion', it proposed that the British Commonwealth be regarded as a model for a new international organisation, based on the 'true principles of national freedom and political decentralisation', that would prevent future wars and advance world peace.[32] The Cabinet decided to present the document to the American president as an expression of Britain's views. Wilson was captivated by it ('He swallowed it whole,' said Lloyd George[33]) and rewrote his own draft of the Covenant of the League to incorporate most of Smuts's proposals.[34]

*

At the Paris Peace Conference, where Smuts was one of South Africa's two official representatives alongside Louis Botha, he continued to press his case for a generosity of spirit towards the Germans. He laboured long and hard to persuade President Wilson and the other Allied leaders – the French prime minister, Georges Clémenceau, Lloyd George, and the Italian prime minister, Vittorio Emanuele Orlando – that imposing crippling reparations on Germany would deepen rather than reduce economic misery throughout Europe. The eventual terms of the peace treaty were harsh, nevertheless: Germany was to give up much of its territory as well as its colonies. Its army and navy were reduced in size and it was not permitted an air force.

Smuts's concerns were shared by Churchill (who was not an official delegate to the Paris conference but had been brought into discussions over the terms of the treaty) as well as by British economist John Maynard Keynes. The latter, with Smuts's active encouragement, wrote his devastating critique of the settlement terms, *The Economic Consequences of the Peace*.

Like Smuts and Keynes, Churchill was unable to persuade Lloyd George, who was by now more vengeful and had the angry mood of the electorate to consider, to moderate Britain's demands for retribution. Clémenceau, the French war leader, was even more intractable. In Britain and France, there were populist cries of 'Hang the Kaiser' and 'Squeeze them [the Germans] until the pips squeak'.[35] If Smuts and Wilson regarded the overriding purpose of the peace conference as being to lay the foundations of the League of Nations rather than bring Germany to its knees, Europe's Allied leaders thought differently.

Churchill had set out his own arguments for opposing over-harsh penalties on Germany in a Sunday newspaper article, in which he wrote:

> The reconstruction of the economic life of Germany is essential to our own peace and prosperity. We do not want a land of broken, scheming, disbanded armies, putting their hand to the sword because they cannot find the spade or the hammer. The power of Britain to guide Germany into a safe channel of development and pacific recovery is considerable. We do not know how great is our power for good these days. It is a considerable opportunity in our hands. Do not let us miss it. Our safety depends on it.[36]

But Churchill had another overriding reason for not weakening the defeated enemy too much. Germany and its army, or what was left of it, might soon be needed as a bulwark against a far more dangerous menace – the spread of Bolshevist collectivism across a badly damaged Europe. As a true libertarian, Churchill had a hatred of the Soviet system even more deeply rooted than his future dislike of Nazism. For the rest of his days, a detestation of Communism was always central to his outlook and political beliefs.[37]

With the war over, Churchill replied to a personal letter from Smuts in tones whose warmth was evidence of their growing relationship:

> I have been keeping your letter by me in my boxes for an opportunity to tell you how deeply I value it. All the many kindnesses and services you rendered to me in the stormy ups and downs of the great struggle have made a lasting impression on my mind. I can never forget your sympathy and comradeship. We shall always look back upon those fierce crowded days and in them I shall always see your friendship and courage and wise counsel.[38]

*

No sooner had Germany capitulated than Smuts resigned from the British War Cabinet. Having eventually signed the Peace Treaty at Versailles with extreme reluctance and against his better judgement because of the harsh terms forced upon the Germans, he said his farewells in London and left to join his wife and family, and an ailing Louis Botha, at home. Not long after his arrival in Cape Town, on 27 August 1919, his 'closest colleague and dearest friend' Botha died from heart disease. Among the many private letters of sympathy Smuts received, one of the most heartfelt was from Churchill:

> Botha came to see me here before he sailed, and I did what I have so far done for no other visitor – escorted him downstairs and put him into his carriage myself. Almost immediately after (as it seemed) while the impression of his presence was strong within me I learned that he has gone. I know what a loss this will be to you, and believe me I felt a keen personal pang as if someone I had known all my life had passed away. He was one of the truly great men of the world, and, thank God, of the British Empire.[39]

CHAPTER 9

Out of favour

Success is the ability to go from one failure to another
with no loss of enthusiasm.
— CHURCHILL[1]

Throughout the 1920s, Churchill and Smuts kept in regular, though distant, touch with each other. In South Africa, Smuts, now the prime minister, found himself under heavy personal attack for the problems that inevitably arise in the aftermath of any war – spiralling food prices, economic hardship and general disillusionment with the government of the day, especially one that had been in power for ten years. Pro-republican Afrikaners never ceased to berate Smuts for his support of the British Empire, accusing him of conspiring with Milner to impede independence for South Africa.[2]

On the Rand, there was turmoil as white miners resisted attempts by mine owners to reduce labour costs by employing black workers instead of whites. Black miners, in turn, resented being paid less than their white counterparts and frequently resorted to strikes. In the general election of 1920, Smuts's South African Party was dealt a debilitating blow when it won only forty-one seats against Hertzog's Nationalists' forty-four. Only by joining forces with Sir Thomas Smartt's Unionists – the party of the despised Rhodes, Jameson and the mining magnates – was the South African Party able to govern, with a minuscule four-seat majority in Parliament.

Churchill's fortunes, by contrast, were on the rise again after the end of World War I. By now he had become known as a first-class parliamentarian, author, journalist and orator, a personality as familiar to the British public as anyone besides the prime minister. The turbulence and novelty of the post-war political climate seemed to draw out the best, and occasionally the worst, in him.[3] He was still distrusted, though – not only by many Conservatives, but also to a growing extent by his once-close colleague, Lloyd George. The coalition leader was on record as saying that his mercurial colleague was more of a weakness to the government than a strength, that he was 'like the counsel a solicitor employs not because he is the best man, but because he would be dangerous on the other side'.[4]

One reason for the widening rift between the two Liberals was their diverging responses to the threat of Bolshevism (as Russian Communism was then known). As War Minister, Churchill was keen to intervene in Russia, to which Britain had committed thousands of troops after the fall of the Tsarist government to prevent war supplies from falling into German hands. After the armistice, the Allies had become embroiled in the civil war between anti-Bolshevik White Russians and the Bolshevist Reds. Neither Lloyd George nor Churchill wanted to risk outright war with the Bolsheviks, but Churchill was keen on arming the Whites, whereas the prime minister thought that cash-strapped Britain's millions would be better spent at home. Lloyd George warned Churchill, who routinely denounced Communism as a 'dangerous and contagious virus', that he had become obsessed by the matter of Russia: '… If you will forgive me for saying so, [it] is upsetting your balance,' Lloyd George told him.[5] Churchill countered by saying that he would 'not submit to being beaten by baboons'.[6] In the end, he had to bow to the inevitable and concede defeat over Russia, which he did with much reluctance.

Although the prime minister and war minister were gradually drifting apart, Lloyd George continued to rely heavily upon Churchill. He trans-ferred him once again to the Colonial Office, in early 1921, to frame policies to deal with Britain's growing difficulties in the Middle East and Ireland, and to resume responsibility for relations with the dominions.

*

In South Africa, notwithstanding its slender hold on power, the Smuts government managed to enact a wide range of economic, industrial, agricultural and social reforms, including legislation for black local councils – a tentative step forward immediately rejected by those affected because they had not been consulted. Afrikaners, for their part, made attempts to bring about *hereniging* (reunification) between their warring factions. Smuts himself declined to attend any of these get-togethers, believing they were aimed at bringing about South Africa's withdrawal from the empire. He concentrated instead on wooing the Unionists, who were sufficiently alarmed at the upsurge of Afrikaner nationalism to agree to join forces with the much larger South African Party.

Encouraged by the successful merger and sensing a reduction in popular support for the Labour Party, Hertzog's parliamentary ally, as news of the Bolshevik atrocities in Russia became more widely known Smuts called another general election in early 1921. This time, the South African Party won seventy-nine seats to the Nationalists' forty-five and Labour's nine, giving the prime minister a comfortable majority of twenty-four. The South African Party's win was hailed throughout the empire as a significant victory for imperialism over inward-looking nationalism. As events were to prove, it was nothing of the kind.

Contrary to the fears of his Nationalist opponents, who claimed that South Africa was becoming ever more closely tied to Empire, Smuts used the Imperial Conference of 1921 to argue for complete freedom from and equality with Britain and her dominions. He was as demanding as any Hertzogite on the issue of South Africa's right to make decisions for itself, but insisted that the country would exercise its influence in the world only in concert with other members of the League of Nations and the British Commonwealth.[7] His opponents continued tirelessly to assert that any consultation with Britain and the dominions implied a diminution of South Africa's sovereignty.

At the Imperial Conference, Smuts found himself under attack from Indian delegates, who insisted that South African Indians should be afforded full citizenship rights.[8] Although his regard for Indians had risen appreciably following their brave contribution to the Allied cause in World War I, he was unwilling to alter his stance on Indian immigration and political representation. He told the conference:

76

Whatever may be the position in the British Empire as a whole, in South Africa we are not based on a system of political equality. The whole basis of our particular system ... rests on inequality and on recognising fundamental differences which exist in the structure of our population ... We have never in our laws recognised any system of equality. It is the bedrock of our constitution ... You cannot give political rights to the Indians which you deny to the rest of the coloured citizens in South Africa.[9]

Such frankness was met with unease by some delegates, but to Smuts's rescue came the colonial secretary himself. In typically forthright fashion, Churchill declared that it would be 'affectation and humbug' to pretend there would be no great changes in the law of Britain if hundreds of thousands of Indians or perhaps millions were to enter the country to compete with the working and clerical classes. He, for one, understood South Africa's position.[10] And that, for the duration of the conference, was that.

An accord – known afterwards as the Smuts-Churchill Agreement – between the South African premier and the colonial secretary transferred responsibility for the land defences of the Admiralty's strategically important naval base at Simonstown to the Union government, subject to the Royal Navy's right as perpetual user. South Africa agreed to keep the naval station in such a state of defence that it would at all times be able to carry out its functions as 'a naval link in the sea communications of the British Empire'.[11] The agreement was to assume a greater importance in the significant 'neutrality or war' debate in the South African Parliament in 1939.

After heeding one further request from Lloyd George, this time to intervene in the impasse in Ireland, Smuts returned from Britain to find his country in deep economic distress. Early in 1922, violence erupted across the Rand as the Chamber of Mines and the trade unions squared up over job losses and reductions in workers' pay packets. At first Smuts declined to intervene, but when a radical group brought workers out on strike and three miners were shot dead in Boksburg, on the East Rand, he declared martial law and called up Citizen Force commandos to help quell the unrest, and restore law and order.

After reporting hurriedly to Parliament in Cape Town, he rushed back to the heart of the conflict in Johannesburg, where he was driven into the city centre amid a hail of bullets. Next day, he ordered the 20 000-strong security forces into action to crush an insurrection in which 210 people died and 534 were injured. Smuts's tough-minded crackdown may have quelled an incipient revolution, but it drove the Labour Party deeper into the arms of the Afrikaner Nationalists and engendered lingering feelings of bitterness, which was to result in the South African Party's loss of power in 1924.

When news of Smuts's narrow escape on the streets of Johannesburg reached London, a concerned Winston Churchill sent him the following telegram: 'Warmest congratulations your escape. Urge you to take greatest care of yourself. Your life is invaluable [to] South Africa and the British Empire.'[12]

*

Smuts had always hoped to incorporate Southern Rhodesia into the Union of South Africa.[13] If he could bring in the Rhodesians, he thought, he might be able to do the same in Mozambique, Northern Rhodesia and possibly East Africa, thereby extending white settlement across the subcontinent. The Nationalist opposition accused him, not without reason, of wishing to create a much larger English-speaking electorate. In July 1922, Smuts announced the terms on which his government would offer Southern Rhodesia the opportunity to become the fifth province of South Africa, promising financial support, improved transport and trading links, and a secure future within a much larger and stronger entity.

His plans were subverted, unintentionally, by none other than the colonial secretary, Churchill, who had previously appointed a committee under Lord Buxton to consider the future of Southern Rhodesia. The committee had recommended that the country be given self-government if a majority of white citizens voted for it at a referendum. Given the choice between self-rule and joining an Afrikaner-led South Africa, 22 000 white Rhodesians opted by a majority of 3 000 to determine their own future as a self-governing colony.[14] Smuts claimed that their decision was not final and protested afterwards to the Tory leader, Bonar Law, that if only Churchill had not seen fit to offer the Rhodesians self-government, they would have already been part of the Union. When it became obvious that this would never happen, a disappointed Smuts predicted, presciently, that a Southern Rhodesia on its own would become an embarrassment to future British governments.

*

Britain's economic difficulties in 1922 and Lloyd George's inability to alleviate them brought about an erosion of confidence in his coalition, especially from the more numerous Conservative MPs, upon whose support the Liberal prime minister depended. Fearing an upsurge in Labour Party votes, the Tories deserted the coalition in October, forcing a general election on 15 November, in which they were returned to power under the leadership of Bonar Law.

By now Churchill's seat in the industrial city of Dundee had become a worker stronghold and his re-election became even more unlikely when he was unable to take to the hustings because of an operation for appendicitis, a more serious medical procedure then than it is today. The ailing member for Dundee was forced to send his wife, Clementine, who had just given birth to their fourth child, to campaign on his behalf. To his disgust, she had to endure much vilification and abuse from working women in the constituency.

The Liberal Party, of which Churchill had become a dissident member, came a poor third in the 1922 poll, behind the Conservatives and the rapidly rising Labour Party, and the sitting member was heavily defeated in Dundee. At the age of 48, and for the first time in twenty-two years, Churchill was no longer in the House of Commons. As he reflected ruefully later, he was 'without an office, without a seat, without a party, and without an appendix'. Conservative newspapers crowed at his departure, but *The Daily Telegraph*, though not an admirer of his, recorded that 'the House of Commons [had lost], for a time, its most brilliant and dazzling speaker. His is perhaps the most sensational defeat of the whole election.'[15]

Among the many letters of condolence Churchill received after his defeat was one from Smuts:

> My dear Churchill, First the news of your serious illness and then the news of your defeat at Dundee have come as great shocks to your friends in South Africa. I am really sorry, whatever view you may take of the

defeat. But perhaps it is as well that you get a short spell of rest after the very heavy labours you have had to bear recently. I trust you will soon be all right and all the better to do the great work which is still before you.[16]

*

Churchill was not to regain a seat in Parliament for two years. The time for a government of national unity in Britain was over and party politics had come into its own again. The 1922 election had weakened both Conservatives and Liberals as the Labour Party had made gains, posing a dilemma for the dissident former Liberal MP. He no longer felt at home in either of his two old parties but instinctively feared the effects of the Labour Party's socialism. He pondered whether he could change allegiance once more. As he confided to a friend, 'Anyone can rat, but it takes a certain amount of ingenuity to re-rat.'[17]

He postponed a resolution to his dilemma by wintering on the French Riviera, where he devoted most of his time to painting and writing. In January 1923, he published the first volume of *The World Crisis*, which he described as 'a contribution to history ... strung upon a fairly strong thread of personal reminiscence'.[18] Volume two appeared only a few months later. The five-volume book (completed only in 1931) was serialised in newspapers at home and abroad, and earned the author a large sum of money, which he used to pay for extensions to his newly acquired country estate, Chartwell, in rural Kent. Former prime minister Arthur Balfour, writing to a friend, waspishly described *The World Crisis* as 'Winston's brilliant autobiography, disguised as a history of the universe'.[19] The book helped, nonetheless, to make the usually impecunious Churchill the highest paid English author of his day.[20]

The World Crisis contained a photograph and an illustration of Smuts, who was described by Churchill as having

> lent incalculable aid to the cause of the Allies, both in connection with
> the conquest of German South West Africa and German East Africa and
> at the council table in London and in Paris. Years must elapse before any
> adequate appreciation of this great and loyal South African can be made.

It may be said that he was a tower of strength to the Allied cause during many a dark hour.[21]

The author sent a copy of his new book to Smuts, with an accompanying letter:

My dear Smuts, I never answered your very kind letter to me when I left office. But I have been looking forward ever since to sending you a copy of my new book about the opening phase of the war. I dwell a good deal in those dazzling, terrible times and I like to think of how we were together in so many important things. As Botha said to my Mother in Westminster Hall in 1907, we have been out in all weathers.

Your friendship is always much cherished by me.[22]

To this Smuts responded with flattery:

My dear Churchill, Thank you very much for your last letter and the most acceptable gift of your Book. I have read the Book with the deepest interest. It is indeed a very brilliant affair and its subject will remain one of the greatest of all time. I envy you the great gift of being a man of action and a great writer at the same time. Julius Caesar was that rare combination. And although you are not as Francophobe as he was, your book will stand comparison with *The Gallic War*.[23]

*

In Britain, Bonar Law's new Conservative government did not last long and in May 1923 Law resigned, to be succeeded by Stanley Baldwin. In an attempt to reduce unemployment, Baldwin decided to impose tariffs on manufactured imports – the very issue over which Churchill had deserted the Tories more than a decade and a half ago. Denouncing Baldwin's policy as a 'monstrous fallacy',[24] Churchill stood for the Liberals once more, but lost to Labour in a by-election in Leicester.

In November 1923, the British Parliament was dissolved again and in the ensuing election the Conservatives, though returning as the largest party, lost their overall majority in the House. Ignoring the pleas of Churchill in particular for Liberals to support the Conservatives in order to keep out Labour, Liberal and Labour MPs joined forces to defeat the Conservatives in the Commons. Baldwin promptly resigned and Labour came to power for the first time, with Liberal support in Parliament. The new government was headed by Ramsay MacDonald, whom Churchill described as a man 'with the gift of compressing the largest number of words into the smallest amount of thought'.[25] Severing his links with the Liberals, a resolute Churchill now put himself forward at another by-election, this time in London's Westminster district, as an Independent Anti-Socialist. For the third time he was defeated, but by fewer than fifty votes only.

MacDonald's marriage of convenience between Labour and Liberals lasted a mere eight months, when there was yet another general election. This time, Bolshevism was the cause. MacDonald had recognised Lenin's regime and lent it money, which prompted the Liberals to withdraw their parliamentary support for Labour.[26] By now, Baldwin had dropped his policy of protectionism, removing Churchill's last reason for not rejoining the Conservatives. He therefore offered himself as a 'Constitutionalist' candidate in the Conservative stronghold of Epping, promising his 'whole support to the Conservative Party'.[27] The Tories chose not to oppose him and he won the seat comfortably with a majority of nearly 10 000. He was to remain MP for the renamed constituency for the next forty years.

The election of October 1924 resulted in an overwhelming victory for Baldwin's Tories. The new prime minister, unlike Bonar Law, decided it would be better to have the indefatigable Churchill inside his tent, rather than outside. Much to the latter's surprise, despite having switched parties for the second time, he was offered the highest of Cabinet positions in Baldwin's new government – Chancellor of the Exchequer. When asked by the prime minister whether he would accept the chancellorship, an emotionally overcome Churchill was tempted to reply, 'Will the bloody duck swim?' Instead, as it was a formal occasion, he replied, 'This fulfils my ambition. I still have my father's robes as Chancellor. I shall be proud to serve you in this splendid Office.'[28]

Many of Baldwin's senior colleagues were seriously displeased by his choice of chancellor, however. In a letter to his wife, the First Lord of the Admiralty, Sir William Bridgeman, wrote: 'I'm afraid that turbulent, pushing busybody Winston is going to split the party. I can't understand how anybody can want him or put any faith in a man who changes sides just when he thinks it is to his own personal advantage to do so.'[29]

Meanwhile, the Liberal-supporting *Guardian* newspaper commented disapprovingly that 'Mr Churchill for the second time has – shall we say? – quitted the sinking ship and for the second time the reward of this fine instinct has been not safety only but high promotion.'[30]

CHAPTER 10

Outside interests

A man is not defeated by his opponents but by himself.
— SMUTS[1]

While Churchill was in the throes of fighting for re-election to Parliament, Smuts attended his last Imperial Conference, in October 1923. Earlier in the year, Germany had defaulted on its reparation payments, causing France to invade the Ruhr Valley in retaliation.

Perhaps sensing that power was slipping from his grasp, Smuts used the opportunity to speak his mind on international issues, in particular what he deemed to be France's illegal occupation of its neighbour and the punishing reparation payments imposed upon Germany after the war. In a headline-making address to an audience in London, he declared: 'Four or five years ago, we were singing our own songs of victory; today we are all marching to certain and inevitable defeat – victor and vanquished.'[2]

The war in Europe, Smuts asserted, had been transferred from the military to the economic sphere. The invasion of the Ruhr was not only an act of economic and political folly, it was contrary to the Treaty of Versailles and therefore illegal. Although he sympathised with France, 'you cannot be a patriotic Frenchman unless you are also a good European,'[3] he said. The time had come, he suggested, for a convocation of powers interested in the repayment of reparations.[4]

The French were incandescent with fury. Who was Smuts, they asked, to tell them how to become patriotic and good Europeans?[5] Yet his proposal for a conference was greeted with warm approval by the German chancellor, Gustav Stresemann, who invited him to visit Germany. The influential American financier Bernard Baruch told Smuts his words had also made a 'profound impression' in the US.[6] Within months the Dawes Plan had been drawn up, recommending an end to the occupation of the Ruhr and a staggered schedule for German reparation payments.

The Imperial Conference provided the Indians with another chance to tackle Britain on the question of self-government and Smuts on the issue of Indian rights in South Africa. He was accused of double standards. It was, they said, 'for the nations of Europe, justice and mercy; for the Indians of South Africa, injustice and humiliation'.[7] In private discussions with Indian delegates, Smuts spoke highly of Gandhi, declared himself in favour of Indian self-determination but once again refused to accept the argument on which India's demands in South Africa were based. The British Crown, he argued, was a 'binding link'[8] between dominions, but not the source of civil and political rights. Equal rights for Indians would mean equal rights for 'natives', and that would be the beginning of the end for his country. 'We are up against a stone wall,' he asserted, 'and we cannot get over it.'[9] His stance on Indian rights played well with the white electorate at home, but South Africa was to pay for his inflexibility at the United Nations some two decades later.

Although Smuts's reputation as an international peacemaker remained as high as ever at the end of 1923, in South Africa, Nationalist-Afrikaner resentment towards him had been mounting steadily. Although the Hertzogites applauded his attitude towards Indians, he was routinely denounced as an imperialist and a puppet of the mine owners by the Afrikaner workers who now predominated in the Labour Party. And just as his own South African Party had been forced to join forces with the Unionists to stay in power, in similar fashion the National and Labour parties came together in an anti-capitalist, anti-government pact. When the South African Party lost the safe seat of Wakkerstroom, in the Transvaal, in a by-election in early 1924, Smuts immediately called a general election, held on 17 June. In a bitterly fought campaign, the Pact government won 27 seats more than the South

African Party. Smuts immediately tendered his resignation and was replaced by Hertzog, who was to remain in office for the next fifteen years.

*

As Britain's new Chancellor of the Exchequer, Churchill set about mastering the essentials of his new portfolio with customary enthusiasm and energy, unable to resist the occasional temptation to poke his nose into the business of other ministers.[10] His first difficult decision was whether Britain should return to the gold standard, which it had been forced to abandon in World War I in the hope of reducing unemployment. Having weighed the arguments of the Bank of England and the Treasury, on the one hand, against influential economists, such as Keynes, on the other, Churchill chose to return to gold, but at the pre-war exchange rate. It was a decision he later described as the worst mistake of his life.

The sharp increase in the value of sterling after Britain went back to the gold standard made British exports more expensive, especially for the coal-mining industry, and Chancellor Churchill found himself in the eye of another political tempest. In 1926, after the failure of lengthy negotiations with the trade unions, a general strike was declared in support of the coal miners' demands. Although personally sympathetic to the mineworkers, Churchill regarded the strike as a threat to constitutional government and argued in favour of tough action against the miners. In the absence of daily newspapers, he prevailed upon the government to produce its own propaganda sheet to make its case to the public. No one wrote for the short-lived *British Gazette* with more enthusiasm than its de facto editor, the chancellor, who revelled in his temporary role as a newspaper magnate.[11] The anti-strike broadsheet inflamed rather than informed, since Churchill characteristically refused 'to be impartial between the fire brigade and the fire'.[12]

Though the strike eventually petered out, resentment among Britain's workers towards the Tories simmered on. By this time, Churchill had become far more conciliatory. He supported, for example, the introduction of a minimum wage and generally found himself at odds with his Cabinet colleagues on social policy. As a champion of working-class welfare, but who detested socialism,

Churchill, in Manchester's words, was 'always mistaking pink for red'[13] – confusing socialism for communism – and once again he found himself beached high and dry in the wrong party.[14] He was saved from further conflict with his fellow Conservatives when they lost the election of 1929, this time won outright by Ramsay MacDonald's Labour Party. Churchill almost doubled his majority in Epping, but was no longer Chancellor of the Exchequer.

Labour was to govern for the next two years, but the party proved incapable of dealing with the economic crisis brought about by the market crash of 1929 followed by the Great Depression. In 1931, MacDonald formed an all-party National Government to deal with the emergency. Churchill, however, was by now considered to be too erratic and divisive a figure to be given a Cabinet post. He remained out of office until the outbreak of war in 1939.

*

In South Africa, Smuts had lost not only the general election of 1924, but also his own constituency, Pretoria West. Another Transvaal seat was hurriedly found for him, at Standerton, and after briefly contemplating a 'period of release from official duties',[15] he returned to Parliament in Cape Town as leader of the opposition, convinced that the new Pact government would not last long.

With more time on his hands, the ever-industrious Smuts turned his attention to metaphysics again, expanding an earlier manuscript into a 140 000-word book, *Holism and Evolution*, described as 'an attempt to devise some simpler scheme to explain the unitary character of time, space, matter and all physical appearances and activities'.[16] The work was published simultaneously in London and New York in October 1926 and attracted special attention because of the author's international stature. Smuts was reluctant to classify the book as either scientific or philosophical, saying that, like all mankind, he was groping for a key to understanding the haphazard world around him:

> We all feel we have to be guided by some light through the maze of life.
> … I have no synoptic vision … I have only an idea … which may to some
> extent guide us through the surrounding difficulties … Holism – the

theory of the whole – tries to emphasize one aspect of thought that has been hitherto a neglected factor.[17]

A forerunner of many modern books on systems thinking, *Holism* ran to three editions in Britain and one in the US and Germany. It attracted mixed reviews in the academic world, but one distinguished philosopher, Gilbert Murray, thought it 'the most interesting philosophical work that he had read for very many years'.[18] Another admirer was the eminent historian Arnold Toynbee. In South Africa the book aroused hostility in some theological circles. As one who preferred to keep his personal views about the deity to himself, Smuts had deliberately avoided bringing God into the discussion, but expressed his agreement with Kant that 'from the facts of nature no inference of God is justified'.[19] That was enough to arouse charges in the Dutch Reformed Church community that holism was an imperialist concept that promoted atheism. The author was mildly disturbed by the allegation, but thought better of trying to refute it, taking comfort instead from the opinion of his Catholic Afrikaner friend Monsignor FC Kolbe, who pronounced *Holism and Evolution* as a 'deeply religious' work.[20]

Smuts also found time to indulge in his favourite pastime – the study of plants, in particular the veld grasses surrounding his austere country farm, Doornkloof. Whenever he could, he took off on botanical expeditions across southern and eastern Africa, into many areas never before visited by collectors. His interest in botany, geology, zoology and palaeontology led to his appointment as president of the South African Association for the Advancement of Science in 1924/25.

Churchill was one of the first people to whom Smuts sent a copy of *Holism and Evolution*. Britain's then chancellor responded by sending Smuts the third part of *The World Crisis*, which covered the years 1916 to 1918, accompanied by the following letter:

My dear Smuts,

Some months ago you sent me a deeply interesting book on Philosophy, into which I have peered with awe. I now venture to retaliate by sending you a couple of volumes in which I am sure you will find yourself much more at home.

I always follow the course of your affairs with that enduring sympathy which springs from wartime comradeship. I hope it will not be long before you pay us a visit. You will find a very warm welcome awaiting you from your many friends, and from none more than those who with you have faced the battle and breeze of the twentieth century of the Christian era.[21]

In 1929 there was another general election in South Africa, which left Smuts, like Churchill, still a Member of Parliament but not in government.

Churchill described the ensuing decade as his 'wilderness years'. Not knowing how to occupy himself, he said, 'My veins threatened to burst from the fall in pressure.' He took refuge in the silent pastime of painting.[22]

He and Smuts ran into each other again at a dinner in London in February 1930, after which Smuts wrote him the following letter:

My dear Churchill

It was deeply thoughtful of you to come to the South African Dinner, and I am most deeply obliged to you for adding distinction to that function by your presence.

I formed the impression in England that things political were in a flux and more unsettled than I had expected. I shall not be surprised to see re-groupings in the near future. I was much interested to see the amount of support that Lloyd George was quietly getting in Conservative circles.

The time for national conciliation is approaching, for the Empire is not holding its own in the industrial war which is going to settle our fate. It seems to me that party lines are getting confused and that the opportunity for a new move may soon come. I don't know how you view the situation but that is how it has struck me.

I was so uninterruptedly occupied in London at the end that the opportunity for a good talk could not be found. But when I am in London next year I hope to have the privilege to see more of you, that is to say if you are not immersed again in the cares of high office.

With kind regards and remembrances to Mrs Churchill

Ever yours sincerely

J C Smuts[23]

By this time, Churchill was devoting most of his time to his increasingly lucrative writing career. He completed *The World Crisis*, published *My Early Life* – an autobiography of his years at school, military college and in the army – and began a lengthy four-volume biography of his ancestor, the Duke of Marlborough. In between, he kept up a steady stream of articles to newspapers and magazines in an attempt to recoup some of the money he had lost in the Wall Street stock-market crash. He also undertook two well-paid lecture tours of the US, during the second of which he nearly lost his life in a motor accident, when he looked in the wrong direction while crossing a New York street.

In South Africa Smuts continued to soldier on as leader of the opposition as the country also began to feel the effects of the economic depression sweeping the world. Internationally, he was much in demand as a speaker, delivering lectures on African and world affairs in the UK, US and Canada. In 1931 he was given one of the scientific world's highest distinctions – an invitation to preside over the centenary meeting of the British Association for the Advancement of Science, a gathering in London of the world's greatest scientists.

Sensing that the Nationalist government was losing support for its obstinate refusal to alleviate South Africa's economic woes by going off gold, as Britain had done, Smuts pleaded with Hertzog to follow Ramsay MacDonald's example of forming a national government to deal with the economic crisis, and thereby build a broader white South African nation. In 1933 the unthinkable came to pass: after years of bickering, Smuts and Hertzog joined hands to form a United Party. The party was in truth more of an arranged marriage than a meeting of minds, but the new Fusion government, headed by Hertzog as prime minister and with Smuts as his deputy, was to survive uneasily for the following six years.

In 1934 Smuts visited London again, where he delivered two weighty speeches on the worsening international climate. He also accepted the rectorship of St Andrew's University, the oldest in Scotland. In his rectorial address, he sided with those sounding the warning bell, and called on Britain to take the initiative in Europe against the destructive forces of Fascism and Nazism.

In response to a telegram from Churchill – 'Hope I'm going to see you before you depart' – Smuts sent a handwritten note in return, addressing Churchill with a growing familiarity:

My dear Winston

It has been a great disappointment to me that in the rush of this last week I have not been able to get [in] touch with you as I had hoped. But I have scarcely had time for the necessary minimum of sleep. Now that I am on the point of leaving, I can only send you a line of farewell and of warmest good wishes.[24]

*

Churchill returned from his extended sojourn in the US to a place on Baldwin's Conservative Business Committee (as the shadow Cabinet was then called), thereby keeping himself at the centre of British political affairs. He set himself the task of rebutting the impression in America that Britain was a nation in terminal economic decline and failing to live up to its international obligations. Two matters were of particular concern to him because he believed they threatened the country's future as the foremost great power: British policy towards India and the spirit of militarism arising in Germany, where he paid a visit in 1932 to gauge matters for himself.[25]

As a reward for its loyal support of the Allies in World War I, India had been promised dominion status by Britain at some unspecified date in the future. As anxious as Smuts was about the implications of this for the British Empire, Churchill refused to contemplate casting away 'that most truly bright and precious jewel in the crown of the King'[26] – even though 'indigenous nationalism', led by Gandhi, was on the rise. In January 1931 he resigned from the Conservative Business Committee in protest at the party's bipartisan support for Labour's mildly liberal Indian policy, and thereafter spoke out vociferously and whenever he could against any moves towards self-government.

The passing of the Statute of Westminster, long advocated by the dominion leaders, had introduced a new element into the debate over India. The dominions were now effectively independent, and Churchill feared that a self-governing India might cut ties with Britain and lead other dominions out of the empire.[27] He positioned himself, accordingly, in the forefront of opposition to the India Bill in Parliament, fighting the legislation clause by clause in committee. When the viceroy, Lord Irwin (later to become Lord Halifax), declared that 'the natural issue of India's constitutional progress ... is the attainment of Dominion status', Churchill was outraged. And when Irwin officially received Gandhi a short while later, Churchill lost his composure altogether. In words that have resonated in India ever since, he denounced Gandhi as 'a seditious Middle Temple lawyer now posing as a fakir of a type well-known in the East, striding half-naked up the steps of the Vice-regal palace ... to parley with the representative of the King-Emperor'.[28] Behind this blimpish rhetoric, Churchill believed that the British Raj was governing India quite capably and argued, not without reason, that if ever Britain were to leave India to its own devices, Hindus and Muslims would slaughter one another mercilessly.[29]

The Indians, understandably, held contrary views about their future, as did most mainstream British politicians. But, after describing Parliament's passing of the India Act in 1935 as 'a monstrous sham erected by pygmies', which would prove to be the 'knell of the British Empire in the East',[30] Churchill finally relented, accepting his political defeat with good grace[31] and moving on to a far more pressing concern – the threat posed by Germany's growing belligerence. He was the first British politician of any consequence to sound the alarm about the pernicious confluence of German national aspirations with Hitler's Nazi ideology.[32]

*

What he foresaw clearly, others failed to see. For Churchill, the growing menace of German rearmament posed an even greater existential threat to Britain than the feeble state of its economy and weakening grip on its empire.[33] In mid-1935, the Conservatives returned to head a National Government under Stanley Baldwin, but the ever-outspoken Churchill, rather pointedly, was again overlooked for a Cabinet post. His successor as Conservative chancellor, Neville Chamberlain, was far more troubled by Britain's straitened

finances than the state of its defences, and did little to encourage re-arma-
ment, denying the Royal Navy new ships, the RAF better aircraft and the
army much-needed equipment.

Aware that there was no appetite in the country for war, Churchill nonetheless continued to speak truth to those in power, warning the House of
Commons that [Britain] could not 'afford to see Nazidom in its present phase
of cruelty and intolerance, with all its hatreds and all its gleaming weapons,
paramount in Europe'.[34] He regarded it as his bounden duty to keep reminding the British people of the gravity of the threat they faced, and exhorted the
government incessantly to shore up the country's defences with much greater
urgency.

Just as his appeals were beginning to gain traction in influential circles,
Britain was distracted by the abdication crisis, into which Churchill inserted
himself as a friend of the king. Unlike much of the establishment, he thought
highly of Edward VIII, who, he once rashly predicted, 'would shine in
History as the bravest and best-loved of all sovereigns who have worn the
island crown'.[35] As an influential backbencher, but against the wishes of his
fellow Tories, Churchill sought a way in which the king could both remain
on the throne and marry his lover, the American divorcée Wallis Simpson. In
so doing, he seriously misjudged the mood of the country, which was firmly
against the prospect of Mrs Simpson becoming queen. Once again, his many
critics contended that he had reinforced his reputation for being 'unsound' in
a crisis, and were less inclined than ever to heed his apocalyptic views about
Germany.[36]

Churchill's outspoken opposition to the 'appeasement'* of Hitler continued until it eventually became clear to almost everyone that he had been
far-sighted all along.[37] In 1937 Baldwin stepped down as prime minister to
be replaced by the appeasers' champion, Chamberlain, who took Hitler's
promises of peace in Munich at face value but was soon to find that he had disastrously misjudged the character of the Führer. In one of his finest set-piece
speeches in the House of Commons, Churchill denounced Chamberlain's

---

* It was Smuts who had put the term 'appeasement' into international use, well before it acquired its pejorative meaning
in World War II. Writing to Lloyd George from Paris in 1919, he pleaded for the appeasement of Germany, by which
he meant demonstrating the magnanimity of the strong for the weak that the British had displayed towards the Boers.
The term came into common use at the Locarno Conference of 1924. (See WK Hancock, *Smuts: The Sanguine Years
1870–1919*. Cambridge University Press, 1962, p 512.)

'Peace with Honour' at Munich as being in reality 'a dishonourable defeat'.

On 3 September 1939, after Hitler's forces had launched an armed assault on Poland and ignored an ultimatum to withdraw, Britain went to war with Germany for the second time in twenty-five years. Chamberlain decided to form a small War Cabinet and invited Churchill to resume his old office as First Lord of the Admiralty. On the same evening, a delighted First Lord wired the Royal Navy to be ready to receive him at six o'clock. The Board of Admiralty flashed the news to all stations and ships: 'Winston is back!'[38]

*

In South Africa, the urgent imperative for Parliament to come to a decision on what had become the most divisive issue in white politics – whether to side with the empire against Germany or remain neutral – was enough to shatter the fragile coalition between Hertzog and Smuts. In a sombre and hushed House of Assembly on Monday 4 September, the prime minister's motion that South Africa should stay out of the conflict was opposed by Smuts, and defeated by a mere 13 votes. Hertzog resigned and Smuts was invited by the governor general to become prime minister again. He accepted without any sense of elation, knowing that war would solve nothing, but seeing no realistic alternative. On 6 September, South Africa declared war on Germany.

One day later, a telegram arrived for 'General Smuts' from Britain's newly appointed First Lord of the Admiralty: 'I rejoice to feel that we are once again on commando together.'[39]

CHAPTER 11

On the back foot

*Never, never, believe that any war will be smooth and easy or
that anyone who embarks on the strange voyage can measure
the tides or hurricanes he will encounter.*

— CHURCHILL[1]

Smuts took South Africa into World War II out of a conviction that the
civilisation of Europe – and indeed of the human race – was under threat
from Hitler's Nazism as well as the false promise of Russian Communism.
It was, as he characteristically phrased it, 'a choice between the Devil and
Beelzebub'.[2] If South Africa, a small nation, were to isolate itself from the
British Commonwealth, it might one day find itself alone in a friendless
world.[3]

Showing a steadfastness under political fire that might, in retrospect, be
described as 'Churchillian', Smuts set about rebuilding the Union Defence
Force, which had been allowed to wither on the vine under the Fusion government's Defence Minister, a politician with Nazi sympathies. As Hancock
records, when World War II broke out, South Africa was 'militarily naked'.[4]
Although Hertzog had insisted throughout his premiership that South Africa
should run its own affairs, he had been prepared to let the Royal Navy defend
the country's coasts and trade routes. As a result, the country had no warships and only a tiny Naval Volunteer Reserve. Two of the main harbours,
Port Elizabeth and East London, had not a single piece of artillery for their
defence.[5] And the Union Defence Force was in no better shape: the army
numbered under 5 000 men, its weaponry was obsolete and it had only two
demo-model tanks and two armoured cars, while the air force consisted of

two bombers and a few fighter aircraft well past their sell-by date. More seriously, there was no munitions industry to speak of.[6]

The beleaguered Smuts had to fight the war not merely on the military but on the (white) political front as well. Nationalist Afrikaners joined forces in mounting an internal resistance, which, on its fringes, was treasonous. While Hertzog, Malan and their supporters confined their opposition to the parliamentary arena, fringe organisations such as the pro-Nazi Ossewa Brandwag resorted to bombings, sabotage and attacks on servicemen to hinder the war effort. Afrikanerdom was split asunder, with many Afrikaners choosing to ignore Hertzog and follow Smuts, who responded to the insurgency in typical fashion by introducing tougher security measures, including detainment without trial in internment camps. At all times, he remained resolutely but serenely single-minded, confident that the decision to go to war against Hitler was morally right and in the country's best long-term interests.

Besides being prime minister, Smuts took on the portfolios of defence and external (foreign) affairs, and set about building South Africa's war machine with a vigour that was quite remarkable in someone on the cusp of seventy. Bomber and other aircraft were purchased from the US, and South African Airways Junkers planes were commandeered for reconnaissance purposes. Trawlers and fishing boats were converted into minesweepers and sent to patrol the coastline, while a National Reserve Volunteer Force of several thousand was enlisted to guard key security installations and internment camps.[7] A fighting force of almost 200 000 volunteers (roughly two-thirds of them Afrikaners) was assembled for service in the Union Defence Force army, navy and air forces 'anywhere in Africa'. Meanwhile, the managing director of the state-owned Iron and Steel Corporation (Iscor), Dr HJ van der Bijl, was given sweeping powers to reorganise the country's manufacturing sector.

As Smuts had foreseen, by virtue of its location, South Africa was drawn into the European conflict almost immediately. With the Straits of Gibraltar now hazardous, Allied troopships were diverted around the Cape where, in the first two years of war, 6 500 vessels would put in for repairs or provisioning.[8] From London, First Lord Churchill wired Smuts to offer him the warship HMS *Erebus* for the defence of Cape Town, a gesture Smuts turned down, as Churchill's wording had made it obvious that the *Erebus* could be more usefully deployed off the coasts of Holland and Belgium.

Even though he had been out of office for a decade on the day war was declared, 3 September 1939, Churchill was asked to speak in the House of Commons soon after the prime minister. In a brief but powerful speech, he said: 'This is not a question of fighting for Danzig or fighting for Poland. We are fighting to save the whole world from the pestilence of Nazi tyranny and in defence of all that is most sacred to man.'[9]

To many Conservatives, especially those in the appeasement lobby who still failed to grasp the threat posed by Hitler, Churchill remained a war-mongering 'outsider', regarded with suspicion and even contempt.[10] Some of his old colleagues, such as David Lloyd George, who might have known better, continued to make the case for a negotiated peace with Germany. On 6 October, in the Reichstag, Hitler made a 'last offer' to the Allies of a peace conference, saying he had no demands on France. Churchill passed on to Lloyd George a secret telegram from Smuts, who, viewing matters from a distance, warned that any peace offer from Germany would be insincere and was not to be trusted.[11]

For the first seven months after war was declared, the British people would have been forgiven for believing that, notwithstanding Germany's invasion of Poland, hostilities might somehow be averted. On 2 April 1940, Prime Minister Chamberlain told an audience that 'Hitler has missed the bus'.[12] Unfortunately, he had not. Five weeks later, after Norway and Denmark had been invaded by the Germans and the danger to Britain was becoming obvious, public pressure grew for another coalition government to oversee the conduct of the war. Labour flatly refused to serve under the indecisive Chamberlain, so the choice of his successor lay between the former leader of the appeasement lobby, Lord Halifax (by now mistrustful of Hitler) and Churchill. Realising his own limitations, Halifax withdrew, so on 10 May 1940, at the age of sixty-five, Churchill became Britain's new prime minister and war leader, despite being distrusted by the Royal Family and many Tories. Earlier that day, Hitler's forces had come storming across the borders of neutral Holland, Belgium and Luxembourg, en route to the French border. World War II had begun in earnest.

In his memoirs, Churchill wrote that he had accepted the premiership with 'a profound sense of relief. At last I had the authority to give directions over the whole scene. I felt as if I were walking with Destiny and that all my past life had been but a preparation for this hour and this trial.'[13] He was well aware however, that his hold on power was tenuous and dependent on his delivering results.[14]

Addressing the House of Commons for the first time as prime minister on 13 May 1940, he asked rhetorically:

> What is our policy? I will say: it is to wage war by sea, land and air with all our might and with all the strength God can give us; to wage war against a monstrous tyranny, never surpassed in the dark lamentable catalogue of human crime. You ask: What is our aim? I can answer in one word: victory – victory at all costs, victory in spite of all terrors, victory, however long and hard the road may be; for without victory there is no survival.[15]

He repeated what he had told all his ministers at Admiralty House that morning: 'I have nothing to offer but blood, toil, tears and sweat.'[16]

That day he also sent the following telegram to Smuts:

> To you my friend of so many years, and faithful comrade of the last war, I send my heartfelt greetings. It is a comfort to me to feel that we shall be together in this long and hard trek, for I know you and the Government and the peoples of the Union will not weary under the heat of the day, and that we shall make a strong laager for all beside the waters at the end.[17]

While Churchill was delivering his speech in the House on 13 May, German panzer divisions were breaking through the French defensive lines in the Ardennes and encircling the British Expeditionary Force stationed across the Channel in northern France. The ease with which the Maginot Line (a series of fortifications intended to defend the French, Swiss and Luxembourg borders adjacent to Germany) was breached came as a rude shock to Churchill, who made the first of several flying visits to France to shore up French resolve and gauge the situation for himself. He found the French government, under Prime Minister Paul Reynaud, in a state of panic. After taking the decision to send no more than ten RAF fighter squadrons urgently to France, leaving only twenty-five squadrons for the defence of the British homeland, Churchill acceded to advice from his military advisers that the British Expeditionary Force – by now cut off from support by land or sea – should be brought home. On 27 May, an evacuation fleet began to bring back British troops from the harbour and beaches of Dunkirk.

The successful withdrawal of almost 340 000 troops from the French coast temporarily lifted the morale of the British people, but Churchill was quick to warn, on 4 June, in what was perhaps his greatest speech to the House of Commons, that what had happened in Belgium and France was a 'colossal military disaster'. Dunkirk had been 'a miracle of deliverance', but he said: 'We must be careful not to assign to this deliverance the attributes of a victory. Wars are not won by evacuations …'[18] In a stirring peroration, he added:

> Even though large tracts of Europe and many old and famous States have fallen or may fall into the grip of the Gestapo and all the odious apparatus of Nazi rule, we shall not flag or fail. We shall go on to the end … We shall defend our island whatever the cost might be. We shall fight on the beaches. We shall fight on the landing grounds. We shall fight in the fields and on the streets. We shall fight in the hills. We shall never surrender.[19]

He did not need to spell out his subliminal message: the French might give in, but the British would never succumb – at least not while he was prime minister.

*

Two days before the evacuation of Dunkirk and three weeks before the Nazis overran Paris, Smuts celebrated his seventieth birthday. In a letter to a close friend in England, he described himself as 'too old for thinking but not too old for doing'.[20] By 'doing', he meant pursuing the struggle against Hitler on two fronts, externally and internally, and making sure that South Africa remained a key contributor to the Allied cause.[21] The fall of France came as no real surprise to him: while not anticipating the suddenness of the country's military collapse, he had always had reservations about the moral conviction and staying power of the French.[22]

Yet, notwithstanding his lack of confidence in France and unaware of the extent of Britain's lack of fighter aircraft, Smuts advised Churchill to be responsive to French appeals for help. However, Britain's war leader must have decided that saving France was a lost cause, for he telegraphed a reply to Smuts in the following terms:

> We are of course doing all we can both from the air and by sending divisions as fast as they can be equipped to France. It would be wrong to send the bulk of our fighters to this battle, and when it was lost, as is probable, be left with no means of carrying on the war. I think we have a harder, longer, and more hopeful duty to perform ... I can see only one sure way through now, to wit, that Hitler should attack this country and in so doing break his air weapon. If this happens, he will be left to face the winter with Europe writhing under his heel, and probably with the United States against him after the Presidential election is over. ... Am most grateful to you for cable. Please always give me your counsel, my old and valiant friend.[23]

Smuts was as hopeful as Churchill about the United States' intentions. As he wrote privately to a friend in England:

> I hope the day is not far off when America will really bear her share of the burden, even if she does not send an army to Europe. If Britain and the Commonwealth win alone, America will never forgive herself; if they are beaten she will be even less able to bear the intolerable stigma. It is a most awkward fix for a really pacific nation ...[24]

On 10 June 1940, Mussolini brought Italy into the war on Hitler's side. The vainglorious Italian dictator was not going to be upstaged by the Germans and hoped that a British defeat would open the way for Italian gains in North Africa and the Middle East. All three combatants were reliant to a greater or lesser extent on supplies of oil from the Gulf to fuel their military machines. While Britain could obtain most of its requirements from America (the world's major oil producer at the time), if Germany and Italy required extra fuel they needed first to seize control of the Mediterranean from the Royal Navy.[25] If Hitler and Mussolini's forces could prevail in the Mediterranean, they would enjoy open access to the Middle East and much of Africa. Egypt, in the south-eastern corner of the region, was the crucial link in Britain's imperial chain, with the Suez Canal being the conduit for shipping to India and Asia. To safeguard the canal, and because its usual base on Malta had become too exposed to air attack from nearby Italy, the Royal Navy had based its Mediterranean fleet in Alexandria.

In the early stages of the war, huge amounts of fuel and munitions passed between Italy and Libya, demonstrating that the Royal Navy was no longer in full control of the Mediterranean. Mussolini's declaration of war had 'transformed the sea into a battle-zone, through which convoys passed at their peril'.[26] Britain's naval and air bases in Malta came under heavy attack.

With France on the point of collapse and Italy now a new threat, Smuts recognised at once the implications of the closure of the sea route through the Mediterranean to all but the most heavily guarded Allied shipping. The Cape sea route was now of great strategic importance, and South Africa – for geopolitical reasons – had become a key member of the Commonwealth.[27] Smuts responded to Mussolini's provocation in two ways: he had South Africa promptly declare war on Italy and took over supreme command of the Union's armed forces himself – to the renewed fury of his Nationalist opponents.[28]

For the Commonwealth forces scattered around Africa and the Middle East, in Kenya, the Sudan, Palestine and Egypt, the outlook was ominous. They were faced by large Italian armies in Abyssinia and Libya, and unable to count any longer on French support. Anticipating an attack on Kenya by Mussolini from bases in Abyssinia, Eritrea and Italian Somaliland, Smuts quickly sent the First South African Infantry Brigade under Dan Pienaar to East Africa. And from its station in Kenya, the tiny South African Air Force launched bombing attacks on Italian targets in Abyssinia.

The fall of Paris to the invading Germans on 14 June 1940 and the subsequent collapse of official French resistance led to the signing of an armistice between Marshal Pétain, former hero of the Battle of Verdun in World War I, and Germany. With Hitler's troops now occupying northern France, Pétain became head of a 'free zone' in central and southern France, with its headquarters at Vichy. The only French leader to call on his countrymen to 'free France' was General Charles de Gaulle. This was made in a radio broadcast from London, to where he had fled on 15 June.

The Vichy government now took its orders from Hitler, who demanded the surrender of the French naval fleet, dispersed around the Mediterranean. British military chiefs were determined to deny these warships to the Germans.[29] When Pétain refused Britain's ultimatum to sail French warships holed up at the naval base at Oran, in Algeria, into British waters or scuttle them, Churchill took the brutally tough decision to attack the ships of Britain's former ally at their moorings. One battle cruiser managed to escape and make its way to Toulon, in southern France, but another was blown up and the rest damaged. Twelve hundred French sailors lost their lives and Britain had suddenly become the sworn enemy of Vichy France. Oran became the symbol of Churchill's 'ruthlessness and determination'.[30] After being received for weeks in an embarrassing silence by the Tories, for the first time he was given warm applause by his own side in the House of Commons.[31] Yet the damage caused by the incident was to linger always in many French minds.[32]

*

With much of France in enemy hands and German troops not far away across the Channel, it was apparent that an assault on the British mainland was imminent. As Churchill wrote later:

> Our fate now depended upon victory in the air. The German leaders had recognised that all their plans for the invasion of Britain depended on winning air supremacy above the Channel and the chosen landing-places on our south-coast ... For the actual crossing and landings complete mastery of the air over the transports and the beaches was the decisive condition.[33]

In Parliament on June 18, he warned the British people about what lay ahead:

> What General Weygand called the Battle of France is over. I expect that the Battle of Britain is about to begin ... Upon this battle depends the survival of Christian civilization ... The whole fury and might of the enemy must very soon be turned on us. Hitler knows that he will have to break us in this island or lose the war. If we can stand up to him, all Europe may be free ... But if we fail, then the whole world, including the United States ... will sink into the abyss of a new Dark Age ... Let us therefore brace ourselves to our duties, and so bear ourselves that, if the British Empire and its Commonwealth last for a thousand years, men will still say, 'This was their Finest Hour.'[34]

On 16 July, Hitler set in motion Operation Sea Lion, his plan for the invasion of Britain. Some 2 500 Luftwaffe fighters and bombers stationed in Belgium and France were to neutralise Britain's air defences and pave the way for German ground forces to cross the Channel. Despite having hurriedly ramped up production, the RAF could muster only 650 Spitfires and Hurricanes to keep the German air force at bay.[35]

There is some dispute today over when the Battle of Britain, as it became known, actually began. During July 1940, there were repeated skirmishes between RAF and Luftwaffe fighters over the skies of southern England. It was in mid-August, however, that the conflict in the air became much more intense. Within twelve days the RAF lost 133 fighter planes in action and 44 to mishaps, against 299 losses for the Luftwaffe.[36] On 24 August, the first German bombs fell on airfields in the English countryside, and the Luftwaffe launched as many as 600 sorties in a day, causing hundreds of civilian casualties.

The turning point in the air battle came on 7 September, however, when the Germans made the strategic error of switching their attack from airfields and production facilities in the countryside to London.[37] Although the East End of the British capital, as well as cities such as Coventry, were devastated in the

Blitz, the pressure on the air bases and radar facilities in south-east England was eased and from then on the survival of the RAF's Fighter Command was never in doubt. Churchill responded with typical far-sightedness by sending a consignment of tanks, no longer needed at home, to Egypt to shore up the defence of the route through Suez.[38]

By 15 September, deterred by Luftwaffe losses and the success of British radar in detecting any advancing bombers, Hitler and his high command had come to the conclusion that Germany could not win control of the skies, and decided to postpone Operation Sea Lion indefinitely. Churchill repeated, in the House of Commons, his much-quoted remark to chief of staff, General Hastings ('Pug') Ismay during the fighting: 'Never in the field of human conflict has so much been owed by so many to so few.'[39]

The Blitz on Britain's major cities continued, however, for another eight months, killing 43 000 civilians and inflicting horrendous damage on homes and buildings. The airborne assault petered out only in May 1941, when Hitler had to turn his attention to a much more important challenge – the invasion of Stalin's Soviet Russia.

CHAPTER 12

Meddling in Africa

Personally, I am always ready to learn,
although I do not always like being taught.
— CHURCHILL.[1]

E ven before World War I, Churchill had been no great admirer of generals. He also thought the World War II crop were 'too cautious, always demanding more and more resources, human and material, before they were prepared to put matters to the test of battle, with the result that, by that time, the enemy had built up his resources too'.[2]

The summer of 1940 provided him with the perfect opportunity of doing what he liked best: directing military matters himself. In no other theatre of operations was he to become more deeply involved than in the Middle East, where his unfortunate desert generals 'came under greater scrutiny and pressure than any other element of the armed forces'.[3] Anthony Eden, British Foreign Secretary at the time, remarked once that Churchill should not meddle in the decision making of his commanders, to which Churchill replied: 'You mean like a great bluebottle buzzing over a huge cowpat?' He disregarded the advice and did exactly what he wanted anyway.[4]

The hyperactive prime minister often clashed with his more cautious military chiefs, who resented his interference in operational decisions which they believed should be left to them. Foremost among them was General Archie Wavell, the commander-in-chief of the British Army in the Middle East, and one of the most intellectually gifted men ever to hold senior rank in the UK's armed forces.[5] Wavell was a most unusual soldier, once writing of a fellow officer that 'his defect as a soldier is probably the same as mine, that soldiering rather bores him and books and art and history interest him more'.[6] Wavell's introverted nature and extreme taciturnity infuriated Churchill, who found him 'aloof and uncommunicative'.[7]

Wavell went to South Africa in April 1940, to consult Smuts about military strategy and the Union Defence Force's involvement in the war in Africa.[8] Churchill was eager to deploy South African troops against Mussolini in the Western Desert as soon as possible, instead of using them to confront the Italians in East Africa. Smuts, on the other hand, who had called up untrained volunteers to defend the Union and was under sustained political attack as a consequence, felt he could hardly move troops further north into the desert until the Italians had been expelled from Abyssinia. He also reckoned that attacking Mussolini on his southernmost flank would inflict significant damage on Italy's East African empire. And Wavell agreed with him.[9]

Worried about the security threat posed by the Italians to East Africa, and eventually to the Union itself, Smuts had previoulsy petitioned Churchill unsuccessfully for British forces to be sent to bolster his volunteer army. The British prime minister replied that it was not the moment to send more troops to Africa:

> The British Eastern Mediterranean fleet is well-placed to resist an attack on Egypt, as well as to cover east coast of Africa. We can also send forces from here by the Atlantic far quicker than any German force can traverse the immense land distances of Africa … Possibility of air attack on South Africa appears remote at present time. We are attacking Germans ceaselessly and heavily in their homeland, and are also being attacked ourselves, so far in a very unskilled fashion.[10]

To his aide, 'Pug' Ismay, Churchill was less diplomatic: 'Where is the South African brigade of 10,000 men?' he wanted to know. 'Why is it playing no part in the Middle East?'[11] Summoning Wavell, whom he had never met before, for face-to-face discussions in London and writing to him afterwards, Churchill noted that the commander-in-chief had explained the situation in Egypt and Somaliland, but they had yet to discuss the position in Kenya and Abyssinia: 'I mentioned the very large forces which you have in Kenya, namely the Union Brigade of 6 000 white South Africans, probably as fine material as exists for warfare in spacious countries …'[12] Two days later, he fired off another memo to Wavell, via Ismay:

> I am not at all satisfied with the Union Brigade and the West Africa brigade in Kenya … Without further information I cannot accept the statement that the South African Brigade is so far untrained that it cannot go into action … I cannot see why the Union Brigade as a whole should be considered in any way inferior to British Territorial units. Anyhow, they are certainly good enough to fight Italians …[13]

Churchill did not have a high regard for Italians. Years before, over dinner with Hitler's future minister Ribbentrop, who had boasted that in any future war with Britain, Germany would have the Italians on its side, Churchill – in a reference to Italy's poor record in World War I – is said to have responded with one of his most devastating put-downs: 'Well, that's only fair – *we* had to have them last time.'[14]

*

On the evening of 21 July 1940, Smuts addressed millions of Britons for the first time in World War II, speaking from South Africa in a BBC radio broadcast. As Hancock records,[15] he was 'not at all dramatic or rhetorical but meditative', as if he were thinking things out as he went along. He spoke, he told his listeners, as a detached observer 'charting the deep oceanic currents which are already flowing in your favour'. His purpose was to reassure the British people they were not standing alone in the world. The next day, Churchill wired him to say, 'We are all deeply grateful for your splendid and inspiring broadcast.'[16]

Smuts was the only dominion prime minister whose opinion Churchill really valued. As Max Hastings observes, 'Throughout the war, [Churchill] treated all the self-governing dominions as subject colonies, mere sources of manpower. Dominion prime ministers visiting London were accorded public courtesy, private indifference.'[17] The best illustration of this was Operation Menace, an attempt inspired by the French leader, the temperamental General de Gaulle, to reconquer French West Africa via the Vichy-held port of Dakar. Churchill did not even bother to inform the Australian prime minister, Robert Menzies, of the imminent Royal Navy attack on what remained of the French fleet holed up in the strongly defended West African port. Menzies learnt about the operation only by reading the newspapers.

On the other hand, Churchill kept Smuts fully in the picture, warning South Africa's prime minister of the dire consequences for the Cape sea route if Dakar were to fall into German hands. In his long message to Smuts on 22 September 1940, Churchill said:

> I have been thinking a great deal about what you said in your various messages about not neglecting the African sphere ... If Dakar fell under German control and became a U-boat base, the consequences to the Cape route would be deadly. We have therefore set about the business of putting De Gaulle into Dakar, peaceably if we can, forcibly if we must, and the expedition now about to strike seems to have the necessary force.
>
> ... Naturally the risk of a bloody collision with the French sailors and part of the garrison is not a light one. On the whole, I think the odds are heavily against any serious resistance, having regard to the low morale and unhappy plight of this French colony, and the ruin and starvation that faces them through our sea control. Still, no one can be sure until we try. ...
>
> Anyhow the die is cast ... It gives me so much pleasure and confidence to be trekking with you along the path we have followed together for so many years.[18]

Churchill also took the precaution of keeping President Franklin D Roosevelt personally informed, telling him that 'there was a reasonable chance of the operation being carried out without heavy casualties on either side'.[19] The president was encouraging and offered to send American warships into the area as a friendly gesture and as a warning shot across the Vichy government's bows.[20]

As it turned out, the Dakar expedition – which Churchill admitted advocating to 'an exceptional degree'[21] beforehand – was a fiasco. Besides a lack of secrecy before the invasion force had even left England, dense fog off the West African coast made visibility difficult and enabled the Vichy French and local partisans to mount a spirited resistance to the 6 000 French Foreign Legionaries, led by De Gaulle, and the Royal Marines, waiting aboard the British aircraft carrier *Ark Royal* and two other battleships before attempting a landing. After several vessels of the invading armada had been damaged in a three-day-long engagement, it became obvious that Dakar would be defended to the death. The War Cabinet quickly concluded that the game was no longer worth the candle and called for Operation Menace to be abandoned.

Although his first offensive operation of the war had been an unmitigated disaster, Churchill refused to blame anyone for its failure, taking the view that this kind of setback was inevitable in battle. It illustrated, he wrote afterwards, the difficulties of combined operations, 'especially where allies are involved'.[22] In the House of Commons, he said that De Gaulle's 'conduct and bearing on this occasion had made [his] confidence in him greater than ever'.[23] This despite the fact the French general had not helped matters by alerting the authorities in Dakar to the imminent arrival of the British.[24]

There was much unfavourable criticism of the Dakar episode in America. Roosevelt's ambassador to Britain, Joseph Kennedy, reported to Washington that Dakar had been a disaster and told the *Boston Globe* off the record that Britain was finished, that the Brits were fighting for the preservation of Empire rather than democracy, and that to think otherwise was 'bunk'. In London, Kennedy became known as 'Jittery Joe'.[25]

The damage done to De Gaulle's reputation in the US was far greater, however. It confirmed the opinion of Roosevelt, never an admirer of the mercurial Frenchman, and others that the Free French* leader was unreliable, unstable and under the thumb of Churchill.[26]

*

---

* The Free French were the forces of France's government in exile, based in London and led by Charles de Gaulle.

In October 1940 Smuts flew to Khartoum to discuss the war in Africa with Britain's Foreign Secretary, Anthony Eden, and generals Wavell and Dill. His own prediction that Hitler would send forces to fight alongside the Italians in an attempt to capture Egypt had proved premature, but Churchill had decided anyhow to keep the fleet at Alexandria and defend the Suez Canal, even if it meant sending to the Middle East Hurricane fighters and military equipment badly needed at home. (It was not until 1941 that Axis forces under Rommel landed on the North African coast at Tripoli.)

At the Khartoum meeting, plans were hatched for two major offensives: Operation Compass, whose purpose was to drive the Italians out of North Africa via Cyrenaica (eastern Libya); and Operation Canvas, to expel them from Abyssinia.[27] Operation Compass was mounted in the greatest secrecy; even Churchill was not informed about it at first, for fear that he would interfere and put pressure on Wavell to speed up the exercise. When Eden told him about Compass, the prime minister purred 'like six cats', exclaiming, 'At long last we are going to throw off the intolerable shackles of the defensive. Wars are won by superior willpower. Now we will wrest the initiative from the enemy and impose our will on him.'[28] But no sooner had the plan been approved, 'without a moment's hesitation', than Wavell felt the prime minister's pressure upon him. Churchill had his own views about how the exercise should be carried out and interfered almost daily in its planning.

It was unfortunate for Wavell that, from the outset, he and Churchill constantly rubbed each other up the wrong way. Churchill wanted to see immediate action in the Middle East, but Wavell insisted on first being given the necessary equipment and resources. A relationship that had begun badly went steadily downhill. Wavell resented Churchill's constant interference and refused to compromise his judgement in order to placate the impatient prime minister.

Their worst conflict occurred over the Italian invasion of tiny British Somaliland, which Wavell thought was not worth defending. He was subsequently accused by Churchill of breaking his pledge to resist the Italians. When Wavell replied that 'a big butcher's bill [in defending Somaliland] was not necessarily evidence of good tactics', the prime minister blew up. Dill told Wavell that he had never seen Churchill so angry; but the prime minister's rage was so much greater because he knew in his heart that Wavell was right.[29]

*

From his bases in Libya, Mussolini had been waiting for Hitler to make good on his promise to invade Britain before sending his forces into action in North Africa. When, in September 1940, it became apparent that no invasion would take place, the Italian leader ordered an attack by his Fifth and Tenth Armies across the western border of British-held Egypt to try to capture the Suez Canal. Driving into Egypt from Italy's only possession in North Africa, Libya, the Italians managed to advance by sixty miles in three days before digging in at the key port of Sidi Barrani (*see map on page 140*) to await supplies and reinforcements.

It was now time for Wavell to counter attack with Operation Compass, which had taken six months of hard training and meticulous planning.[30] But before that, it was necessary to cut Italian supply lines in the Mediterranean. On the night of 12 November, 21 torpedo-equipped bombers from the British aircraft carrier HMS *Illustrious* inflicted severe damage on the nucleus of the Italian fleet anchored at its main naval base at Taranto, southern Italy. The strike succeeded in scattering the Italian navy, reducing the threat to British convoys and restoring the pre-eminence of the Royal Navy.[31] Churchill was delighted: according to Sir John Colville, his reference to 'this glorious episode' at Taranto in the House of Commons was met 'with enthusiastic cheers from an assembly hungry for something to be cheerful about'.[32] 'By this single stroke,' Churchill wrote later, 'the balance of naval power in the Mediterranean was decisively altered.'[33]

Compass began in the early hours of 9 December, when Lieutenant General Richard O'Connor's Western Desert Force, only 31 000 in number but equipped with the latest tanks and artillery pieces, and supported by the RAF and Royal Navy, caught Mussolini's Tenth Army by surprise with a lightning-fast twin-pronged attack at Sidi Barrani and along the Egyptian coast. Mussolini's generals proved to be 'epic bunglers'.[34] Within two days, the Italians' line of fortifications had been overrun and 39 000 prisoners taken. Reinforced by Australian troops, O'Connor's army pushed the Tenth Army back into Libya and captured the isolated but strategically vital deep-water port (and fortress) of Tobruk on 21 January 1941.[35] For the next two months the Western Desert Force kept Mussolini's men on the run until Churchill ordered the advance to be stopped, so the British could redeploy troops to East Africa and to the defence of Greece.

Operation Compass resulted in the capture of 130 000 Italian prisoners of war, 400 tanks and 1 290 guns, and eliminated the Tenth Army as a fighting force.[36] As Eden remarked gleefully, 'Never has so much been surrendered by so many to so few.'[37] The devastating setback for the Italians forced Hitler to send Rommel's Afrika Korps to Libya on 6 February 1941 to save Mussolini's face.

Though he still disapproved of Wavell, a delighted Churchill sent the commander-in-chief a congratulatory signal praising his 'glorious service to the Empire and to our cause. We are deeply indebted to you, Wilson [Officer Commanding British troops in Egypt] and other Commanders whose fine professional skill and audacious leading have gained us the memorable victory of the Libyan Desert. Your first objective now must be to maul the Italian Army and rip them off the African shore …'[38]

In another telegraphed message, this time to Smuts, Churchill said: 'Great credit is due to Wavell and Wilson for brilliant planning and execution. … Wickedness is not going to reign.' The Italians were 'corn ripe for the sickle … Let us gather the harvest,' he declared triumphantly.[39]

Year of destiny

I never 'worry' about action, but only about inaction.
— CHURCHILL[1]

O n New Year's Day 1941, Smuts broadcast once more to the British people. He began in philosophical vein, quoting the ancient saying 'the
Gods lavish on those they love infinite sorrow and infinite joy', before pre-
dicting that 1941 would be a year of trouble for Hitler. He also, says Hancock,
gave voice to what every British statesman fervently hoped but did not dare
say: 'I feel convinced that in the last resort, America will not, as indeed she
cannot afford to, stand out [from the war].'[2] Surveying the globe, and developments in the US, Germany and Russia in particular, Smuts said he felt sure
of only one thing: 1941 would prove to be a 'year of destiny'.

So far, the war had gone badly in France but reasonably well for the British
and Commonwealth forces in North Africa. That was soon to change nearby,
however, as the Axis powers went on the offensive in Yugoslavia and Greece.
In March 1939, Chamberlain had made a pledge of support to the Greeks if
they were attacked, and although Britain could ill afford it, Churchill decided
to honour the commitment because he feared that a failure to act would send
the wrong message to Roosevelt. There could not be a repeat of Munich.[3]

In one of the most controversial decisions of his premiership, Churchill
disregarded the advice of his military chiefs and drew down on Wavell's
slender resources in the Western Desert. By diverting troops from Libya to
Greece, he overlooked the much greater strategic imperative of driving the

Axis armies out of North Africa. It was a disastrous miscalculation on his part – one that not only had a heavy cost in terms of men and equipment, but more importantly in the loss of the initiative won by Wavell's desert army.

In March 1941 the Germans invaded Greece, whose forces were already exhausted from trying to keep Mussolini's army at bay during a winter campaign in neighbouring Albania.[4] 50 000 out of 62 000 recently landed imperial troops had to be hastily evacuated from the Greek mainland, 26 000 of them to Crete, which was overrun by German paratroops in June. In a mini reprise of Dunkirk, 18 000 men, mostly New Zealanders, had to be taken off Crete and trans-shipped to Egypt by the hard-pressed Royal Navy. A 17 500-strong invading German army had defeated a British and Commonwealth force twice as large, while for the Royal Navy, the defence of Crete proved to be Britain's single costliest naval campaign of World War II.[5]

The diversion of part of Wavell's army to aid the embattled Greeks gave Rommel the opportunity he was looking for. His Afrika Korps began a strong counter-attack in Libya, landing a mechanised force at Tripoli, driving the British from Benghazi and regaining most of the territory lost in Operation Compass. A garrison of Australians was left holding on to Tobruk, aptly described as 'a bleak and unforgiving place, more heavily populated by scorpions, mosquitoes, flies and sand fleas than people'.[6]

Changing his mind again, Churchill now decided that Greece and Crete were less important than stopping Rommel's advance across North Africa. He kept up the pressure on his generals to relieve the besieged Tobruk. In mid-May 1941, Wavell launched the unfortunately named Operation Brevity, which lasted just one day but during which he lost ninety-six badly needed tanks. In mid-June, he tried once more to relieve Tobruk by means of Operation Battleaxe, which lasted for three days and also ended in failure.

By now, the ever-demanding Churchill had had enough: the time had come, he decided, to replace the popular Wavell as commander-in-chief with a general for whom he had a higher regard, the introverted Sir Claude Auchinleck, who would 'infuse a new energy and precision into the defence of the Nile Valley'.[7]

Meanwhile, further south, General Alan Cunningham's East Africa Force had overcome extreme conditions and tropical disease to march nearly 4 000 kilometres, drive Mussolini's forces out of Abyssinia and restore Emperor

Haile Selassie to his throne. After Addis Ababa had been occupied by the Allies on 6 April 1941, the Italian governor general, the aristocratic Duke of Aosta, surrendered a few weeks later. Later, in his official report on the successful East Africa Force operation, Cunningham made special mention of the assistance of the Union Defence Force, 'without which the campaign could not have been undertaken. ... Through the personal interest of Field Marshal Smuts, I was at the start able to knit the Force into a whole and all the many resources which the Union placed at my disposal were pooled for the common good of the whole Force ...'[8] The rout of the Italian naval and air forces, and the flight of the army opened up the Red Sea to Allied shipping once again.

In March, Smuts had flown to Cairo, via Nairobi, to deliberate again with Eden and the Chief of the Imperial General Staff (CIGS), General Dill. On learning that he was about to meet Eden, Churchill cabled Smuts to inform him of the decision to give assistance to the Greeks:

> I look forward to receiving your personal views upon this after your conference. The decision makes it most necessary to reinforce Egypt and Libya, and I hope you will arrange with Wavell and Dill to bring 'Acanthus' [the 1st South African Division] forward to the Mediterranean at the earliest moment ... Our affairs are helped by rapid successes gained in East Africa.[9]

The main topic on the agenda in Cairo was the situation in Greece, and in particular whether Australian and New Zealand troops should be sent into the Mediterranean to aid the embattled Greeks. Eden telegraphed Churchill to convey the meeting's view that the collapse of Greece, 'without any effort on our part to save her by intervention on land ... would be the greatest calamity ... In the existing situation we are all agreed that the course advocated should be followed and help given to Greece. We devoutly trust therefore that no difficulties will arise with the dispatch of Dominion forces, as arranged.'[10]

Having already had matters his own way as usual, Churchill was relieved to hear that the Cairo group had endorsed the decision to aid Greece, later writing for the record rather disingenuously: 'There was no doubt that their hands had not been forced by any political pressure from home ... Smuts, with all his wisdom and from his separate angle of thought and fresh eye, had concurred. ... Nor could anyone suggest we had thrust ourselves upon Greece against her wishes.'[11]

Diligent in keeping the US president abreast of developments, Churchill conveyed Britain's decision to Roosevelt:

> Our Generals, Wavell and Dill, who accompanied Mr Eden to Cairo ... believe we have a good fighting chance. We are therefore sending a greater part of the Army of the Nile to Greece and are reinforcing to the utmost possible in the air. Smuts is sending the South Africans to the Delta. Mr President, you can judge these hazards for yourself.[12]

Churchill was later to admit that his decision to support the Greeks had been a strategic blunder, but Commonwealth leaders, such as Smuts and Robert Menzies, felt on the other hand that he had made the right decision at the time. Smuts was supportive of intervention because of his deep admiration for Greece and its classical history. He also agreed with Menzies that reneging on a promise and abandoning the Greeks to their fate would give the wrong impression of Britain's resolve, especially in the US.[13]

By this time, Churchill was eager to talk to Smuts in person. In a message he sent to Eden in Cairo, he asked him to 'tell Smuts how glad I should be if, now he is so near, he could come and do a month's work in the War Cabinet as of old'.[14] Preoccupied with affairs at home, however, Smuts felt he could not afford to be away for so long and turned down the invitation.

*

Germany's betrayal of Stalin and invasion of Soviet Russia on 22 June 1941 was one of the turning points of the war. Though the British had long been aware of Hitler's intentions, an astonishingly complacent Stalin – despite being alerted to the danger – had chosen to ignore every warning. More than 3 million German troops in 150 divisions, supported by 3 400 tanks and 2 000 aircraft, swarmed across a 1 000-mile front into the Soviet Union, catching the Red Army unawares. Within the first six months of Operation Barbarossa, the invading

Germans had occupied present-day Belarus and most of Ukraine, and had laid siege to Leningrad (now St Petersburg). Vastly superior in ability to Stalin's forces but far fewer in number, Hitler's army found its progress slowed significantly by stiff resistance and determined Soviet counter-attacks. And, in a repeat of Napoleon's invasion of 1812, the German invaders fell foul of the Russian winter and were further hampered by the defenders' scorched-earth strategy of burning villages and crops to prevent them falling into German hands.

Since well before the Nazi–Soviet non-aggression pact of 1939, most of Britain's ruling class, and Churchill in particular, had viewed Stalin's Soviet Union with deep distaste.[15] After Hitler's betrayal of Stalin, however, Churchill set aside his aversion of Communism and welcomed the Soviet Union as a new ally, displaying his remarkable ability to think strategically and set aside long-standing prejudices when circumstances required. Explaining his new-found support for Stalin, Churchill told the US ambassador and others over dinner at Chequers that 'if Hitler invaded Hell, I would at least make a favourable reference to the Devil in the House of Commons'.[16] He then had to consider the tricky question of how much military hardware Britain could afford to dispatch to Stalin in Moscow.

Smuts distrusted Stalin as much as Churchill did, but consoled himself in the knowledge that the Soviet Union was now successfully absorbing the main impact of the German war machine.[17] In fact, as he wrote to a friend in Britain, the Russians were 'doing far better than knowledgeable observers had forecast'. The Americans, by contrast, he believed, were proving themselves 'the real disappointment' of the war.[18]

*

Throughout 1941, Churchill's foremost aim had been to draw the US into the conflict. He knew that without American help, Britain might keep the Axis powers at bay, but was unlikely to achieve victory. The newly re-elected US president, Franklin Roosevelt, had recognised the threat that Hitler posed to America's national interest, and was eager to assist Britain, but was hamstrung by having to honour his election campaign commitment to Congress and the people that American troops would not be sent to Europe.

From the outset of the war, Churchill had gone to great lengths to cultivate a close personal relationship with the American leader, updating him regularly on the military situation and impressing upon him the need for the US, in its own interest, to come to Britain's aid. It was an uphill battle, in which there was still no sure sign, by late 1941, that America would abandon its neutrality. In Max Hastings's words, 'it would be hard to overstate the bitterness that many people in Britain, high and low, felt about the US's abstention from the struggle'.[19]

Britons deeply resented American visitors telling them how to run the war, while the US remained unwilling to fight.[20] From the American perspective, though, as historian Michael Howard explained, the British did not realise that a very large number of Americans, if they thought about the British at all, did so 'with various degrees of dislike and contempt'. In Howard's view, in the early 1940s 'the Americans had some reason to regard the British as a lot of toffee-nosed bastards who oppressed half the world and had a sinister talent for getting other people to do their fighting for them'.[21]

Despite having his hands tied by Congress, Roosevelt did as much as he could to give Britain 'all aid short of war'.[22] His imaginative Lend-Lease scheme, which he forced through a reluctant Republican Congress and announced in 1941, enabled the US to send warships, tanks, aircraft and other military equipment across the Atlantic in return for the right to establish US bases on imperial soil.

Smuts may have played a small part in Roosevelt's decision making. In Jack Fishman's book *My Darling Clementine*, there is an account by General Sir Frederick Pile of a discussion over lunch with the Churchills about the difficulties the British were having with the Americans. Lend-Lease came at a high cost, and Churchill was distressed at the price being asked for fifty elderly warships; he felt the Americans were driving too hard a bargain. Out of the blue, Clementine Churchill is said to have asked her husband:

> 'Why don't you get Mr Smuts to talk to Roosevelt about this?' Winston jumped up at once and said, 'I will.'
>
> He put a call through immediately to Smuts in South Africa and asked him if he would talk to Roosevelt about the various points of disagreement between us. He did, and things improved. Mrs Churchill ... was

the one person sufficiently detached to see sometimes the whole picture from a quite different angle. It was genius [Sir Frederick continued] because Roosevelt was a person of world importance ... General Smuts was just the right stature and he was a tremendous friend of both of them – they both admired his statesmanship.[23]

Though Lend-Lease was more of a business deal than an altruistic gesture,* it provided Britain with a financial underpinning for the rest of the war.[24] Never one to understate matters, Churchill later described the scheme as 'without question, the most unsordid act in the whole of recorded history'.[25] 'From then on,' he wrote later, 'our relations with the US grew steadily closer.'[26]

In August 1941, Churchill braved the hazards of an Atlantic crossing aboard the battleship HMS *Prince of Wales* to meet Roosevelt at Placentia Bay in Newfoundland. They had not met face to face since 1918, when Roosevelt had not been impressed by Churchill, calling him 'a stinker'. At this, the first of their nine wartime meetings, the prime minister was intent on pleasing the president. And Roosevelt, fascinated by what he had heard about Churchill, 'was ready to be pleased'.[27]

High on the agenda of both leaders was the danger posed by Japanese aggression in the Far East. Britain, for its part, would be unable to respond if Tokyo were to attack its territories while America maintained its neutrality. The Americans, having embargoed supplies of oil and raw materials to the military government in Tokyo to protect their ally, China, also had good reason to fear Japanese bellicosity.

The outcome of the Newfoundland meeting was the Atlantic Charter, which affirmed the US and Britain's belief in the right of all people to 'choose the form of government under which they will live' (a ringing commitment that Churchill, and Smuts, would later have cause to regret). In the view of British military historian Walter Reid, the charter was not an idealistic statement of common intent, but a highly political document designed to constrain Britain's imperial activities and reassure Roosevelt's domestic critics.[28] The Anglo-American declaration also demanded the withdrawal of

---

* Lend-Lease required the selling of British assets in the US and the shipping of $120 million in gold bullion from South Africa to cover any shortfall. Churchill said at the time 'it was like a sheriff collecting the assets of a helpless debtor'. (See Walter Reid, *Churchill 1940–1945: Under Friendly Fire*. Birlinn, 2012, p 152.)

Japanese troops from Indochina and warned Japan against advancing further into the south-west Pacific[29] Noticeably absent, however, was any sign of America's intention to enter the war. As Churchill's military secretary noted, 'not a single American officer has shown the slightest keenness to be in the war on our side'.[30]

*

In August 1941, Smuts paid another visit to Cairo, this time accompanied by his wife, to inspect South African troops in the Western Desert holding a forward position at Mersa Matruh and preparing the defences at El Alamein. From the British Embassy in Cairo, he wrote letters to Churchill and Roosevelt to emphasise, once again, the dangers of neglecting the war in North Africa in favour of action elsewhere.[31]

A few weeks later, on 21 September, Britain's Governor General in South Africa, on behalf of King George VI, conferred on Smuts the rank of field marshal, describing him as 'a great rock in a weary world'.[32] Churchill had written to him earlier to offer him the honour:

> I wonder whether you would care for me to suggest to the King your appointment as an Honorary Field Marshal of the British Army. It seems to me that the great part that you are playing in our military affairs and the importance of the South African Army would make this appropriate in every way, and I need not say how pleasing it would be to your old friend and comrade to pay you this compliment.[33]

Smuts replied via Britain's Acting High Commissioner in the Union:

> I cannot tell you how much I appreciate your kind thought to suggest to the King my appointment as Honorary Field Marshal of the British Army. Personally I would value the honour most highly but the people of South Africa would also appreciate the compliment to them. That the honour should come from your hands moves me most deeply of all.[34]

If Smuts was pleased by his new rank, his Afrikaner Nationalist opponents, and especially their political cartoonists, were equally delighted. It was further proof that their prime minister was now more British than South African. From then on, they referred to him with mock respect not as 'General' Smuts, which he preferred, but by his honorary British title of 'Field Marshal'.

*

Both Churchill and Smuts were concerned that the Allied army in the Western Desert had not been able to take better advantage of the diversion presented by Operation Barbarossa in Russia to go on the offensive against Rommel's Afrika Korps. Wavell's replacement as commander-in-chief, the ever cautious Auchinleck, had persuaded Smuts if not Churchill that he needed more resources before his planned Operation Crusader could be launched.

To replace the Army of the Nile, 'the Auk' reorganised his forces in the Western desert into the Eighth Army, comprising troops from the UK, Australia, New Zealand, India and South Africa, commanded by Lieutenant General Alan Cunningham. On 18 November, Crusader got under way, with the Eighth Army driving west from Egypt along the coast of Cyrenaica (eastern Libya). Despite suffering a heavy defeat at Sidi Rezegh, the Allied army was able to outflank Rommel's forces and relieve the besieged Tobruk. The occupation and defence of this port by Australian troops had lasted for 241 days and denied the Axis armies access to key naval and airfield facilities on the Mediterranean coast. It was the first victory by British-led ground forces over the Germans in the war. By this time, both armies had overstretched their supply lines and, while they regrouped, there was a temporary lull in the fighting.

*

A few months earlier, in July, Smuts had predicted that the clash of interests between the US and the Japanese in the Pacific would eventually draw America into the war: 'Japan is at last coming into the open,' he wrote.

'Germany's attack on Russia was the first great surprise after the fall of France. Now Japan moves in the Far East and the repercussions may be even more serious. The USA will now be forced to take action which will sooner rather than later lead her into the war ... So Evil defeats itself, and however powerful and clever, works its own undoing ...'[35]

On 7 December 1941, he recorded that 'destiny is writing a new chapter in our tangled human story'.[36] That very night, the Japanese attacked Malaya and bombed America's Pacific fleet at anchor in Pearl Harbor. Next day, the US and Britain both declared war on Japan, and three days later Germany and Italy both declared war on America.

Churchill's immediate reaction to the news of Pearl Harbor, which reached while he was at dinner with American envoys, Gil Winant and Averell Harriman, was incredulity – and then relief and elation. 'We had won the war,' he wrote afterwards. 'England would live; Britain would live; the Commonwealth of Nations and the Empire would live ... Once again in our long island history we should emerge, however mauled and mutilated, safe and victorious.'[37]

When Britain's ambassador to Tokyo described Japan's assault on British territories in the east as 'a disaster for Britain', he was sharply admonished by the prime minister. 'On the contrary,' said Churchill, 'it is a blessing ... Greater good fortune has never happened to the British Empire.'[38]

Earlier in the day, Roosevelt had telegraphed to say, 'Today all of us are in the same boat with you and the people of the Empire and it is a ship that cannot and will not be sunk.'[39]

America's entry into the war prompted Churchill to make another visit to Washington to deliberate with Roosevelt. As usual, he wrote to Smuts beforehand:

> I thought it my duty to cross the Atlantic again, and hope to confer with President Roosevelt on the whole conduct of the war. I hope of course to procure from him assistance in a forward policy in French North Africa and in West Africa. This is in accordance with American ideas, but they may well be too much with the war in Japan. I will keep you informed.[40]

After a storm-tossed ten-day sea voyage, Churchill was Roosevelt's guest at the White House for the next three weeks, during which the prime minister suffered a mild heart attack, which only momentarily diverted his attention from war business. He and the American president laid plans for a joint Anglo-American war strategy, a key element of which was an Allied invasion of French North Africa, to which each country would commit 90 000 troops, to free the Mediterranean for Allied shipping.[41] Before Churchill left Washington, he and Roosevelt signed a declaration that led to the establishment, after the war, of the United Nations Organization.

*

Pearl Harbor was not the only Allied naval disaster to occur in the dying days of 1941. Having landed an invasion force in northern Malaya, the Japanese advanced relentlessly south towards the British Crown Colony of Singapore, defended by 85 000 British, Indian and Australian troops. On 8 December, on the eve of Churchill's departure for Washington, Japanese warplanes sank the British warships *Repulse* and *Prince of Wales*, with a terrible loss of life. Churchill deemed the shock to Britain of losing these ships to be as devastating as Pearl Harbor was to the Americans. His anguish was all the greater for his having overruled advice from the Admiralty – and from Smuts as well – that it was tempting fate to base Britain's naval presence in the western Pacific in inadequately defended Singapore.[42]

CHAPTER 14

Madagascar

Although Madagascar is separated from Ceylon by the breadth of
the Indian Ocean, the possibility of a Japanese descent or
a Vichy betrayal is a constant fear.

— CHURCHILL[1]

On 16 December 1941, the exiled leader of the Free French, General Charles de Gaulle, wrote to Churchill proposing the capture of the Vichy-held Indian Ocean island of Madagascar. The large land mass, one of the biggest island nation states in the world, lies along the shipping routes around the Cape of Good Hope to India and the Far East. After Pearl Harbor, the fear of Japan's intentions in the Indian Ocean made the seizure of Madagascar one of Britain's most immediate air and naval priorities.[2] Churchill and his military strategists were worried that the Vichy government might either cede the French colony to Japan or allow the Japanese to establish a naval base at the port of Diego Suarez (now Antsiranana), from where their submarines could threaten Allied shipping.

There was good reason for this concern among the Allies. In Indochina, Vichy had allowed the Japanese to take over bases and airfields in southern Vietnam and Cambodia without offering any resistance. Churchill did not believe, however, that Britain had the necessary resources to capture Madagascar and, after the fiasco in Dakar, he was not going to allow British forces to mount a joint operation with the Free French again. Instead, he turned to Roosevelt for naval assistance, which was forthcoming despite America's existing diplomatic relations with Vichy France.

In South Africa, Smuts had also become concerned that a Japanese presence on Madagascar might threaten supply lines to the Eighth Army in Egypt. On 12 February 1942, he telegraphed Churchill to say:

> I look upon Madagascar as the key to the safety of the Indian Ocean, and it may play the same important part in endangering our security there that Indo-China has played in Vichy and Japanese hands. All our communications with our various war fronts and the Empire in the East may be involved.[3]

On 5 March, Churchill sent the following reply:

> We have now carefully considered General de Gaulle's proposals for the occupation of Madagascar by Free French forces. Plan is dependent on support by British naval and air forces, and we are doubtful whether the necessary Free French forces are available. We are anxious not to reject De Gaulle's plan out of hand, but we cannot afford to risk a failure, particularly in view of the present attitude of the Vichy Government.[4]

In Volume IV of *The Second World War*, Churchill quotes, without attributing the source, from a conference held at Hitler's headquarters on 12 March 1942, at which the German naval chief reported to the Führer that the Japanese had recognised how strategically important Madagascar was for their naval warfare:

> According to reports submitted, they are planning to establish bases on Madagascar in addition to Ceylon, in order to be able to cripple sea traffic in the Indian Ocean and the Arabian Sea. From there they could likewise successfully attack shipping around the Cape. Before establishing these bases, Japan will have to get German consent. For military reasons, such consent ought to be granted. ... However ... such action on the part of the Japanese may have repercussions in the French homeland and the African homeland as well as in Portuguese East Africa.[5]

According to Churchill, Hitler had said 'he did not think France would give her consent to a Japanese occupation of Madagascar'.[6]

After Dakar, however, the British were taking no chances. Operation Ironclad, as the invasion plan to take control of the French colony was code-named, was mounted in the strictest secrecy lest Vichy got wind of it beforehand and sent reinforcements to Madagascar. To the fury of De Gaulle, the Free French were kept out of the loop and told about Ironclad only after the landings on Madagascar had begun. Major General Robert Sturges of the Royal Marines was in command of Force 121, made up of three infantry brigades; and Rear Admiral Edward Syfret was in charge of a naval armada of over fifty ships, which included an elderly battleship, two aircraft carriers taken from Gibraltar, two cruisers, eleven destroyers, four minesweepers, eight U-boat-hunting corvettes and various auxiliary ships.

On 24 March, Churchill telegraphed Smuts, surprising him with the news that an invasion force was already on its way, and would be sailing via Durban:

> As arrival of Japanese in Madagascar would not be effectively resisted by the Vichy French and would be disastrous to the safety of our Middle East convoys and most menacing to South Africa, we have decided to storm and occupy Diego Suarez. Assaulting force leaves tonight, intermingled with a convoy of 50 000 men for the East. Operation is, we believe, on a sufficiently large scale to be successful …[7]
>
> We cannot allow French troops from Dakar to reinforce Madagascar. There has been no leakage of our plans, but of course we cannot prevent German-Vichy suggestions or British newspaper surmises, since the strategic significance of this island harbour is obvious. Nonetheless, if we stop this Dakar crowd, we can get there first and if the operation is successful an enormous advantage will be gained.

Churchill continued:

> Our plans have been studied for many weeks, but until President Roosevelt had given us the naval replacements we needed we could not take decisions. It was only late this week that this was settled and I have been seeking an hour in which to tell you all about it. … Therefore I must beg you to favour this enterprise and facilitate our indispensable arrest of the French ships, should it be necessary to catch them at the Cape. We

will show them every possible consideration but of course they cannot on any account be allowed to go to Madagascar ...[8]

To this communication Smuts immediately replied:

> Your message alters whole situation. From previous correspondence I had concluded that the Madagascar operation had been postponed till the Ceylon situation had stabilized. In that case, interception of Vichy convoy now might have precipitated a crisis with French prematurely, with added risk of misunderstanding with America. Both these risks now disappear, and I shall give all necessary support for interception of convoy.[9]

Smuts was extremely keen to support Operation Ironclad, and offered a battalion of South African troops to occupy the whole of Madagascar, including the ports of Majunga and Tamatave. However, Churchill demurred. In a message to his chief of staff, General Ismay, he said that too much emphasis should not be placed on 'gaining control of the whole island. It is 900 miles long and all that really matters are the two or three principal centres, and above all Diego Suarez. We are not setting out to subjugate Madagascar, but rather to establish ourselves in key positions to deny it to a far-flung Japanese attack.'[10]

*

Madagascar was defended by some 8 000 French, Malagasy and Senegalese troops under the command of the pro-Pétain governor general, Armand Léon Annet. The local Vichy French had a few naval ships and aircraft, and some strategically positioned coastal batteries. Most of their defences were concentrated around the superb natural harbour at Diego Suarez, located in a bay entered through a narrow mile-wide gap between two high cliffs. The bay was large enough to contain the entire Japanese fleet, and fortified by a series of coastal batteries and a web of mines. France had last re-equipped the base in the 1930s.

At four o'clock in the morning on 5 May 1942, after extensive reconnaissance by South African Air Force planes from East Africa, Operation Ironclad was launched. A force of 13 000 Allied troops was landed in the dark on beaches near Diego Suarez, in what Churchill described as 'our first large-scale amphibious assault since the Dardanelles twenty-seven years before'.[11] Under a strong air and naval bombardment, the Vichy French force – though taken by surprise – resisted fiercely. After two days of intensive fighting, Diego Suarez and its dockyard fell to the Allied invaders. Elsewhere on the huge island, however, Annet's forces had yet to capitulate.

In the Madagascan countryside, hostilities were to continue intermittently for several months. On May 19, two British brigades on the island were withdrawn and dispatched to India, to be replaced by troops from South Africa and East Africa. Smuts, however, remained eager to extend operations. On 28 May he telegraphed Churchill:

> Tamatave and Majunga, as well as other ports, have been regularly used by French submarines and can be so used by the Japanese. Madagascar authorities are violently hostile, though not the population. After capture of Diego, no material resistance likely at present, but if time is given to organize resistance, we may have a stiff job. Control of Madagascar is all-important for our lines of communication in Indian Ocean and no risk can be run.[12]

Only days later, Smuts's fears were realised when the British flotilla off Diego Suarez came under surprise attack from three Japanese midget submarines. An oil tanker was sunk and the battleship HMS *Ramillies*, the flagship of the fleet, severely damaged. South Africa's prime minister sent another message to Churchill, expressing condolences 'on [the] Diego mishap':

> It all points to necessity of eliminating Vichy control completely from the whole island as soon as possible. Appeasement is as dangerous in this case as it has proved in all others, and I trust we shall soon make a clean job of this whole business. My South Africa brigade stands ready and simply awaits transport.[13]

After another lull in the fighting – during which, according to Churchill, the

French governor general was 'given a chance to amend his pro-Vichy attitude ... but remained obdurate'[14] – the second phase of Operation Ironclad began on 10 September, ahead of the rainy season. Allied troops, mainly from South Africa and Rhodesia, carried out amphibious landings at Majunga in north-west Madagascar, and Tamatave on the east coast.

With Diego Suarez now secure, Britain had more important military challenges in the Far East to worry about than subjugating the rest of the island's inhabitants. The French settlers in the capital, Tananarivo, were keen on settling matters so they could get back to making money, but knew that capitulating to the British would arouse the displeasure of Annet and the Vichy authorities. Through diplomatic channels, they let the British know that if they wanted the whole of Madagascar, they should apply enough force to make a Vichy surrender 'honourable'.

By this time, the remaining Vichy troops on the island had lost heart, as the following anecdote from Colin Smith's *England's Last War Against France* illustrates:

> Major Jones of the SAAF [South African Air Force] and four colleagues, one of whom was his navigator, 'Bull' Malan, younger brother of the famous RAF air ace 'Sailor' Malan, had crash-landed an aircraft some-where on the east coast of Madagascar. The well-built Malan had taken along with him a heavy Vickers machine gun from the plane's rear turret. Walking through a narrow path in the thick bush, Jones heard the approach of what turned out to be a French officer and eight Malagasy riflemen. He told his colleagues to hide.
>
> 'You are my prisoner,' said the Frenchman to the South African, in English.
>
> 'No, No, Monsieur le capitaine, you are *my* prisoner,' said Jones. At which point, he broke into Afrikaans, *'Bull, los maar 'n paar skote* (Bull, let off a few shots). 'Bull' obliged with a short burst into the air with his Vickers.
>
> 'Monsieur, I am your prisoner,' agreed the Frenchman, and the party adjourned to a nearby lighthouse where they were all picked up by a naval vessel.[15]

When Tananarivo and the nearby town of Ambalavao surrendered in late September, and Tuléar, in the south, had also fallen, the British-led forces declared victory. Yet sporadic fighting went on until 8 November, when Annet finally surrendered near Ilhosy in the south and was sent into comfortable internment in Durban.

Six months to the day after it had begun, the Madagascar exercise was over. The Allies had sustained 620 casualties; Vichy French and Malagasy casualty numbers were unknown. It later transpired that Germany and Japan had not valued Madagascar as a submarine base nearly as much as the British – and Smuts – had feared. After the Allied forces had been withdrawn, the island was left in Free French hands, as 'a recognition of De Gaulle's claim to constitutional authority'.[16] Churchill telegraphed Roosevelt to reassure him that the island would remain French and would receive all the economic benefit accorded to French territories 'which have already joined the United Nations'.[17]

The prime minister described the Madagascar campaign, 'in its secrecy of planning and precision of tactical execution [as] a model for amphibious descents'.[18] It was also for many months, 'the only sign of good and efficient war direction of which the British public were conscious', he said.[19]

CHAPTER 15

Trouble in the east

So far we have not failed. We shall not fail now. Let us move forward
steadfastly together into the storm and through the storm.
— CHURCHILL[1]

The devastating postscript in the Far East to the attack on Pearl Harbor came as no surprise to Smuts, who had warned seventeen years earlier, when a naval base was mooted for Singapore, that it would be a strategic error for Britain to divide its fleet.[2] He kept silent in public, but writing privately to his confidante, Margaret Gillett,* Smuts pointed out that he'd predicted almost everything that had occurred in the Far East, but his comments had been 'pigeon-holed'.[3]

After meeting Admiral Tom Phillips, commander of a naval force of several ships including HMS *Prince of Wales*, who was en route to the Pacific via Cape Town in late 1941, Smuts wired Churchill to warn him of the Royal Navy's vulnerability: 'If the Japanese are really nippy, there is here opening for a first-class disaster.'[4]

Smuts had always maintained that the huge danger zone extending from Malaysia to New Zealand ought to be a combined American-British responsibility. He wrote later:

If the British fleet at Singapore and the American fleet at Pearl Harbor had been together somewhere in the Pacific, Japan might never have

---

* Margaret Gillett was the granddaughter of radical Quaker John Bright. She was a close friend in whom Smuts confided for most of his adult life.

entered this war and ... both we and America would still have had our
big battleships, now at the bottom, and the prospect before Hitler would
have been one of unrelieved gloom.[5]

Despite the swiftness of Japan's conquest of Malaya, Singapore, the
Philippines, the Solomon Islands, northern New Guinea, Burma and Hong
Kong, Smuts did not believe the Japanese could withstand the might of
America indefinitely. He told Parliament in March 1942 that the Japanese
had committed the greatest act of national folly in history, and it was better
that way, for Japan was an evil influence and if there had to be a showdown
with evil, 'let it be worldwide'.[6]

Smuts was gratified to learn that on Churchill's visit to Washington
immediately after America's entry into the war, he had managed to persuade
Roosevelt that, notwithstanding Pearl Harbor, victory over Germany was
the immediate aim and, after that, victory in Asia over the Japanese. Smuts
agreed with the prevailing British view that it was of greater importance for
the Allies to take control of the North African coastline from Tunis to Egypt
and the Levant (including France's African territories) than open a second
front in Western Europe – as many Americans and Stalin were proposing.
Until US war materiel could reach Europe on a massive scale, which, by his
reckoning, would take at least a year, Africa should be given priority. In a letter to Roosevelt, Smuts wrote: 'To me, the all-important consideration is our
time-table. It is 1942 that matters most. No doubt we can develop and deploy
huge resources in 1943 and 1944, but we must first pull through 1942.'[7]

Smuts's thinking, at the time, was that even if Hitler defeated the Russians,
victory in Africa would give the Allies time to establish a firm base from
which to counter any German thrust towards the oilfields of the Persian Gulf
and Middle East. And if Hitler became bogged down in Russia, there would
be an opportunity to attack the weaker 'hangers on of the Axis' across the
Mediterranean from Africa, before launching a cross-Channel attack from
Britain on Germany.[8]

For Churchill, 1942 began badly. On 15 February Singapore's more numerous
but grievously under-resourced defenders put up only perfunctory resistance

to the invading Japanese. In and around the city, and in nearby Malaya, 9 000 British troops were killed and more than 130 000 taken prisoner. It was the biggest British-led wartime surrender ever, which meant that the great waterways of the Pacific were now vulnerable.[9]

Although the loss of Singapore was less the fault of its defenders than Britain's military establishment, which had diverted munitions destined for the Far East, and Singapore in particular, to Russia and the Middle East, there is little doubt that the badly trained and underequipped British-led army had given in too easily. As British newspapers pointed out, the implications for the empire were alarming: Australasia was now under threat and the Middle East might conceivably follow.

A mortified Churchill wrote to Roosevelt: 'We have suffered the greatest disaster in our history at Singapore and other misfortunes will come thick and fast upon us.'[10] He was forced to admit to himself that, time and again – in Norway, France, Greece, Crete, Libya and now at the tip of the Malay Peninsula – British forces had been badly beaten. As General Alan Brooke confided to his diary in great despair: 'If the army cannot fight better than it is doing at the present, we shall deserve to lose our Empire.'[11] To anyone who questioned how he kept his morale up, Churchill would explain that there was no alternative but to 'KBO – Keep Buggering On'.[12]

By early March 1942, the global outlook for the Allies had worsened. Java, Sumatra, Timor, Borneo, New Guinea and the entire Dutch East Indies had fallen to the Japanese; the conflict in North Africa had stalled; and the US Navy and Royal Navy were in danger of losing the war at sea to the Germans.[13] To add to Churchill's mortification, two German battleships, the *Scharnhorst* and *Gneisenau,* and the cruiser *Prinz Eugen* were able to slip out of Brest harbour, on the north-western French coast, and sail through the English Channel in broad daylight, despite being pursued by the Royal Navy and RAF, to reach the safety of German ports in the North Sea. This 'Channel dash', a publicity coup for the Germans, upset the British public even more than the fall of Singapore, according to diarist Henry 'Chips' Channon. For the first time in the war, comments critical of the government and Churchill began to appear in British newspapers.[14]

The burden on Britain's leader was immense, and only someone of extraordinary mental toughness could have coped with the heavy workload, high levels of stress and the regular setbacks from the battle front. To add to the pressure, Churchill found his conduct of the war coming under attack in Parliament. He responded by taking the fight to his critics and demanding a vote of confidence in his leadership. One who felt deeply for him was Smuts, who wrote: 'Democracy does really involve a cruel waste. How can a man find time and proper concentration for some of the hardest and most fateful problems of all time, when he has continually to pause and prepare for and make speeches which surely involve an immense amount of physical and mental energy?'[15]

Smuts need not have worried. In the House of Commons, the combative prime minister gave as good as he got. During a two-hour speech, he declared:

> There has never been a moment, there could never have been a moment when Great Britain, or the British Empire, single-handed, could wage the Battle of Britain, the Battle of the Atlantic and the Battle of the Middle East – and at the same time stand thoroughly prepared in Burma, the Malay Peninsula and generally in the Far East against the impact of a vast military Empire like Japan.[16]

The subsequent vote of confidence he insisted upon went in his favour by 364 votes to one. As he wrote to his friend Smuts: 'Just now I am having a very rough time, but we must remember how much better things are than a year ago, when we were all alone. We must not lose our faculty to dare, even in dark days.'[17]

*

One of the crosses Churchill had to bear during World War II was what to do with his erstwhile friend the Duke of Windsor, the former Edward VIII, whose side he had taken in the abdication crisis. Now in exile in Portugal (having fled France when it fell to the Nazis) and suspected of having pro-Nazi sympathies, the Duke had been packed off to the Bahamas as governor, as a means of getting him out of harm's way in Europe. In May 1942, a deciphered 'most secret and personal' message reached Smuts from Churchill:

The Duke of Windsor is anxious to have a wider sphere of activity than that presented by Nassau. As you will imagine, his affairs and well-being are important to the State. I have been wondering whether the Governorship of Southern Rhodesia which is again vacant might not afford him the scope he seeks ... I should be grateful to know your personal views as to how such a solution would affect the Union.[18]

Smuts responded immediately:

I am most grateful to you for consulting me about Viscount [*sic*] Windsor. Frankly I cannot but feel that his presence in [an] official capacity anywhere in Southern Africa, and particularly the adjacent Union, might have the most awkward consequences on public opinion both Afrikaans and British ... There is an open republican movement here and it is therefore all the more important to keep personnel of the Royal Family out of public and private discussion here. Actions or inactions of His Royal Highness and his wife in Rhodesia could not be kept from such people in the Union. I may add that the presence of an ex-King of England in subordinate capacity in Africa, responsible to the Secretary of State, would be very difficult to explain to the millions of natives here and in the neighbouring British territories as the Crown has a special significance in their mind ... I appreciate your anxiety and personal sympathy for His Royal Highness, whose difficult position I understand, but I cannot, as you have invited my opinion, refrain from stating that his selection for the post might be embarrassing to the best friends of continued co-operation of South Africa in the Commonwealth under the Crown.[19]

The troublesome royal stayed put in the Bahamas until the end of World War II, his defeatism and supposedly pro-German views a constant source of concern to Churchill, and at times Roosevelt, who asked the Federal Bureau of Investigation, established by Edgar Hoover before the war, to keep a close eye on the Windsors.[20]

*

As if Churchill did not have enough on his mind in early 1942, he also had to deal with the imminent threat of a Japanese advance on India. 'India is vital to our existence,' Field Marshal Auchinleck had told him. 'We could still hold India without the Middle East, but we cannot hold the Middle East without India.'[21] Even before the fall of Singapore, Britain's deputy war leader, Clement Attlee, had been arguing in favour of 'an act of statesmanship' towards India. A new political initiative was needed, he told the War Cabinet, to get Indian political leaders to unite in defence of their country against the marauding Japanese.[22]

Gandhi, whose tactic of non-violent resistance was often a catalyst for the violence of others,[23] had precipitated matters by going on a well-publicised 'hunger strike to the death' on 9 February. A furious Churchill informed the king that 'the old humbug, Gandhi' was so healthy 'one wonders whether his fast is bona fide?'[24] He cabled the viceroy, Lord Linlithgow, saying: 'I have heard that Gandhi has glucose in his water when doing his various fasting antics. Would it be possible to verify this?'[25] When Linlithgow reported that the allegation was untrue, Churchill urged the viceroy to remain 'steadfast and unflinching'. He ordered his ambassador in the US, Lord Halifax, to tell any uneasy Americans that they may 'be certain there will be no weakness here'.[26]

On the sixteenth day of Gandhi's hunger strike, Churchill cabled Smuts: 'I do not think Gandhi has the slightest intention of dying and I imagine he has been getting better meals than I have for the last week. It looks now highly probable that he will see his fast out. What fools we should have been to flinch before all this bluff and sob-stuff.'[27]

Next day, he wired the viceroy: 'It now seems certain that the old rascal will emerge all the better from his so-called fast. The weapon of ridicule, so far as it is compatible with the Government of India, should certainly be employed.'[28]

Lord Linlithgow was of a similar mind to Churchill. 'I have long known Gandhi as the world's most successful humbug and have not the least doubt that his physical condition and the bulletins reporting it from day to day have been deliberately cooked so as to produce the maximum effect on public opinion,' he wrote.[29] Whatever the case, on 3 March 1942, Gandhi ended his fast and soon afterwards was released from prison.[30]

Attlee and his Labour colleagues had been insisting that it was time to send a single representative from the British government to negotiate with all parties in India, including the Muslim League.[31] Their proposed envoy was fellow socialist Sir Stafford Cripps,[†] an austere vegetarian, like Gandhi, and known to be sympathetic to the Indians' cause. Churchill, whose idiosyncratic views on India were well known, reluctantly agreed. Added pressure for political negotiations came from the anti-imperialist Americans, who needed India as a base from which to supply President Chiang Kai-shek's forces in China. Roosevelt worried that Indian resistance against the Japanese might falter unless Britain could come to some new constitutional arrangement, such as a 'temporary government', that would satisfy India's fractious politicians.[32]

Cripps took with him to India an offer of independence from Britain, dominion status and the right to leave the Commonwealth after the war, as well as freedom for Indian parties to draw up their own constitution, in return for military cooperation during the war. To placate the Muslim League, he also announced that any province opposed to a new constitution would be able to secede. To Cripps's astonishment – and mortification – his offer was resoundingly rejected on all sides. Gandhi scornfully dismissed it as 'a postdated cheque on a bank that is going bust'.[33] So Cripps, Roosevelt's envoy to India, Louis Johnson, and Congress had hurriedly to cobble together an alternative arrangement whereby Indian ministers would oversee the defence of India – only to have this proposal also vetoed by Gandhi, who feared Muslim secession and the fragmentation of India.[34] Only six days earlier, Japanese bombs had fallen near Calcutta.[35] Gandhi was one of the very few who maintained that the Japanese did not wish to conquer India, having convinced himself that once the British left, the reason for Japan to attack his country would disappear.[36]

The future of India was one issue, according to Roosevelt's right hand, Harry Hopkins, on which the president and Churchill's minds could never meet.[37] As Roosevelt came to realise, Churchill deeply resented any American interference

---

[†] It was said of Cripps that he was, like other men, in favour of short skirts for women, but unlike them his reason was the need to save textile material. (See Peter Clarke, *A Question of Leadership: From Gladstone to Thatcher*. Penguin, 1992, p 203.)

in Indian affairs. Knowing this, he once mischievously invited a vocal supporter of Indian independence, Ogden Reid, to lunch with the British leader in Washington. 'What are you going to do about those wretched Indians?' Mrs Ogden Reid wanted to know of Churchill, who replied, 'Before we proceed further, let us get one thing clear: are we talking about the brown Indians in India, who have multiplied alarmingly under benevolent British rule? Or are we speaking of the Red Indians in America who, I understand, are almost extinct?' Mrs Ogden Reid was speechless; Roosevelt roared with laughter.[38]

Churchill was quietly relieved that the Cripps mission had failed because, this time, it was the Indians, and not the British, who had stood in the way of what America had been asking for. He echoed Cripps's words in his final report: 'Now we get on with the job of defending India.'[39]

Gandhi, however, remained an obstacle by continuing to insist that the presence of the British was an invitation to the Japanese to invade India.[40] This made even the tough-minded Indian Congress leader, Nehru, uneasy; in his view, Gandhi was being hopelessly naive.[41] After Cripps had departed, Nehru said, 'We are not going to surrender to the invader. In spite of all that has happened, we are not going to embarrass the British war effort in India. The problem for us is how to organise our own.'[42] Most other Indian Congress politicians, however, preferred the pacifism of Gandhi.[43]

In August 1942, Gandhi launched his 'Quit India' movement, a campaign of civil disobedience aimed at forcing an orderly British withdrawal from India. The country was plunged into 'a state of ordered anarchy' in which there were riots, strikes, damage to public buildings and the looting of property. Not all Indians were supportive of the movement and the British government cracked down hard on those involved, imprisoning Gandhi, Nehru and other Congress leaders, most of them for the rest of the war.

Gandhi had overestimated his followers' appetite for martyrdom this time, and his campaign soon petered out. Churchill noted wryly in his memoirs that Congress's agitation had not hampered recruitment into India's armed forces. By the end of 1942, the largest volunteer army in history had been enlisted: no fewer than 34 divisions had signed up to keep the Japanese out of India.[44] Before that, the American Navy's victory at the Battle of Midway in the central Pacific in June 1942 had inflicted irreparable damage on the Japanese fleet and brought an end to Japanese naval domination of the Pacific region.

CHAPTER 16

Changing commanders

I myself was prepared to go even to the gates of hell! We were going to release our boys captured at Tobruk and bring them home.

— SMUTS[1]

While Britain's dominoes were falling in the Far East, the battle for control of North Africa resumed in earnest in mid-1942. Immediately at stake was the security of Malta, the strategically important island base for British air and naval operations in the Mediterranean and North Africa. Malta had already become a byword for courage and endurance, sentiments exemplified by the axiom mounted on the door of the RAF's air commodore, Hugh Lloyd: 'Less depends on the size of the dog in the fight than on the size of the fight in the dog.'[2]

Under siege from the Axis powers since 1940, Malta was one of the most intensively bombed targets in World War II: over a two-year period, German and Italian warplanes had flown an estimated 3 000 bombing raids over the island in an attempt to knock out RAF air bases and Royal Navy ports. It was little Malta that stood in the way of the Axis armies making amphibious landings along the North African coast and taking control of North Africa.[3]

On the question of Malta's significance to the North Africa campaign, Churchill found himself at odds once more with his commander in the Middle East. He and Auchinleck held diametrically opposing views. The prime minister believed the recapture of Cyrenaica in Libya and neutralisation of the port of Tripoli were essential to winning the Desert War. The 'Auk', also responsible for the strategically important Persian oilfields to the east,

Mediterranean Theatre

viewed Cyrenaica and Malta 'only peripherally'.[4] Churchill wanted action, but Auchinleck would not move until his forces were ready. 'The bloody man doesn't seem to care about the fate of Malta,' Churchill fumed.[5] Once again, he had begun to lose confidence in an obdurate general, who compounded matters by refusing to travel to London to review the situation in the Middle East with the impatient prime minister.[6]

*

From February to May 1942, Auchinleck and Rommel's forces had taken up positions opposite each other along the Gazala Line, a series of defensive fortifications in the Cyrenaican Desert, about thirty miles west of Tobruk (*see map*). Rommel struck first, and yet again the British-led forces, under General Ritchie, dithered. By mid-June, Rommel had seized control of the Gazala Line, as well as the approaches to Tobruk, rendering the port inaccessible. Major General HB Klopper of the 2nd South African Infantry

Division, in command of British, South African and Indian troops garrisoned at Tobruk, was ordered to defend the fortress but was unable to hold out against Rommel's superior forces.

Auchinleck had regarded the defence of Tobruk as non-essential and had told Ritchie the base was not to be held at all costs. By 20 June, Klopper had lost all his tanks and half his guns, and on 21 June, realising there was no point in fighting on, he surrendered. Besides a huge store of food, fuel and weaponry, 33 000 Allied prisoners of war were given up to the Germans, 10 000 of them South Africans. On 25 June, a triumphant Hitler promoted Rommel to Field Marshal, while Auchinleck fired Ritchie and took personal command of the Eighth Army to try to halt Rommel's seemingly unstoppable drive towards Egypt, and Suez. By the end of June, the Eighth Army had fallen well back into Egypt, holding a thirty-mile line between the impassable Qattara Depression and an insignificant coastal port 240 kilometres west of Cairo, known as El Alamein.

The siege of Tobruk in 1941 had given the Allied-held fortress an iconic status, which made its fall to the Germans all the more devastating.[7] Churchill was given the news during another of his visits to President Roosevelt in the White House. 'Defeat is one thing,' he said. 'Disgrace is another.' As he wrote afterwards, 'This was one of the heaviest blows I can recall in the war. Not only were its military effects grievous, but it had affected the reputation of the British armies.'[8] It was the latest in a long series of British military failures.

If news of the fall of Tobruk came as a shock to Churchill, to Smuts it arrived with the force of 'a thunderbolt from the north'.[9] He recovered his equanimity quickly, though, and at the country's premier horse race, the Durban 'July', arranged for armoured cars to race around the track bearing placards carrying the words 'Avenge Tobruk'. Within a week of this recruitment drive, 5 000 more young men, including his eldest son, Japie, had volunteered for service 'up north'. Smuts also sent messages to Churchill and Auchinleck, saying it was not the time for post-mortems, but for securing what could be held. As Auchinleck struggled to hold the line against Rommel at the (according to D'Este, misnamed) First Battle of El Alamein,[10] Smuts sent the beleaguered general another message, expressing his confidence and saying he would be with him 'heart and soul' in the forthcoming battle for Egypt.[11]

With his mind on so many other matters, it took Churchill a few days to send Smuts a message about Tobruk, which he eventually did on 4 July:

> I have been so much harried by the weaker brethren in the House of Commons since my return from America last week that this is the first chance I have had of telling you how deeply I grieve for the cruel losses you have sustained in your gallant South African divisions, and how I admire the indomitable manner in which you have inspired South Africa to face this heavy blow.
>
> We have been through so much together and are so often in harmony of thought that I do not need to say much now about lamentable events of the last three weeks. The President gave me three hundred of their latest Sherman tanks ... a hundred gun howitzers as anti-tank weapons ... and up to one hundred Liberators [bombers]. Two heavy Halifax bombing squadrons from England will be in action during the next ten days. Another sixty American fighters are being rushed across the Atlantic, via Takoradi. All this is in addition to our regular reinforcement of the air. As you probably know, the 8th Armoured Division with 350 tanks ... is landing now. The 44th British Division should land July 23, and the 51st a month later. Whether these forces will be able to play their part depends upon the battle now proceeding at Alamein.[12]

Smuts replied three days later:

> What with your most heartening message and news from Middle East foreshadowing that tide [which] is turning at El Alamein, yesterday was one of my happiest days. I do believe Rommel has overstretched himself, and if Auchinleck remains in personal charge, not only will Tobruk be avenged, but our counter-stroke may carry us right on to Tripoli and save both Egypt and Malta. ...
>
> As America is now our great strategic reserve for the final blows, much of your time will have to be devoted to wisely guiding Washington in its war effort and not letting vital war direction slip out of our hands. I think your service in this respect can now be at least as great as your Empire war service. Your contacts with Roosevelt are now a most valuable war asset,

and I hope your weaker brethren with their purely domestic outlook will be made to realise this.[13]

*

Earlier, in April 1942, Roosevelt had dispatched two of his most trusted aides, Harry Hopkins and General George C Marshall, to try to persuade Churchill and his advisers of the need to undertake an early Allied landing in France, by mainly British forces. A 'second front', it was argued, would divert Hitler's attention from the 'first front' in Russia, and ease the burden on Stalin. Churchill and Co. were incredulous: here were the Americans, latecomers to the war, impatient for action that would entail another major sacrifice of British troops. Outwardly, Churchill responded enthusiastically to the president's plan, describing it as 'masterly'; inwardly, he had no intention whatsoever of approving another invasion of Europe before Allied forces were battle-ready.[14]

It took another visit by Churchill to Roosevelt, at which the former was at his most persuasive, and further discussions between British generals and the senior US officer in Europe, General Dwight D Eisenhower, before the Americans understood that they could not plan an invasion that depended almost entirely on the further loss of British lives.[15] Instead, and with much reluctance, General Marshall agreed to commit his forces to Operation Torch, an invasion by the Allies of Vichy-controlled Algeria and Morocco, to take place later in 1942. Smuts approved wholeheartedly of Torch. The time had come, he said, 'to end this African see-saw once and for all'.[16]

In the meantime, the loss of Tobruk had caused an avalanche of criticism to descend upon the head of Churchill and his government. The prime minister was hurt by his Labour bête noire Aneurin Bevan's cruel taunt in the House that he 'wins debate after debate, but loses battle after battle'.[17] To Bevan, he responded with wry humour: 'I do not resent criticism, even when, for the sake of emphasis, it departs from reality.'[18]

In another exchange with his opponents over the unreliability of British weapons, including a new tank named after him, he replied that the tank had indeed many defects and teething problems, but only when these became apparent had it been christened the 'Churchill Tank'. Another motion of no-confidence in his government was easily defeated by 475 votes to 25. Roosevelt telegraphed to say, 'Good for you.'[19]

From their different vantage points, Smuts and Churchill had been conducting their own post-mortems into what had gone wrong in North Africa. The fall of Tobruk had caused Churchill to lose even more confidence in his generals, who were proving no match for Rommel. Auchinleck's message that he would not be able to take the offensive against the Afrika Korps until mid-September 1942 proved to be the last straw for the prime minister.[20] There was nothing wrong with British soldiers that better leadership could not rectify, he believed.[21]

Smuts, for his part, agreed that a lack of leadership was the main shortcoming, but he also thought that the commander-in-chief of the Eighth Army had far too great an area of responsibility.[22] Though supportive of Auchinleck while his army was on the retreat, he believed it was time for the 'Auk' to show more aggression. Smuts had no time for defeatist rumours of a possible British withdrawal from Egypt. Earlier, his representative, General Frank Theron, had tipped him off about an emergency fall-back plan for South African forces to retreat to Palestine.[23]

On 23 July, Smuts let Churchill know that his confidence in the military leadership in North Africa had been gravely shaken by the talk of withdrawal. Churchill responded by inviting the South African leader to join him for 'a grand inquest' in Cairo, and then to accompany him to Moscow to explain British-American thinking to Stalin (the latter an invitation that Smuts had to decline).

In early August, Smuts flew to meet Churchill in Cairo for their first face-to-face meeting in more than a decade. King George VI had written to his prime minister wishing him *bon voyage* on a visit that would be, in his words, 'epoch-making' because of 'two people with whom you will make personal contact, Smuts and Stalin. Two great men in their own spheres, utterly different in character but with a single aim to win the war.'[24] In reply Churchill said: 'I am looking forward to meeting my old friend Smuts again. His wisdom and courage will be a comfort in these serious days that lie ahead.'[25]

*

After a long and uncomfortable trip via Gibraltar in an elderly Liberator bomber with only shelves for beds, Churchill arrived in Cairo, accompanied by General Sir John Dill's replacement as Britain's Chief of the Imperial General Staff, General Sir Alan Brooke*, the tough-minded, brusque Northern Irishman, whose candid *War Diaries* were later to become a source of friction between the two men.

Brooke had been looking forward to meeting Smuts for the first time. After their get-together on 2 August, with Churchill present, Brooke recorded in his diary that Smuts, who had just flown in from Pretoria, had been 'astounding good value, and full of wit in answering the PM's remarks'.[26] He and Smuts found themselves in agreement that changes in the Eighth Army command, though regrettable in Auchinleck's case, were desirable because Auchinleck selected his subordinates badly. 'Most of the changes he suggested coincided with my own views. He is the most delightful old man with a wonderfully clear brain,' Brooke noted.[27]

Two crucial decisions emerged from the Cairo deliberations. First, the Middle East command would be divided into two, with General Harold Alexander brought in to take command of Middle (i.e. Near) East, with Persia (now Iraq) split off into a separate command; and, secondly, General William Gott would take over the Eighth Army from Auchinleck.

Both Churchill and Smuts had wanted Brooke to assume the crucial Near East command, which included the Eighth Army, but the Irishman refused after what he described as 'one of the most difficult days of my life'.[28] Certain that it would be the wrong move because he knew nothing about desert warfare and believing he could be of more value at Churchill's right hand, the unselfish Brooke turned down the tempting offer.

Smuts then tried to exercise his own power of persuasion. Brooke describes this attempt in his diary:

> Telling me what importance he attached to my taking [the command], and what a wonderful future it would have for me if I defeated Rommel, I repeated exactly what I had said to the PM. Thanked him for his kindness but said he did not really know me well enough to be so assured I should make a success of it. At last I got him to agree that Alexander was a better

---

* Later Lord Alanbrooke

selection than me.[29]

Before any changes could be announced, however, Gott's plane was shot down by German fighter aircraft on 7 August as he was on his way to take up his new post. After further discussion with Smuts, a shaken Churchill appointed General Sir Bernard Montgomery, who had been earmarked to lead British forces in Operation Torch later in the year, to head the Eighth Army in Gott's place. On 8 August, Churchill sent Auchinleck a letter offering him the Persia/Iraq command. When an acutely disappointed Auchinleck turned down the offer, Sir Henry (Jumbo) Wilson was appointed to the Baghdad post. Churchill later described disposing of the generally well-regarded Auchinleck as like 'killing a magnificent stag'.[30] Yet the decision was the right one – as events were to prove: many people, including Brooke, considered Montgomery to be Churchill's best appointment of the war.[31]

Dictating a letter to Clementine on 9 August, Churchill described how he, Brooke and Smuts had been in continual discussion with 'the necessary people' in Cairo, collecting opinions from all quarters. 'Smuts was magnificent in counsel,' he wrote. 'We could work together with the utmost ease. He fortified me where I am inclined to be tender-hearted, namely in using severe measures against people I like.'[32] He continued: 'Smuts, I'm sorry to say, has gone. He has promised to come to England in September to stay at least a month so I shall convene a formal session of the Imperial War Cabinet then.' Announcing the changes in the Middle Eastern command before leaving Egypt, Churchill acknowledged 'the massive judgment of Field Marshal Smuts, who flew from Cape Town to Cairo to meet me.'[33]

*

Churchill's physician, Lord Moran, was another to pen some acute observations of his own about Smuts in Cairo:

> While they [Churchill and Smuts] talked I kept asking myself what kind of a man is Smuts? Is he the Henry James of South Africa? Does he think of his fellow Boers as James came to think of the American scene as

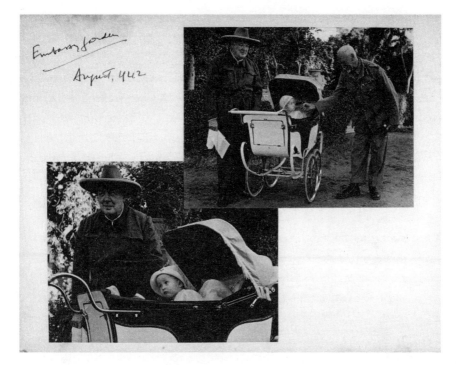

*Churchill and Smuts enjoy some distraction from the cares of war, Cairo, August 1942.
The infant in the pram is the present Lord Killearn, son of Sir Miles Lampson,
Britain's High Commissioner in Egypt.*

PHOTO BY KIND PERMISSION OF LORD KILLEARN

perhaps a little primitive? A South African here speaks of him as remote; even to his own people he is a stranger. No one really knows him. It appears that this solitary, austere Boer with his biblical background lives in a world of his own. It is as if he had been cut off from his kind.

He lives to get things done. Anyone who steps in his path is ruthlessly pushed aside. As for his colleagues in the Cabinet, they are kept at arm's length. The whole political apparatus is just a necessary nuisance. He is taken up with the war and with world events; social affairs in South Africa mean little to him: he is not interested in the slums of Johannesburg. Like Winston, he is sure that there is nothing in the world which he could not do as well as anyone. There is nothing that cannot be thought out. Certainly he has an extraordinary mind, thinking out everything for himself. And yet in the end, human nature being what it is, I am fearful that his arrogance will trip him up.[34]

From Cairo, Churchill and Brooke flew on to meet Stalin in Moscow. On his return, Brooke recorded his impressions of the two leaders he had only recently met:

It has been very interesting meeting men like Smuts and Stalin. Such a contrast! Smuts I look upon as one of the biggest of nature's gentlemen that I have ever seen. A wonderful clear grasp of all things, coupled with the most exceptional charm. Interested in all matters, and gifted with the most marvellous judgment. Stalin, on the other hand a crafty, brilliant realistic mind, devoid of any sense of human pity or kindness. Gives one almost an uncanny feeling to be in his presence. But undoubtedly a big and shrewd brain, with clear-cut views of what he wants and expects to get.[35]

CHAPTER 17

The tide turns

It is the cleanest, neatest, most sudden and spectacular victory
of the war and in size is quite comparable to the German
defeat before Stalingrad.

— SMUTS[1]

Having reorganised Britain's Middle East command to his satisfaction, the seemingly tireless Churchill undertook the long flight to Moscow from Cairo for his first meeting with Joseph Stalin, whom he described as 'the great Revolutionary Chief and profound Russian statesman and warrior with whom for the next three years, I was to be in intimate, rigorous but always exciting, and at times almost genial, association'.[2]

The purpose of Churchill's visit was to reassure Stalin that Britain was making a significant contribution to the war against Germany, which Russia might otherwise have been fighting alone.[3] The Russian leader had already been tipped off by his spies in Britain that Churchill was bringing some unwelcome news: the Allies were not about to launch Operation Sledgehammer, the cross-Channel invasion of Europe to open a 'second front' – at least not in 1942.[4] Plans were being made, however, Churchill explained to Stalin, for 'a very great operation in 1943', by which time a million American troops would have reached the UK.[5] Stalin affected displeasure at the disclosure: 'A man who is not prepared to take risks,' he taunted Churchill, 'cannot win a war.'[6] But the Russian leader perked up when told that the bombing of Germany was one of Britain's leading military objectives.[7] He was further mollified by news of the imminence of Operation Torch, the Allied invasion of North Africa. If the Allies could win possession of Axis-controlled territory along the North African coast by the end of 1942, Churchill explained to him, they could threaten the 'soft belly' of Hitler's Europe before attacking 'his hard snout' in 1943.[8]

After four days of intense and often unpleasant exchanges with his host, Churchill returned to Cairo, having established a limited rapport with Stalin but nevertheless satisfied that he had achieved as much as he could in difficult circumstances. Averell Harriman, the American envoy who accompanied him, was full of admiration for the prime minister's forbearance in the face of Stalin's rudeness, and for not once being tempted to refer to the Russian leader's ill-judged and ill-fated 'devil's bargain' (non-aggression pact) with Hitler in 1939.[9]

Back in Cairo, Churchill was impressed by the personnel changes Montgomery had already made among the leaders of his new command. He was even more delighted with Monty's explanation of how he proposed to drive Rommel and his forces out of Egypt and Cyrenaica. As Walter Reid describes him, Monty was 'arrogant, cocksure, untruthful, ruthlessly ambitious and unpleasant in his dealings with senior fellow-officers, but he [Churchill] loved his vulgar showmanship, and it worked very well with most, if not all, on whom it was deployed. He put new heart and confidence into junior commanders and other ranks.'[10]

Although disappointed that it would take another six weeks to prepare the Eighth Army for the offensive, Churchill sensed that in Montgomery he at last had a commander who might make good on his promises.[11] The prime minister's high spirits were dampened only by physical exhaustion as well as news of the failure of Mountbatten's raid on the port of Dieppe in occupied France. The incursion on the French coast had been intended as a trial run to demonstrate Britain's seriousness about launching a second front, but the exercise cost the lives of 1 000 troops, mainly Canadians, and the loss of 2 000 prisoners of war.

In Cairo, Churchill received a congratulatory message from Smuts:

> I have read your Moscow messages with interest, and congratulate you on a really great achievement. Your handling of a critical psychological situation was masterly ... and you have achieved even more than you appear to realise and finally bound Russia to us for this war at least. The

quarrelsome interlude was evidently a clumsy attempt by Stalin to save appearances for himself while really accepting 'Torch' as a better alternative for 'Sledgehammer' … After reading your account of talks, I feel much happier about Russia than I had felt before. There appears now to be a good prospect of Hitler having to spend another winter in Russian mud, while we clear [the] Mediterranean and establish a firm base for Second Front next year. … After your Herculean labours, I implore you to relax. You cannot continue at the present pace. Please follow Charles Wilson's [his doctor Lord Moran's] advice as you expect [the] nation to follow yours.[12]

*

In mid-October 1942, as promised, Smuts visited Britain – his first during World War II. After talks with military commanders in Cairo, he boarded the Liberator bomber sent specially by Churchill and flew over Rommel-occupied North Africa to Gibraltar, and on to London. He was put to work immediately, attending meetings of the War Cabinet twice daily, the Defence Committee, the Privy Council and the Pacific War Council. He was the only dominion leader invited to these high-level meetings.* He also met with King George VI, the kings of Yugoslavia and Greece, as well as several prime ministers and foreign ambassadors. After an audience with Queen Wilhelmina of the Netherlands, Smuts broadcast a message to her people in Dutch.

Perhaps remembering Smuts's success with the Welsh miners at Tonypandy in World War I,[†] Churchill enlisted him to exhort 3 000 coal miners to support the war effort at a meeting in Westminster. The highlight of his visit, however, was his address on 21 October to the combined Houses of Lords

---

* See JC Smuts, *Jan Christian Smuts*. Cassell, 1952, p 422. This involvement on the part of Smuts would have been resented by Prime Minister Robert Menzies of Australia, who had argued for an Imperial War Cabinet in which all the dominions would be consulted on war strategy. At first a critic of Churchill, Menzies was to become as much of an admirer of Britain's war leader as Smuts (See John Ramsden, *Man of the Century: Winston Churchill and His Legend Since 1945*. HarperCollins, 2003, pp 486–489.)

† Smuts had been sent by Lloyd George to Tonypandy in the Welsh coalfields in late 1917 to address a huge crowd of disaffected miners. He managed to avert a strike by asking his hostile audience to sing to him – a visitor from afar who had heard that the Welsh were among the world's greatest singers. His invitation broke the tension and enabled him to persuade the crowd to go back to work and defend the 'Land of My Fathers', of which they had sung so well. (See Richard Steyn, *Jan Smuts: Unafraid of Greatness*. Jonathan Ball, 2015, pp 86–87.)

and Commons, an honour never before accorded to a Commonwealth prime minister. The gathering in the historic Royal Gallery of Parliament was presided over jointly by Churchill and Lloyd George, and broadcast live by the BBC to 15 million people. In his speech, which was preceded by a two-minute standing ovation, Smuts declared that the 'defensive phase' of World War II was over and that the 'offensive phase' was about to begin.[13] Thanking Smuts for his speech afterwards, Churchill said:

> The wisdom which he brings, the knowledge which he has of all those matters which he has touched in his broad survey, are invaluable to those of us who are charged with executive responsibility, and is a comfort and an inspiration. All that he has said arises from profound reflection – full of knowledge and resolute, unflinching, inflexible conviction and courage.[14]

Yet not everyone was as impressed. Harold Nicolson MP wrote in his diary that Smuts, who looked 'bronzed and vigorous and spoke for 55 minutes', had 'uttered every commonplace that we have all been trying to avoid for years'.[15] A Conservative, Leo Amery, on the other hand, described the speech as 'finely-phrased and inspired by a lofty conception of what the British Commonwealth is today'.[16]

The timing of Smuts's address to Parliament was propitious. In the Western Desert, Montgomery had repelled an attempt weeks earlier by Rommel's forces to break through the key Alam Halfa Ridge, outside El Alamein. He had since been trying Churchill's patience by waiting for October's full moon before launching Operation Lightfoot, his long-awaited counter-attack on the Axis army.

With a massive advantage of roughly two to one in men, tanks, anti-tank guns and artillery pieces, and after two weeks of the most savage fighting of the Desert War, the Eighth Army succeeded in overcoming Rommel's half a million mines laid across five miles of desert[17] and driving the Afrika Korps out of Egypt and across the Libyan desert back into Vichy-held Tunisia. It was the first and last significant land victory of British Commonwealth forces in World War II – from then on, every major battle was fought as part of an alliance.[18] On 13 November 1942, Churchill ordered church bells in Britain to be rung in celebration of victory at Alamein. 'This is not the end,' he declared with undisguised relief. 'It is not even the beginning of the end. But it is perhaps the end of the beginning.'[19]

While the Battle of Alamein was still raging, Operation Torch got under way at the western end of the North African coast on 8 November. A joint American and British force under General Eisenhower landed near Casablanca in Vichy-held Morocco, and at Oran across the border in Algeria (*see map on page 140*). Brooke noted in his diary: 'If Torch succeeds, we are beginning to stop losing this war.'[20]

On the Russian front, there were even more crucial developments. The five-month-long battle for Stalingrad (now Volgograd) – the most savagely fought in history, and far more costly to the Nazis than El Alamein – had begun to turn in Stalin's favour. Hitler had committed some 190 divisions to the subjugation of Stalingrad, but only three to Alamein.[21]

Eisenhower's Torch invasion force of 117 000 men (35 000 of them British) was half the size of Montgomery's 200 000-strong Eighth Army, but there was immense symbolic significance to the commitment of so many American ground troops to the fight against Hitler.[22] As always, Churchill involved himself deeply in the planning of Torch, which was directed from both Washington and London. He, Eisenhower and American General Mark W Clark would sit up into the early hours of the morning fretting over and questioning every aspect of the operation. On occasions, Smuts would also be present. Brooke confided to his diary that he often had to tone down his excitable chief's 'excessive demands', but recognised that he could never have as much influence as Smuts. To bring an end to one interminable late-night meeting, he recorded, 'Smuts sent the prime minister to bed, like a small boy, and he went off obediently, as though despatched by his mother.'[23]

The invading Allies encountered a confusion of loyalties among the 125 000-strong French forces defending North-West Africa. Some supported Pétain's Vichy regime; others were sympathetic to the Allies.[24] In Morocco, Casablanca fell without resistance to US General George Patton but in Algeria there was some opposition in Oran. An attempted coup by soldiers in the capital, Algiers, delivered the city to the invading Allies. In both countries, French resistance proved to be less of a military problem than a temporary inconvenience.

In neighbouring Tunisia, the resistance was much more vigorous, however. A furious Hitler had ignored Rommel's advice that North Africa was a lost cause and ordered some 100 000 additional German and Italian troops to be sent to Tunisia to reinforce the battered Axis army. After a British-led thrust was stopped about forty miles from the capital, Tunis, any further Allied advance was held up by the new Fifth Panzer Army, supported by the Luftwaffe, and compounded by the onset of the rainy season. In mid-January 1943, the Eighth Army succeeded in capturing the key port of Tripoli, in adjoining Libya. Ten days later, Rommel's retreating forces reached Tunisia and took up a defensive position along the Mareth Line, a formidable system of fortifications built by the French before World War II.

Buoyed by the Eighth Army's successes in North Africa, Churchill now sought a summit of the 'big three' to settle on an Allied strategy for bringing about Hitler's defeat. Stalin declined to leave Moscow, so Churchill invited Roosevelt to meet him in Casablanca in January 1943. After ten days of discussions, the two leaders had surveyed the 'whole vast war scene' and reached agreement on what should be done in five or six different theatres around the world. 'It is in every respect as I wished and proposed,' a well-satisfied Churchill wrote to his wife. 'The triumphant arrival of the Eighth Army in Tripoli has made it possible for us to obtain practically all the solutions we wished from our American friends.'[25]

The Casablanca summit, the most important Anglo-American strategic conference of the war,[26] was the last meeting at which the British prime minister's opinions would prevail. Up to then, most operations had been dependent on Britain's military strength, but the success of Torch had put an end to that. As the US became more directly involved in the war, and Britain's resources declined, Churchill's influence with Roosevelt and Stalin began inevitably to wane – a development he gradually but reluctantly came to realise.[27]

At Casablanca, it was agreed that the next priority for the British and American forces was the capture of Tunis, as the precursor to an invasion of Sicily and thereafter mainland Italy. By now, Hitler's decision to rush reinforcements to Tunisia to forestall the loss of his precarious North African foothold had rendered an Allied cross-Channel invasion of France in the

Smuts and Churchill with Mrs Clementine Churchill after the two premiers
had addressed mining delegates on 31 October 1942.

CENTRAL ARCHIVES REPOSITORY

summer of 1943 impossible. That would now have to take place in 1944. Stalin, as might be expected, was highly displeased.

Under pressure from Hitler, Rommel had not abandoned his efforts to establish an Axis foothold in Tunisia, however. In mid-February 1943, his troops and the Fifth Panzer Army under General von Arnim launched surprise attacks on Allied positions in the Atlas Mountains, causing heavy American losses during the Battle of Kasserine Pass. In early May, the Eighth Army broke the French-fortified Mareth Line and joined with the other Allied forces in Tunisia. On 7 May, the Afrika Korps at last surrendered and its 250 000 troops were taken prisoner. General Alexander cabled Churchill saying, 'It is my duty to report that the Tunisian campaign is over. All enemy resistance has ceased. We are masters of the North African shores.'[28]

*

Cartoonists in the Nationalist Afrikaner press in South Africa delighted in
portraying Smuts as Churchill's puppet.

TO HONIBALL/DIE BURGER

Churchill would have liked Smuts to stay on in London well beyond the five weeks he had committed to in late 1942. He wanted him to go and see Roosevelt in America to persuade the American president of the need for the Allies to carry the war across the Mediterranean and into Italy, before planning for any 'second front' in France. Smuts had obligations in South Africa, however, and wrote Roosevelt a long letter instead.

Back home, Smuts noted with satisfaction what had been decided at Casablanca but was apprehensive about the slow pace of the Allied armies' attempts to oust the Axis forces from Tunisia. He was also concerned about Churchill's health. After Casablanca, the peripatetic British prime minister had criss-crossed North Africa and visited Turkey before coming down with a severe bout of pneumonia, which confined him to bed for a fortnight. From his sickbed, Churchill followed closely the course of the battle for Tunisia.

When the Tunisian campaign reached its triumphant climax in early May, Smuts was euphoric: 'It is the cleanest, neatest, most sudden and spectacular victory of the war. And in size quite comparable to the German defeat before Stalingrad. In Africa it is a crowning mercy as Cromwell would have said … I am a happy man and deeply thankful for this great "mercy" …'[29]

Smuts was also not about to let a promising political opportunity go by. With South Africa's Parliament coming to the end of its five-year term, and the victory in North Africa bringing many wavering white voters to his side, he called a general election for June 1943 and won with a comfortable majority of sixty-seven seats over the anti-war Afrikaner Nationalists. It was the greatest political triumph of his career. The successful outcome in North Africa – to which South African forces had made a proud contribution – and Germany's travails in Russia had undermined his opponents' confident predictions of an Allied defeat; and it encouraged voters who now wished to be on the winning side.

As the South African prime minister noted drily, there are 'none so keen as those who come up when the fight has [already] been won'.[30]

CHAPTER 18

A demanding man

Of course I'm an egoist. Where do you get if you aren't?
— CHURCHILL[1]

Whenever Smuts came to England during World War II, Britain's prime minister would set aside his other business and make time to see him. As Churchill's private secretary, Sir John (Jock) Colville recorded, the PM would 'listen attentively to the accented words of wisdom spoken in high staccato tones, which poured from the South African patriarch on all the issues of present and future policy ... There were few of Churchill's colleagues in the British Government whose words carried the same weight.'[2]

Smuts was often invited to spend weekends at Chequers, the country retreat of Britain's prime ministers. It was there that he encountered his host's egocentric working habits at first hand.

In his memoir of World War II, Churchill explains how he was able to maintain his exhausting daily schedule: it was a 'method of life' forced upon him at the Admiralty during World War I, which greatly extended his capacity for work. Every day, he would take to his bed for at least an hour after lunch, and fall into a deep sleep. By so doing, he wrote, he was able to work late into the night and compress a day and a half's work into one:

> Nature had not intended mankind to work from eight in the morning until midnight without that refreshment of blessed oblivion which, even if it only lasts twenty minutes, is sufficient to renew all the vital forces. I

regretted having to send myself to bed like a child every afternoon, but I was rewarded by being able to work through the night until two or even later – sometimes much later – in the morning and begin the new day between eight and nine o'clock. This routine I observed throughout the war, and I commend it to others if and when they find it necessary for a long spell to get the last scrap out of the human structure.[3]

This regime may have worked well for the prime minister, but it imposed a severe strain upon those who had to attend to him, especially in the early hours of morning. After the war, there were many vivid accounts of what it was like working for Winston Churchill. No day, it was said, was ever normal when he was around. He had to be awoken at 8.00 am because that was when the daily intelligence report arrived. After a full English breakfast, washed down by black tea or the occasional glass of white wine, he would remain in his pyjamas – surrounded by a retinue of assistants – puffing on a cigar and attending to papers, which came in a large black dispatch box. After a hot bath, in which he wallowed about 'like a pink, plump porpoise', summoning secretaries on the other side of the closed bathroom door to take dictation while he splashed about, he would leave to attend daily meetings of the War Cabinet or other committees.[4]

Lord Alanbrooke, in his celebrated *War Diaries*, paints a colourful portrait of Churchill in the mornings:

> The scene in his bedroom was always the same and I only wish some art-ist could have committed it to canvas. The red and gold dressing gown in itself was worth going miles to see, and only Winston could have thought of wearing it! He looked rather like some Chinese Mandarin. The few hairs were usually ruffled on his bald head. A large cigar stuck sideways out of his face. The bed was littered with papers and despatches. Sometimes the tray with his finished breakfast was still on the bed table. The bell was continually being rung for secretaries, typists, stenographers, or his faithful valet, Sawyers.[5]

Churchill always focused intently on the job at hand. On one memorable occasion at Chequers, he was propped up in bed, smoking his usual cigar while dictating to a stenographer, when the bedclothes began smouldering and were about to burst into flames. The stenographer excused herself to sound the alarm. A private secretary rushed in to find Churchill wreathed in cigar and other smoke. 'Sir, I think you are on fire,' he said.

'So I am,' replied Churchill.

'Would you like me to put you out?' the aide enquired.

'Yes, please do,' said the unruffled prime minister, who went on working as if nothing out of the ordinary had happened.[6]

Churchill's sense of humour seldom failed him. On his way to the Yalta Conference, he was laid up in bed. He shouted to his valet, 'Sawyers, where is my hot water bottle?' Sawyers answered: 'You're sitting on it, Sir, not a very good idea.'

'It's not an idea,' retorted the PM. 'It's a coincidence.'[7]

Churchill's morning meetings would always be followed by an extended lunch, never eaten on the run because any meal was an opportunity for serious conversation or discussion. The food would be accompanied by a bottle of Pol Roger champagne, one or two brandies perhaps, and a glass of port. After lunch, there would be the 'Cuban siesta', another bath, and then it was back to work again.

Food, and especially drink, were extremely important to Churchill, who ignored all dietary rules and for some reason was able to get away with it. Boris Johnson puts it well: 'It is as if his body was itself a physical symbol of the nation's ability to soak up punishment.'[8] He had a great fondness for red meat and believed that, by consuming beef, the British soldier was being far more sensible than any nutritional scientist. He once told his Minister of Food, 'Almost all the food faddists I have ever known, nut eaters and the like, have died young after a long period of senile decay.'[9]

He drank whatever alcoholic drink he felt like, whenever he wished to. When told, at a splendid banquet for King Ibn Saud of Saudi Arabia, that the king's religion meant there could be no smoking or drinking in his presence, Churchill replied that his religion prescribed, as an absolute sacred rite, the smoking of cigars and drinking of alcohol 'before, after and if need be during, all meals and the intervals between them'.[10] The Saudis surrendered meekly.

When the American envoy, Harry Hopkins, came across him enjoying a bottle of wine for breakfast, Churchill explained that he hated canned milk, but had 'no deep-rooted prejudice about wine' and had 'resolved the conflict in favour of the latter'.[11] A glass of weak whisky and soda was at his side throughout the day. He held all this liquor remarkably well; it was only late at night that he was occasionally the worse for wear.

Dinner, served at 8.00 pm, was his favourite meal – invariably soup, fish, roast beef and Yorkshire pudding, followed by ice cream – accompanied once more by champagne, brandy and port, as well as cigars. At 10.00 pm or even later, he might chair a committee, or call in a Cabinet minister or civil servant to discuss an aspect of the war. He would usually go to bed at between one and three in the morning.[12]

The demands of this abnormal routine on his staff, who had to be up early in the morning and could not, like him, enjoy a siesta after lunch, were considerable. As Geoffrey Best observes, grumbling about their chief was endemic among those around him, yet serving such an extraordinary leader was a form of war service that most regarded as a privilege: 'Submission to his will was a tribute paid to genius.'[13]

Churchill much enjoyed the sound of his own voice and would subject his guests at the lunch or dinner table to long monologues and rambling reminiscences. Lord Moran wrote:

> Winston feeds on the sound of his adjectives. He likes to use four or five words with the same meaning as an old man shows you his orchids; not to show them off but just because he loves them. The people in his stories do not come to life; they are interred in a great sepulchre of words ... So it happens that his audience, tired by the long day, only wait for a chance to slip off to bed, leaving Winston talking to those who have hesitated to get up and go.[14]

The hyperactive prime minister had a very low boredom threshold: he disliked having to stand in line to shake the hands of strangers at official receptions or sit through long films. He once told a friend that his favourite evening was to enjoy fine food in the company of friends, and then to move on to a good discussion – 'with myself as chief conversationalist'.[15]

His energy late at night was unflagging. Alanbrooke records being called in after midnight to Chequers to discuss aspects of the war in North Africa. At 2.15 am, Churchill suggested they adjourn to the hall for some sandwiches. He then put on a 'gramophone', and in his multicoloured dressing gown, with sandwich in one hand and watercress in the other, trotted round the hall giving occasional little skips in time to the music. 'On each lap,' wrote Alanbrooke, 'he would stop at the fireplace to release some priceless quotation or thought.' At ten minutes to three, they were allowed to go to bed.[16]

Churchill's generals, like Wavell and Auchinleck, did not know what to make of him. 'Pug' Ismay once wrote to Auchinleck to say that while the 'Auk' and the prime minister might be temporarily at loggerheads, this would be a passing phase:

> You cannot judge the PM by ordinary standards; he is not in the least like anyone you and I have ever met. He is a mass of contradictions. He is either on the crest of a wave, or in the trough; either highly laudatory or bitterly condemnatory, either in angelic temper, or a hell of a rage; when he isn't half asleep, he is a volcano. There are no half-measures in his make-up ...[17]

Perhaps the best description of what it was like to work for Churchill came from Sir George Mallaby, an undersecretary in the Colonial Office and thereafter High Commissioner to New Zealand:

> Anybody who served anywhere near him was devoted to him. It is hard to say why. He was not kind or considerate. He bothered nothing about us. He knew the names only of those very close to him and would hardly let anyone else into his presence. He was free with abuse and complaint. He was exacting beyond reason and ruthlessly critical. He continuously exhibited all the characteristics which one usually deplores and abominates in the boss. Not only did he get away with it but nobody really wanted him otherwise. He was unusual, unpredictable, exciting, original, stimulating,

provocative, outrageous, uniquely experienced, abundantly talented, humorous, entertaining – almost everything a man could be, a great man.[18]

*

On his wartime visits to Chequers, Smuts would often be accompanied by his younger son and aide, Jannie (jnr), a serving officer in the Union Defence Force. There Jannie was able to observe at first hand the personal chemistry between Churchill and his father. In the biography he wrote after his father's death, he emphasises the 'warmth of feeling and mutual admiration that was touching to behold. ... In public, it was "Prime Minister" and "Field Marshal", but otherwise it was simply "Winston" and "Jan". ... In each other's company, they seemed to cast the cares of the world from their shoulders and to assume a new animation. They were a tonic to each other.'[19]

Churchill ruled his entourage 'with a rod of iron and a stern peremptoriness,' Jannie observed. 'His personal physician had no more influence over him than his valet, Sawyers. My father was the only man he listened to with respect.'[20]

Churchill's bodyguard, Edmund Murray, endorsed this observation: 'It wasn't surprising that these two great statesmen always got on harmoniously, for I think the Old Man had greater respect and admiration for the Field Marshal than for any other man living at that time.'[21]*

The abstemious Smuts,† who once complained that his host would be asleep when he (Smuts) was working, and working when he (Smuts) wanted to be sleeping,[22] was one of the few people who were able to influence Churchill. In Cairo, the future British prime minister, Harold Macmillan, wrote of Smuts in his war diary: 'He is going to stay there [in England] more or less permanently. This is most fortunate for us all. He has all the qualities which will make him

---

* During the war, there had been gossip that in the case of accident Smuts might step into Churchill's shoes. Churchill's private secretary, Sir John Colville, records that in 1940 a colleague suggested to him that if anything should befall Churchill during the war, he should be succeeded by Smuts. Colville put the idea to his mother, lady-in-waiting to Queen Mary, in the expectation that she would mention it to her son, the King. See John Colville, *Downing Street Diaries: The Fringes of Power:* Sceptre, 1985, p 319. And Jannie Smuts recorded in his notebook on a visit to Chequers in 1943 that Churchill wanted Smuts to take over his job while he (Churchill) was away at the Tehran conference. (See JC Smuts, *Jan Christian Smuts.* Cassell, 1952, p 342.)

† Smuts's severely simple living quarters and spartan lifestyle were a source of wonderment to visitors to his wood and corrugated-iron residence at Irene, aptly described by his son as 'an ideal refuge for Stoics'.

an admirable addition to the PM. And it will be very good for Winston to have a colleague older than himself whom he cannot browbeat.'[23]

Churchill's personal physician held a similar view: 'Smuts is the only man who has any influence with the PM; indeed he is the only ally I have in pressing counsels of common sense on the PM. Smuts sees so clearly that Winston is irreplaceable, that he may make an effort to persuade him to be sensible,'[24] Lord Moran recorded in his diary in exasperation.

Time meant nothing to Churchill; he could just as easily phone an aide at two o'clock in the morning as two o'clock in the afternoon. He took it for granted that someone would be around to attend on him at any time of day or night. Public holidays were working days, and he once convened a meeting at 1.45 am on a bank holiday.[25] Military chiefs were often summoned from London to Chequers for an after-dinner discussion, late at night. Nothing was allowed to stand in the way of winning the war.

In America, Roosevelt's invitation to Churchill 'to treat the White House as his home' was taken literally by the prime minister, who would use his host's state home to summon the likes of General George Marshall to his presence. The Americans had difficulty adjusting to their visitor's unorthodox schedule. Roosevelt's secretary once minuted the following observations after Churchill had departed after one of his extended stays in Washington: '[It] must be a relief to the Boss, for Churchill is a trying guest – drinks like a fish and smokes like a chimney, irregular routines, works nights, sleeps days, turns the clocks upside down ... Churchill has brains, guts ... and a determination to preserve the British Empire.'[26]

Much as Smuts revered Churchill, he was not, like most people, intimidated by him, even at Chequers, where he (Smuts) preferred to be in bed by his usual ten o'clock. After the war, Earl Mountbatten of Burma, Britain's commander in South East Asia, would dine out on the story of the only night he saw Churchill defeated. Mountbatten explained that there had been a long and drawn-out dinner at Chequers, during which the prime minister held the floor in his usual way, interrupted only by some teasing from Smuts. This had been followed by a film show, which ended well after midnight:

At about 1 am, Churchill said to the gathering, 'Well, Gentlemen, now we will start work ...' 'No,' said Smuts, 'I am not going to start work. I am not going to be party to killing your Chiefs of Staff. Here they are; they have to be back in the office by 9 o'clock in the morning, ready for meetings at 9.30; you will still be lying in bed with a fat cigar, dictating to your secretary. They will have to work all morning and all afternoon; in the afternoon you have a siesta. You bring them down here and make them work all night as well; you will kill them and I am not going to be a party to that.'

With that, Smuts got up and went off to bed. ... There was a stunned silence for a minute or two; nobody spoke. After a long pause, Winston stood up and said, 'Well, Gentlemen, perhaps we'd better go to bed.'[27]

'That was the only time he let us off,' Mountbatten recalled.[28]

CHAPTER 19

A meeting of minds

*It would be a disaster if it afterwards appeared that Russia had won
the war. It would make her the master of the world and this
might go to her head.*

— SMUTS[1]

The Allied victory in North Africa did more than change the course of the war in Europe. It immediately reduced South Africa's strategic significance. With the Mediterranean open to shipping once again, the importance of the sea route around the Cape suddenly decreased. As Hancock observed, 'it was the irony of fate that Smuts and his country should find themselves so much diminished by victories they had done so much to win'.[2] Like Churchill, Smuts deeply resented the diminution of his influence.

While the British war effort was at its peak, Churchill was able to speak with authority to the Americans and Russians, and would regularly consult Smuts, who needed little encouragement to turn his mind to matters of grand strategy.[3] Ever since World War I, Smuts had insisted that political decisions should always come first and military planning second. Although he agreed, as did Churchill, that the Allies should go all out for victory in 1944, unlike the Americans he believed the route to victory should be through southern Europe and then, with the Axis forces divided and stretched, by an invasion of France across the English Channel. His reason for insisting on an attack via the Mediterranean was his concern for the state of European civilisation after the war, and mounting concern over the growth of Russian power.[4]

The Americans, under the direction of General Marshall, were much less concerned than the British about the fate of Europe. To the impatient

Marshall, any operations in the Mediterranean were a diversion from the more important exercise across the English Channel, and would also prolong the conflict in the Pacific. It took a further meeting between Roosevelt and Churchill, at the White House in May 1943, before a compromise was reached. Operation Overlord, the invasion of France across the Channel, would begin on a target date of 1 May 1944. In the interim, an American – in the person of General Eisenhower – would take overall command of Allied operations in the Mediterranean.

In July, the Allies' Italian campaign began with an airborne and amphibious attack on the Axis-held island of Sicily, as a prelude to the invasion of the Italian mainland. The operation, known as Husky, was a complex exercise requiring close collaboration between the various air, naval and land forces. It revealed some immediate shortcomings in Anglo-American cooperation and implementation. Preliminary aircraft and glider incursions turned out to be, according to D'Este, a 'first-class disaster',[5] though the Eighth Army's amphibious landing was much more successful. In Sicily, the Italians offered feeble resistance, but the German army put up a spirited fight before withdrawing across the Straits of Messina onto the Italian mainland. Within six weeks, Husky was over and the way had been opened to the invasion of Mussolini's Italy.

From South Africa, Smuts cabled Churchill to urge that the next step should be the capture of Rome, 'whose possession,' he said, 'may mean the transformation of the whole war situation this year and the chance of finishing it next year'.[6] Churchill replied that a decision had to be made whether to invade mainland Italy immediately or not:

> I believe the President is with me: Eisenhower in his heart is naturally for it. I will in no circumstances allow the powerful British and British-controlled armies in the Mediterranean to stand idle ... In all this there is great hope provided action is taken worthy of the opportunity. I am confident of a good result, and I shall go all lengths to procure the agreement of our Allies. If not we have ample forces to act by ourselves.[7]

In the end, it was not necessary to go to 'all lengths': on 17 July a message from Marshall to Eisenhower proposed a direct amphibious assault on Naples. A delighted Churchill telegraphed Marshall: 'Post Husky, I am with you heart and soul.'[8] To Smuts, he cabled: 'General Marshall's view is a great relief to me ... We all go the same way home.'[9] Eisenhower, however, was not satisfied with the air cover mooted for the navy and called off plans to attack the key port of Naples in order to cut off the Axis forces in Sicily. Instead, he decided the Allied army should establish a firmer toehold on the mainland, before proceeding northwards.

The fall of Sicily prompted the dismissal, arrest and detention of Mussolini, and the appointment – by King Victor Emmanuel III – of himself and Marshal Pietro Badoglio to govern Italy. Within weeks, the new leaders opened secret negotiations with the Allies, at which point Churchill persuaded Washington that yet another summit was necessary to settle the future of Italy. On 5 August the prime minister left with an entourage of 200 aboard the *Queen Mary* for a meeting with Roosevelt and his American advisers in Quebec. There, at the conference, code-named Quadrant, more serious differences of opinion emerged between US and British military chiefs over Allied strategy. The Americans, under pressure from Stalin, were insistent on inflicting a direct body blow on Germany by carrying out Operation Overlord in May 1944, as planned, whereas Churchill and his generals argued that, if the Germans were capable of mustering fifteen mobile divisions in France in the two months following an invasion, the landings should be postponed.[10] To the chagrin of the Americans, it appeared as if the British were reneging on a prior commitment.

This was not the case, however. Unlike Churchill (and Smuts), as well as Stalin, America's military establishment had given no consideration to any post-war settlement in Europe, and were not intending to remain on the continent for any longer than was necessary.[11] Whereas Churchill had already foreseen the likelihood of Stalin pushing as far as he could into western Europe after the war, the Americans had not thought that far ahead. They looked with suspicion upon Churchill's eagerness to take the offensive in the Mediterranean, as well as in the Balkans, Greece and the Middle

Churchill met President FD Roosevelt in Quebec again in 1944 to agree, inter alia,
on a policy for the treatment of Germany after the war.

East, in preference to mounting the risky Channel crossing, regarding it as a
reversion to Britain's 'traditional imperialism', to which they remained resolutely opposed.[12] Harry Hopkins told Anthony Eden that Roosevelt loved
Churchill 'for the war, but [was] horrified at his reactionary attitude ... after
the war'.[13] The president's anti-colonial stance seemed not to extend, however,
to America's own overseas colonies and dependencies – in the Philippines, the
Virgin Islands and Puerto Rico.

After much heated discussion between the two sides, the Quebec conference
eventually reached two firm decisions: the main strategic priority in 1944
would be Overlord, and the commander on D-Day, the Allied invasion of
France, would be an American. At the meeting, Roosevelt and Churchill also
discussed the imminent production of the atom bomb, likely to be ready for
use by August 1945.[14]

The pace of events in Italy now quickened. The new Badoglio government's readiness to capitulate had made it unthinkable that the Allies could leave a vacuum on the Italian peninsula for the German army to fill.[15] On 3 September, while Italian representatives were signing surrender documents in Sicily, Eighth Army troops landed on the mainland, north of Reggio. On 8 September, Eisenhower announced the terms of an Italian armistice. That night German forces began to occupy Rome.

In South Africa, Smuts was most dissatisfied with the outcome of the Quadrant deliberations, both the limited scale of the proposed Allied operations and the leisurely timetable envisaged. He replied to a conference summary sent to dominion prime ministers with two cables to Churchill, which are quoted at length in the latter's memoirs.

The nub of Smuts's objection was that instead of Allied urgency after the Tunisian and Sicilian landings, there had only been dithering:

> To compare the Anglo-American effort, with all our vast resources, with that of Russia during the same period, is to raise uncomfortable questions … Our comparative performance on land is insignificant and its speed very unsatisfactory. There is much and constant boasting of our production effort, especially of the colossal American production. And after two years of war the American fighting forces must be enormous. But still, the Russians account for the vast bulk of the German army on land. … Surely our performance can be bettered and the comparison with Russia rendered less flattering to us. To the ordinary man, it must appear that it is Russia who is winning the war. … If this impression continues what will be our post-war world position compared with Russia? A tremendous shift in our world status may follow, and leave Russia the diplomatic master of the world.[16]

Smuts expanded upon his concerns in another cable a few days later:

> I must frankly express my disappointment with this Quebec plan as being an inadequate programme for the fifth year of the war … It does no justice to the real strength of our position, and may gravely affect public morale as well as future relations with Russia. We are capable of a much greater effort, and should face the position with greater boldness …

In effect, the plan merely proposes to continue and increase the present bombing and anti-U boat campaigns, to take Sardinia and Corsica and the South of Italy and bomb northwards from there. We are then to fight our way northwards through Italy over difficult mountainous terrain in a campaign which may take much time before we reach Northern Italy and the main German defence position. Next spring we shall cross the Channel in force if the air and military situation is favourable and we may invade France from the south if only as a diversion ... I feel convinced we can and should do much more and better than the Quebec plan, which would unduly drag out and prolong the war.[17]

This gave pause for thought to Churchill, who wrote later that he 'found great comfort in feeling that our minds were in step. The cables that passed between us throw a true and intimate light upon the main issues of the war at this milestone.'[18]

He responded to Smuts's strictures, also at length, referring to the situation in Italy, the Balkans and Turkey, before going on to say:

These projects in Europe, together with the air offensive and sea war completely absorb all our resources of man power and of ship power. This fact must be faced. There is no comparison between our conditions and those prevailing in Russia, where the whole strength of a nation of nearly two hundred millions [*sic*], less war losses, long organised into a vast national army is deployed on a two-thousand-miles land front. This again is a fact which must be faced ... I think it inevitable that Russia will be the greatest land Power in the world after this war, which will have rid her of the two military Powers, Japan and Germany, who in our lifetime have inflicted upon her such heavy defeat.

'Believe me, my dear friend,' Churchill concluded, 'I am not at all vexed at your two telegrams of criticism. I am confident that if we were together for two or three days I could remove such of your anxieties as are not inexorable facts ... I expect to be at home when Parliament meets, and hope to find you at least approaching our shores.'[19]

As Churchill records, Smuts was somewhat reassured by these words, which made it clear that the Italian invasion force of twenty divisions was intended to cover the whole peninsula and constitute another 'real front', but when he suggested, in another cable a day later, that Italy and the Balkans should be given precedence over Overlord, Churchill was quick to correct him:

> There can be no question however of breaking arrangements we have made with the United States for Overlord ... I hope you will realise that British loyalty to Overlord is keystone of arch of Anglo-American co-operation. Personally I think enough forces exist for both hands to be played, and I believe this to be the right strategy.[20]

Despite Churchill's assurances of progress, while Allied negotiations with the Italians were going on, the Germans were steadily building up their forces and taking up critical defensive positions in south-central Italy, the Balkans and the area around Rome, which fell to Field Marshal Kesselring's army on 11 September. The next day, German Special Forces released Mussolini, who immediately set up a new Fascist government in northern Italy. Twenty-five German divisions were sent south to Cassino to keep the Allies away from Rome.[21]

*

On 27 September 1943, Smuts left on his second wartime visit to London, via another stopover in Cairo to inspect troops and to see what remained of the surrendered Italian fleet at Alexandria. From Cairo, he flew across the Western Desert battlefield in an RAF plane to Tunis to meet, for the first time, General Eisenhower. Churchill had paved the way for the visit, cabling Eisenhower to say that Smuts

> possesses my entire confidence, and everything can be discussed with him with the utmost freedom. He will stay some months in London, taking up his full duties as a member of the British War Cabinet. He will carry great weight here with the public. I shall be grateful if he is treated with the utmost consideration. He is a magnificent man and one of my most cherished friends.[22]

Smuts spent a day in conference with Eisenhower, British General Harold Alexander and Arthur Tedder, the Commander of Air Forces in the Western Desert. From Tunis, he flew to Sicily to inspect South African Air Force personnel and then to London, via Malta, Algiers and Rabat.

Smuts continued to share Churchill's concerns about the decision taken at Casablanca to invade western Europe across the Channel. This essentially American plan was already weakening the Allied advance in Italy, where the Germans had an advantage in numbers. He also harboured deep suspicions about Russia's intentions in the Balkans, and was in favour of the occupation of Yugoslavia and Greece.[23] To anyone in England who would listen, he pressed the case for a more vigorous Allied assault on southern Europe, instead of an invasion in northern France.

Smuts found an anti-Overlord ally in King George VI. Over lunch on 13 October, he and the king 'worked each other up over the rashness of the operation'.[24] On the following day, George VI sent a letter to Churchill saying he was so impressed with Smuts's argument that Britain should go on fighting in the Mediterranean theatre of war – and not engage in Overlord – that he hoped the three of them could discuss the matter over dinner that evening. Churchill complied, but not before writing a firm reply to the King: 'There is no possibility of our going back on what is agreed. Both the US Staff and Stalin would violently disagree with us. It must be remembered that this country is the only base from which our Metropolitan Fighter Air Force can make its weight tell, I think there are resources for both theatres.'[25]

As Roy Jenkins observes, Churchill was privately sympathetic to Smuts and the king's views, but could hardly say so to the Americans. Their joint concerns arose not out of cowardice, but were based on a real fear that the German army might still be strong enough to foil an invasion of the French coast by Allied forces – a scenario that would give Hitler a better chance of winning the war or at least postponing its end. In due course, Churchill passed on these concerns 'gently' to Roosevelt, but the Americans were not to be deflected.[26]

In London Smuts was invited to attend regular meetings of the War Cabinet, whose members were greatly concerned at intelligence reports of an imminent threat of German rockets and glider-bombs raining down on English cities. Unbeknown to the general public, launching pads for these missiles were being set up along the French coast. Perhaps it was the fear of these weapons, Jannie Smuts (jnr) wrote, that prompted his father to emphasise the need for haste in a speech he addressed on 19 October to an audience of 1 500 in London's Guildhall, with a further 3 000 listening on loudspeakers outside.[27] Smuts began the speech with a warm tribute to Churchill:

> The British people are united to a man behind the greatest leader they have ever had – the leader of whom, it is now amusing to recall, a gentleman prominent in your public life told me only a couple of years before this war … had no party, no followers, and no hope of future leadership!
> …
> We are now in the autumn of 1943 … We have climbed out of the depths and moved forward, and by the coming winter we shall have closed in upon Hitler's central fortress of Europe and be making our dispositions for the grand assault by our armies next year … The time is short. The time-factor in this fifth year of the war has become all important and from now on every moment counts …[28]

As usual, Smuts's focus was on the future: 'The last battle in the West – for our Western civilisation – [is one] our race must win or die … Let the greatest war in human history become the prelude to the greatest peace. To make it such will be the greatest glory of our age and its noblest bequest to the generations to come.'[29]

Smuts made one further speech of note before leaving for home. On 25 October he gave 300 parliamentarians in the House of Commons his 'Thoughts on a New World'. In his address, he expressed his belief that, in future, peace had to be backed by power. Matters had gone wrong in the past, he asserted, because the League of Nations had lacked powerful leadership:

> If we leave the future security of the world merely to loose arrangements and to aspirations for a peaceful world, we shall be lost … Great Britain, the United States and Russia now form a trinity fighting the cause of humanity … And as it is in war, so will it have to be in peace. We shall

have to see to it that in the new international organisation, the leadership remains in the hands of this great trinity of Powers.*

More controversially, he floated the idea of the Commonwealth and British Empire uniting with Europe's 'smaller democracies' to balance the unequal power of America and Russia. 'Should we not cease as Great Britain to be an island?'[30] he asked rhetorically. At the end of his 'Explosive speech', as it became known, there was complete silence and not a single question. The chairman, Viscount Cranborne, described the speech as 'profound and thought-provoking ... probably the most remarkable that most of us had ever heard'.[31]

On his way home, Smuts spent three days in Cairo, where Roosevelt, Churchill and their chiefs of staff were meeting once more to discuss joint strategy on the eve of the 'big three' summit in Tehran. He kept in close touch with Churchill and dined privately with Roosevelt, whom he had met in Paris, bending the president's ear on the importance of the Middle East and warning against the premature diversion of troops to the European theatre. All he would say about his encounter with Roosevelt afterwards was that 'we two Dutchmen got on splendidly'.[32]

---

* See JC Smuts, *Jan Christian Smuts*. Cassell, 1952, p 442. On its publication, Smuts's speech infuriated the French, who had resented his involvement in European politics ever since the post-World War I peace treaty negotiations at Versailles. Thinking that he was addressing a closed meeting at Westminster, Smuts declared that France was no longer a great power and it would be 'a hard and long upward pull' for it to recover. 'France has gone, and will be gone in our day and perhaps for many a day,' he said (see Ockert Geyser, *Jan Smuts and his International Contemporaries*. Covos Day, 2001, p 198). No one took greater offence at his remarks than the hypersensitive leader of the Free French, General de Gaulle.

CHAPTER 20

Doubts set in

If I die, don't worry, the war is won.
— CHURCHILL[1]

Despite the consensus on Operation Overlord reached at the Quadrant conference, a chasm had since opened up between Americans and British over grand strategy. Each side viewed their war aims 'through different spectacles'.[2] And, as the war progressed, the strategic divide between the two countries grew wider. American military planning was based on the notion of a concentration of forces. The British (especially Churchill, although not Brooke), preferred smaller, more focused operations – raids carried out by commandos and special forces.

This was partly because of the prime minister's romantic belief, which he had held since the Boer War, that feats of daring uplifted the morale of the people, but mainly because Britain's deep aversion to further casualties after its experiences in World War I meant that flanking operations were often preferred to direct engagement.[3] On the American side, there was always the strong suspicion that Churchill's strategy, particularly in the Far East, was aimed at preserving and advancing Britain's imperial interests after the war. As an article in *Life* magazine in 1942 declared: 'One thing we are sure we are not fighting for is to hold the British Empire together.'[4]

In October 1943 Churchill began to have even deeper reservations about the proposed timing of a cross-Channel invasion and was concerned about the negative effect that preparations for Overlord were having on progress in the Mediterranean. According to Brooke, the prime minister felt that by landing in north-west France, the Allies 'might be giving the enemy the opportunity to concentrate, by reason of his excellent roads and rail communications, an overwhelming force against us and to inflict on us a military disaster greater than that of Dunkirk. Such a disaster would result in the resuscitation of Hitler and the Nazi regime.'[5]

Churchill also argued that the opportunity should not be lost to expel Germany from the Balkans and the Greek islands, in the hope of bringing neutral Turkey on to the Allied side. Before Smuts left London for home, he attended the prime minister's staff conference on 19 October, at which he declared that the events of the last year in North Africa, Sicily and Italy 'now offered a clear run in to victory provided we did not blunder'.[6] Smuts supported the view that a cross-Channel operation could be 'a very dangerous one', unless large German forces were diverted from north-western France to other areas of conflict, such as Italy or the south of France.[7] Churchill would later record in his war memoirs that his chiefs of staff had agreed that Britain should reinforce the Italian theatre to the full, enter the Balkans and hold the position in the Aegean islands. Unfortunately, Churchill noted, 'we could not take a unilateral decision regarding the future strategy of the Allied nations. A further meeting with the Americans would therefore be necessary.'[8]

Ever since Gallipoli in World War I, Churchill had maintained a particular interest in the Aegean region. Now, in World War II, he claimed that the sea route through the Turkish-held Dardanelles would be a better way of supplying Russia than by means of Arctic convoys. He also had a bee in his bonnet about the Axis-held Dodecanese island of Rhodes, believing it was the island's proximity to the Turkish coast that had prevented Turkey from joining the Allies.[*] His growing impatience with the slowness of the Allied advance in Italy made him call more insistently for a British-led invasion of Rhodes.

---

[*] In 1943 Churchill had sent Anthony Eden on a mission to draw Turkey into the war on the Allied side. Eden wired him to say: 'Progress slow. What more can I tell Turkey?' To which Churchill replied, 'Tell them Christmas is coming.' (See Dominique Enright, *The Wicked Wit of Winston Churchill*. Michael O'Mara, 2001, p 93.)

To the Americans, this smacked of yet another excuse for postponing Overlord. Churchill's proposal led to 'the most acute difference I ever had with Eisenhower',[9] who did not believe the Allied forces in the Mediterranean were large enough to fight on two fronts. 'We must therefore choose between Rhodes and Rome,' the general declared. 'To us, it is clear we must concentrate on the Italian campaign.'[10] After stubbornly pressing his case with Roosevelt, Churchill was told firmly that there would be no diversion of forces that might imperil either the Italian campaign or Overlord. If the British wished to go ahead, they should do so on their own.

So Churchill decided to follow his own instincts and do exactly that. He gave orders for Operation Accolade, an assault on the islands of Karpathos and Rhodes, with ancillary action on Kos, Leros, Samos and other Greek islands. He had not reckoned on Hitler and his powerful air force in the Aegean, however, which was not going to let Turkey fall into the Allied orbit without a fight.

Operation Accolade was a failure. It cost greatly in lives (many of them South African airmen), ships and equipment, and presented the Germans with one of their last victories in World War II. It was a 'case study in folly', observes Max Hastings, 'an example of the consequences of the prime minister's capacity for rash boldness'.[11] Montgomery summed up the feelings of most of his fellow generals in a letter to Brooke: 'It has puzzled me for a long time as to why we want to start frigging about in the Dodecanese. The party has ended in the only way it could end – complete failure.'[12]

Churchill's setback in the Aegean resulted in the further waning of his influence with the Americans, which became evident at the two conferences, code-named Sextant, held in Cairo immediately before and after the Tehran summit of the 'big three'. The first get-together, from November 22 to 26, was the most contentious between British and American military strategists to date.[13] The British were irritated by Roosevelt's insistence on regarding China as one of the great powers and having its leader, Chiang Kai-shek, at the meeting in Cairo. They had not forgotten the president's bizarre suggestion, a few months earlier, that the imperial outpost of Hong Kong might be ceded to the Chinese as a 'gesture of goodwill'.[14] On this occasion, Smuts had come to Roosevelt's defence:

We are inclined to forget the President's difficulties. There is a very strong undercurrent against him. The things the Americans do are based partly on ignorance, partly on the determination to get power. We have learned hard lessons in the four years of the war. They have had no hard lessons. Yet we do not want to wait another four years while they learn them.[15]

To general bemusement, Churchill continued during the Sextant conference to press the case for an invasion of Rhodes. The arguments 'got hotter and hotter',[16] General Marshall recalled. A furious Churchill shouted: 'His Majesty's Government can't have its troops standing idle. Muskets must flame.' At which point Marshall also lost his composure. 'Not one American is going to die on that goddamned beach,'[17] he bellowed.

Sextant had been called primarily to discuss the progress of the war in the Far East as a prelude to the meeting with Stalin in Tehran. Roosevelt, by this stage, was determined to forge a personal relationship with the Soviet leader without Churchill by his side, and spent most of his time in Cairo with Chiang Kai-shek, trying to avoid being drawn into tactical discussions with his British counterpart. Churchill was puzzled by the president's reluctance to hold bilateral discussions before the all-important meeting with Stalin. Having counted on engaging Roosevelt on matters of strategy, Churchill and his advisers were left thoroughly exasperated.

*

The 'big three' meeting between Roosevelt, Churchill and Stalin in Tehran at the end of November 1943 caused Smuts to alter his plans to travel to Washington and Ottawa before returning home after a month's absence. Churchill felt more comfortable if South Africa's prime minister were to be present at meetings of the War Cabinet while he was away, and prevailed upon him to extend his stay in Britain. But how was Smuts to explain away his extended presence in London? He called in one of his closest confidants in the media, David Friedmann, of the South African Press Association, an accredited war correspondent stationed in London. Smuts trusted Friedmann, who was about to accompany him to North America, and often gave him information in confidence, knowing he would not be let down.

He told Friedman that Churchill had asked him to postpone his trip across the Atlantic for as long as the British prime minister was out of the UK, to which he had agreed. Although wartime censorship restrictions prevented Friedmann from disclosing the reason for Smuts's extended stay in London, Britain's Chief Censor allowed him to send the following carefully worded report to the South African Press Association, for publication in South African newspapers:

> To what extent was the decision taken by General Smuts to extend his stay in London into December dictated by plans made for the meeting in the Middle East of President Roosevelt, Winston Churchill and Marshal Stalin? Events in the course of time will provide the answer to this question, but meanwhile in South African circles in London and in Whitehall it remains an interesting topic of discussion. The most popular view at the moment is that Mr. Churchill would automatically turn to General Smuts with his unrivalled worldly knowledge and ask him during his absence to take over a considerable part of the responsibilities he normally bears when in residence at No. 10. Soon after General Smuts arrived early in October, SAPA's correspondent learned on good authority that Mr Churchill had passed to General Smuts several important war and post-war plans and problems, which had previously solely occupied the attention of the British Prime Minister as leader of the War Cabinet. Those duties have grown considerably since then – so much so that recently General Smuts had to apologise publicly for his inability to see his friends as often as he would have liked. He told a gathering of the Royal Empire Society when it was still a closely-guarded secret that Mr. Churchill had left for his meetings with President Roosevelt and Marshal Stalin [and] that 'if I do not appear very much in public, or if I do not meet my friends as often as I should like to do, remember I am here on duty. I am a soldier in uniform and I am here to do my best to help us in this vast business in which we are engaged – the biggest business this country or any of us has ever seen in history.[18]

Friedmann was prompted to file his report, he recorded later, because of indications from South Africa that Smuts's long absence from the country without obvious reason was drawing unfavourable comment not only from his political opponents, but also from some of his own MPs. The correspondent wrote:

> My report was scrutinised by a succession of senior censors and was eventually referred to Admiral G. P. Thomson. He got in touch with No. 10 Downing Street and also General Smuts, to whom my message was read. He approved of it and No. 10 too, had no objection. No factual mention was to be made that General Smuts was occupying Mr. Churchill's chair at the War Cabinet meetings. Admiral Thomson telephoned me to say that he had been given the all clear for the report to be transmitted to SAPA in Johannesburg and told me, not for publication, that he had been in touch with both No. 10 and General Smuts. In fact he was kind enough to congratulate me on the phrasing of the report, which, while showing that General Smuts was handling many of the responsibilities passed to him by Mr. Churchill, did not specifically say he was acting as Prime Minister in the absence of Mr. Churchill. I subsequently learned that Mr. Clement Attlee, then the deputy Prime Minister, was 'delighted' that General Smuts had taken over the duties of Mr. Churchill.[19]

According to the *Smuts Papers*, on 18 October 1943, South Africa's prime minister sent his deputy, Hofmeyr, a confidential message saying he might be detained in London until December, as 'Churchill declines to let me return earlier'.[20] On 11 November 1943 Smuts wrote to Hofmeyr again to say, 'everything has gone uncommonly well with my work and my reception has been very good. I think I have been helpful in regards to the larger questions of our future strategy which has been and continues to be, very difficult.'[21]

In his unpublished memoirs, made public years later, Friedmann claimed that while Churchill was away in the Middle East, Smuts had actually taken over his duties at No 10 Downing Street and, as acting chairman of the War

Cabinet, had been the de facto prime minister of Britain for more than a week – 'a wartime secret unparalleled in British and Commonwealth history, mention of which could not be made at the time because of military censorship and secrecy restrictions'.[22] 'I am happy to record these facts for posterity,'[23] wrote Friedmann, who seems in this instance to have let his imagination run away with him.†

When Friedman eventually presented his papers to the University of the Witwatersrand and the Smuts Library at Doornkloof, South African newspapers latched on to the 'revelation' that Smuts had secretly acted as prime minister of Britain several decades earlier. No one at the time saw fit to challenge this remarkable claim, which – posterity reveals – is not borne out by the minutes of the War Cabinet, now available for public inspection at the National Archives in London.

These records disclose that while Churchill was out of the UK in November/December 1943, every meeting of the War Cabinet attended by Smuts was chaired by the deputy prime minister, Clement Attlee. On reflection, it could scarcely have been otherwise: Churchill was always a stickler for constitutional correctness and would never have tried to pass on his executive responsibilities to someone who was not an elected British MP. Even if he had contemplated doing so, he would have discussed it with the king first, and then with Attlee himself. The news of his doing so would not have remained a 'wartime secret' for very long.

*

At the Tehran conference, held from 28 November to 1 December, Roosevelt went out of his way to dispel any impression Stalin might have that America and Britain had formed a cabal against him. He even agreed to stay in the

---

† Another, more plausible, disclosure by Friedmann is that in 1943, and again in 1944, Churchill urged Smuts to formally annex the League of Nations mandate of South West Africa to the Union, while the war was still in progress. (During World War I, the British War Cabinet had secretly agreed that South West Africa should become part of South Africa, but the US and others had intervened at Versailles.) Smuts declined to act on Churchill's advice, says Friedmann, because of his 'unshaken belief in the proprieties of international settlements' and his confidence 'that South West Africa would be handed over ... at the peace conference to settle the fate of the post-Hitler Germany'. (See David Friedmann, *Unpublished Memoirs*, Vol 4, Ch 3, p 1.)

Soviet compound, while Churchill was put up in the British Embassy.[24] At his first (informal) encounter with the Soviet leader, Roosevelt advised Stalin not to bring up the subject of India with Churchill (who was not present at that meeting), using his own disapproval of Empire as a way of ingratiating himself with the Russian.

Stalin was brimming with confidence at the summit, having achieved several major victories over the Germans along the Eastern Front. At the top of his agenda were two matters: a firm Anglo-American commitment to a second front in 1944; and an agreement on redrawing the boundaries of Poland to the Soviet Union's advantage. On the issue of the second front, Churchill rose to the occasion by promising, portentously, that 'it would be our stern duty to hurl across the Channel against the Germans every sinew of our strength'.[25] But Stalin said he refused to take the promise of an invasion seriously until a commander of Operation Overlord was appointed. He was assured by Roosevelt that the choice of commander would be made public within the next few days.

The British delegation was discomfited at the American president's willingness to endorse almost every proposal of Stalin's, particularly where the borders of Poland were concerned. No attempt was made to obtain Soviet recognition of Poland's government-in-exile, based in London, in return for Anglo-American acceptance of that beleaguered country's redrawn borders. Roosevelt blithely ignored Churchill's warnings that the Soviets were preparing to install a communist government in Warsaw, believing that he could trust 'Uncle Joe'. Privately, Churchill was most upset at his 'desertion' by Roosevelt. He deprecated the climate of opinion in the American camp, 'which seemed to wish to win Russian confidence even at the expense of co-ordinating the Anglo-American war effort'.[26]

Churchill left Tehran visibly depressed: he had been made to realise that the 'big three' had become the 'big two and a half'. In his memorable phrase: 'There I sat with the great Russian bear on one side of me, with paws outstretched, and on the other side the great American buffalo, and between the two sat the poor little English donkey, who was the only one who knew the right way home.'[27]

*

From Tehran, the now ailing Roosevelt and a fatigued and ill Churchill went back to Cairo to discuss strategic issues, including British plans in the Far East and negotiations with Turkey. Before leaving for Washington, Roosevelt informed Churchill that he could not spare General Marshall from Washington and had decided to appoint Eisenhower as Overlord commander. On the president's last afternoon in Cairo, Churchill took him to see – for the first and last time – the Pyramids and the Sphinx.

Stopping on the way home to consult General Eisenhower at his headquarters in Tunis, Churchill suffered one of the most severe of his many medical setbacks. First, he developed pneumonia, and then had a heart attack. From his sickbed, however, he continued to entertain a string of visitors, including his daughter, Sarah, to whom he said, 'If I die, don't worry, the war is won.'[28] By 27 December he was well enough to fly to Morocco, where he recuperated for a fortnight in Marrakech before being allowed to fly home. He had been away from England for nine weeks and received a rapturous welcome upon his return, unannounced, to his seat in the House of Commons.

While Churchill lay ill, General Alexander's ground forces in Italy were being gradually reduced in numbers as preparations for Overlord got under way. By late 1943 the Allied advance had been halted some ninety miles from Rome, where the German General Kesselring's troops had dug in along the Gustav Line,‡ not far from the old town of Cassino, with its medieval Benedictine monastery. As Churchill began to recover, he switched his attention from Overlord to the Anzio operation, a plan to liberate the Eternal City, Rome.[29]

Eisenhower and Alexander had previously discussed mounting an indirect assault on Rome, from the Anzio-Nettuno region on the west coast of Italy, about thirty-five miles from the Italian capital. There was little enthusiasm for the idea among Allied air and naval commanders, until Churchill enthusiastically threw his weight behind it, proposing Operation Shingle, an amphibious landing at Anzio behind the Gustav Line. By personally appealing to Roosevelt, and overriding Marshall's objection, he managed to secure American support for the landing. The overall Anzio plan called for US General Mark Clark's army to draw Kesselring's forces southwards along the Gustav Line, while the

---

‡ A defensive line across Italy, south of Rome.

VI Corps, commanded by US General John Lucas were to land at Anzio and drive north-east through the Alban Hills towards Rome.

Despite the misgivings of senior commanders that the two Allied armies were undermanned and underequipped, Shingle was launched on 22 January with the successful landing of 36 000 troops at Anzio. The invasion took the Germans by surprise. Seeking to establish a beachhead, Lucas delayed taking the offensive immediately, enabling Kesselring to rush troops to the marshy terrain. A week later, the German commander had amassed 70 000 men, tanks and artillery to form a tight ring around the beachhead. This was a decisive moment in the fight for Italy: what had been intended as the triumphant liberation of Rome had become a huge embarrassment to the Allies, who were forced to rush troop reinforcements to Anzio to avoid being driven into the sea.[30] Churchill ruefully remarked: 'I thought we were landing a wild cat; instead all we have is a stranded whale.'[31]

The Germans fought with great skill and, on 16 February, Kesselring mounted a huge counter-offensive. The battles for the Anzio beachhead on the coast and the heights of Monte Cassino further south were among the most brutal and bloodiest clashes of the entire war. The Allies narrowly managed to avoid another Dunkirk, but Lucas lost his command to the more aggressive General Lucian Truscott.

The beachhead at Anzio was besieged for 125 days. In the fighting, the Allies lost 7 000 killed and 36 000 wounded or missing, while on the German side 5 000 were killed, 30 500 were wounded or missing and 400 captured.[32] To the American commanders, Shingle had been a badly planned reprise of Churchill's ill-fated attempt to take the Dardanelles in 1915.

In May 1944, after months of stalemate at Anzio and Cassino, a huge build-up of Allied forces enabled Alexander to launch a two-pronged offensive against Kesselring. Realising he was outnumbered, the German commander withdrew northwards from Rome, ready to fight another day. On 5 June, Rome was taken by the Allies, but the joyous tidings of its liberation were all but drowned out by news of the invasion of France on the very next day.

Churchill continued to persuade himself that Anzio had failed only because of Lucas's tardiness in marching on Rome. Unburdening himself in a long cable to the ever sympathetic Smuts, he said:

> Naturally I am very disappointed at what appears to be a frittering away of a brilliant opening ... I do not in any way however repent at what has been done. ... As a result the Germans have now transferred into the south of Italy eight more divisions, so that in all there are eighteen south of Rome. It is vital to the success of Overlord that we keep away from that theatre and hold elsewhere as many German divisions as possible, and hard fighting in Italy throughout the spring will provide for the main operation a perfect prelude and accompaniment.

'Here at home,' he continued, 'all goes fairly well, though the little folk are more active. However their chirrupings will be stilled before long by the thunder of the cannonade. Most earnestly do I look forward to seeing you, and I rejoice that you will be at my side in momentous times.'[33]

CHAPTER 21

Overlord – and beyond

Complete unity prevails throughout the Allied Armies. There is a
brotherhood in arms between us and our friends of the United States.
— CHURCHILL[1]

Smuts paid his third wartime visit to Britain in April 1944, where secret preparations for the D-Day landing in Normandy were in full swing. He found Churchill still unsure whether the invasion of France should go ahead or not. As Churchill later recorded in his war memoirs:

> I was not convinced that this was the only way of winning the war, and I knew that it would be a very heavy and hazardous adventure. The fearful price we had had to pay in human life and blood for the great offensives of the First World War was graven in my mind. Memories of the Somme and Passchendaele and many lesser frontal attacks upon the Germans were not blotted out by time or reflection.[2]

His military advisers were equally apprehensive: 57 per cent of troops to be deployed on D-Day would be British.[3] Sir Alan Brooke confided to his diary that he was 'torn to shreds with misgivings … The cross-Channel operation is just eating into my heart … It might prove the most ghastly disaster of the war.'[4]

Meanwhile, the prime minister had many other matters to agonise over: Poland's disputed frontiers; the progress of the Anzio landing in Italy; the proposed Operation Anvil in southern France; the bombing offensive in

Germany; and Britain's attempt to recapture Burma.[5] He was also aware that control of Overlord was no longer in his hands but in those of the Supreme Allied Commander, General Eisenhower, and the man whom he (Churchill) had nominated to command the Allied ground landings on the French shore, General Montgomery.

The chief reason for Smuts's visit to England this time was to attend the Commonwealth prime ministers' conference. En route to London, via Cairo as usual, Smuts was preoccupied with the situation in Greece, where mutinies had broken out in the Greek army and naval units stationed in Egypt. Accompanied once again by his son, Jannie, as his aide, he spent his first weekend in Britain at Chequers being briefed on developments by Churchill, who was 'looking none the worse from his recent severe bout of pneumonia'.[6]

The two-week-long Commonwealth conference was opened on 1 May by the British prime minister, who confided to the delegates 'in the utmost secrecy' that the British were having difficulties extracting enough landing craft from the Americans, who were more concerned about the war with Japan in the Far East than the situation in the Mediterranean.[7] He told the dominion leaders he 'would have preferred to roll up Europe from the south-east, joining hands with the Russians. However, it had proved impossible to persuade the United States to this view. They had been determined at every stage upon the invasion in North-West Europe, and had consistently wanted us to break off the Mediterranean operations.'[8] Churchill ended his *tour d'horizon* of the war with a reference to Operation Overlord: 'Great forces are about to be set in motion, and all we can do now is to await results.'[9]

The dominion prime ministers present, notably Mackenzie King, the Canadian premier, and Smuts, fully supported delaying the invasion of France until the time was right. Like Churchill, they were most reluctant to risk any more ventures of the likes of Gallipoli, Dieppe or Somme.[10] Underlining the dangers that a cross-Channel invasion might pose, Smuts expressed concern that, as the British and dominion troop numbers were dwindling, the conduct of the war was now in the hands of the Americans. 'Last time, we had at our side the veteran French army, extremely well led. Now we should be fighting alongside troops who had no experience of battle and would be pitted against a veteran army. We could not regard the situation lightly,'[11] he said.

Smuts lamented the switch of focus from east to west in Europe, which, he said, had deprived them 'of the means of exploiting our victories'.[12] By losing the Greek islands and giving too little help to the partisans (underground movements), they were 'in danger of leaving the whole field clear in the south-east of Europe to the Russians'.[13]

Both Mackenzie King and Smuts paid tribute to Churchill's good sense in putting off the invasion of northern Europe for as long as possible. King said that perhaps the greatest of the many great things Churchill had done was to withstand the pressure until the time was ripe.[14] With his eyes firmly on the future, Smuts repeated his conviction that military strategy should not be allowed to hinder political strategy. He realised that what he referred to as the 'switch-over' of forces to the north-west had been because of Russian pressure on America, but believed the outcome might prejudice post-war policy in south-east Europe.[15] Agreeing with Smuts, Churchill admitted that, if he'd had his way, the conduct of the war would have been different.[16]

Much of the conference was taken up with post-war financial concerns. Smuts remarked privately to his son that he and his colleagues were 'chasing shadows' because, before the war was over, conditions would have changed so radically that all their present decisions would count for nothing. 'It was the same in the last war,' Smuts said, 'when all the lofty ideas and resolutions were proved to be quite worthless.'[17]

The latter part of the meeting was taken up by inspections of troops and naval vessels making preparations for Overlord, and concluded with a briefing on plans for D-Day at Montgomery's headquarters at St Paul's School in London. The king and Smuts, who had both doubted the wisdom of the cross-Channel operation, were present, but a representative of the Free French was not. With Eisenhower also in attendance, Churchill declared, 'I am hardening on this enterprise.'[18]

On 16 May, Churchill bade farewell to the dominion leaders, saying with his usual rhetorical flourish, 'We do not know how long history will be denied, or what tribulations we shall have to ask our people to endure, but we are absolutely sure that they will not be found unequal to the tests and the trials, however long and heavy.'[19] Smuts's son noted that the conference had been 'a great success' in many ways, particularly in avoiding any controversy.

The Commonwealth prime ministers' conference, May 1944. From left: Canadian Prime Minister Mackenzie King, Churchill, New Zealand Prime Minister Peter Fraser, Commander-in-Chief of the US Forces in Europe Dwight Eisenhower, Southern Rhodesian Prime Minister Sir Godfrey Huggins, Smuts.

'There has been much mutual patting on the back. So we are all happy and beaming,' he wrote.[20]

On 19 May Smuts was given the Freedom of Birmingham, the heart of Britain's armaments industry, where he addressed a crowd of 2 800 people in the City Hall. Stressing the need for the war to be brought to a quick end, he repeated his belief in a federal Europe and an international body with enough powers to maintain world peace. He indicated his concern about the spread of Communism after the war by urging his largely working-class audience to 'rather follow the Russia of Tolstoy, not of Karl Marx'.[21]

*

By the end of May, there were more than 1 500 000 American troops in Britain and the south of England looked like a vast military camp 'filled with men trained, instructed and eager to come to grips with the Germans across the water'.²² The scale of the planned invasion of enemy-held north-western France – the largest-ever amphibious operation – had no parallel in history.

As Churchill told the House of Commons, the plan involved 'tides, winds, waves, visibility, both from the air and the sea standpoint, and the combined employment of land, air and sea forces in the highest degree of intimacy and in contact with conditions which could not and cannot be fully foreseen'.²³

Patience was required, as inclement weather caused days of tense inaction to go by. The most favourable dates for a Channel crossing, according to the moon cycle, were 2 to 6 June, failing which there would have to be a further twelve-day postponement. On 3 June Smuts drove to Portsmouth with Churchill to inspect troops already embarking for Normandy. On the way back, they went to see General Eisenhower, who was wrestling with the momentous decision of whether to brave the poor weather and launch Overlord without further delay. Despite the meteorological report, Smuts urged going into action. According to Jannie, his father pressed Eisenhower to be more audacious: 'We must be prepared to sacrifice a few thousand additional men at the start, for it would pay off handsomely later,'²⁴ he said. Easier said than done, the American commander must have thought.

The younger Smuts also recorded how, at this moment of extreme tension, Eisenhower seemed the most unruffled of everyone, sitting in his caravan calmly playing poker with his staff. At dinner on the way home by train, Churchill recorded that 'Field Marshal Smuts' was 'at his most entertaining pitch', regaling his listeners with an account of his role in the Boers' surrender at Vereeniging, when he had been 'assailed as a coward and a defeatist by his own friends, and had spent the most difficult hour of his life'. Smuts went on to describe how, at the outbreak of World War II, he 'had had to cross the floor and fight his own Prime Minister, who wished to remain neutral'.²⁵

Operation Overlord was launched in the early morning of 6 June, involving 160 000 American, British and Canadian troops, transported by 5 000 ships and supported by 13 000 aircraft, who successfully stormed five beaches

Winston Churchill with Field Marshal Jan Smuts (right) and
Field Marshal Sir Alan Brooke, Chief of the Imperial General Staff (second from left),
on board a destroyer conveying the party to Normandy, 12 June 1944.

AAI/FOTOSTOCK

along a fifty-mile stretch of the heavily fortified Normandy coast. Less than a week later, over 326 000 troops, 50 000 vehicles and about 100 000 tons of war equipment had been conveyed across the Channel; the five beaches had been secured and five bridgeheads established. By the end of the month, the Allies had transferred no fewer than 850 000 men and 150 000 vehicles to Normandy and begun moving east across France. Despite Churchill's earlier misgivings, losses on the Allied side, though considerable, were far less than anticipated.

On 12 June, only four days after the invasion, Churchill took Smuts and Brooke with him across the Channel on a British destroyer to visit Montgomery at his new headquarters at Bayeux, five miles inland from the coast. General Marshall and Admiral King accompanied the British party, but crossed on an American warship. The media were asked to keep Smuts's presence at Churchill's side a secret because any news of it would deeply

Operation Overlord: Churchill looking at enemy and British aircraft engaged overhead with Smuts, Field Marshal Sir Alan Brooke, General Sir Bernard Montgomery and others, Normandy, 12 June 1944. The officer on the left is Lieutenant General Sir Richard O'Connor.

CAPT. HORTON AND SGT MORRIS/IWM VIA GETTY IMAGES

offend the uninvited and hypersensitive General de Gaulle, to whom Smuts was 'like a red rag to a bull'.[26]

In *Churchill's Wizards*, his book about British intelligence's genius for deception in World War II, Nicholas Rankin describes an incident on the visit to 'Monty'. As senior officers stood outside with the prime minister,

Field Marshal Smuts 'sniffed the air and said, "There are some Germans near us now ... I can always tell."' Two days later, two fully armed German paratroopers emerged from a rhododendron bush where they been hiding all along. Had they used their weapons on Churchill and his party, the course of history might well have been changed.[27]

The success of Overlord dealt a severe blow to Hitler, preventing the transfer of his forces to Eastern Europe to counter the advancing Soviet army, which, as Stalin had promised, had begun an offensive from the east. On 24 August, the Allies reached the River Seine and entered the outskirts of Paris. De Gaulle, whom Roosevelt – with reluctance – and Churchill had permitted to return to France, made a triumphant entry into the capital down the Champs-Elysées the following day.

*

In Britain, meanwhile, the intelligence services had been warning for some time of a new threat emerging from Hitler – the launch across the Channel from Axis-occupied Europe of unmanned V-1 flying bombs. For some strange reason, Churchill's scientific adviser, Frederick Lindemann (Lord Cherwell), had discounted the rumours as enemy propaganda. In the War Cabinet, when Smuts was asked his views about the possibility of such bombs and long-range rockets, he gave the sensible advice: 'Well, the evidence may not be conclusive, but I think a jury would convict.'[28]

One week after D-Day, the first V-1 bombs, known as doodlebugs or buzz bombs, landed on London, supposedly in retaliation for the invasion at Normandy. The Smutses, father and son, watched from their hotel window in the West End as the missiles rained destruction and devastation on the streets of London. On 18 June, a V-1 missile landed on the Guards' Chapel during a service, killing sixty people. The building was just 300 yards from Churchill's study.[29]

Over a twenty-four-hour period in mid-June, the Germans launched 200 V-1 missiles from bases on the France and Dutch coasts; 3 000 more were to follow in the next five weeks.[30] Churchill recorded grimly: 'The blind, impersonal nature of the missile made the person on the ground feel helpless.

There was little he could do, no human enemy he could see shot down.'[31]

It took a redeployment of fighter planes and anti-aircraft batteries, as well as barrage balloons, to slow down the bombing onslaught, which did not cease until 1945, when the last launch site within range of Britain was overrun.

After the V-1s came the longer-range V-2 rockets, the first-ever guided ballistic missiles. Some 3 000 of these were launched, mainly from The Hague, at Allied targets in Britain, France and Belgium, in apparent retribution for the carpet-bombing of German cities (about which even Churchill had become uneasy). Each of these rockets caused on average twice as many casualties as a flying bomb, and killed over 2 700 people in Britain alone[32] before Allied attacks on Peenemünde and other launch sites in Germany brought their use to an end.

*

It did not take long after D-Day for tensions between the British and Americans to surface again. Once more, the bone of furious contention was future Allied policy in the Mediterranean. Churchill, Smuts and the British chiefs of staff were determined there should be a follow-up to General Alexander's victories in Italy with an immediate advance north towards Germany. That would entail three armies converging on Berlin: Eisenhower's from the west; Stalin's from the east; and the British and American forces via Italy in the south-east.[33]

The Americans, on the other hand, were equally insistent on proceeding without delay to implement Operation Anvil, a plan to invade France from the south to complement the Normandy invasion. The original plan had been to synchronise Anvil with Overlord in order to compel the Germans to split their forces in France, but time had not permitted this. To divert troops to France now, the British argued, would take six weeks and give the Germans precious breathing space, while also diluting the Allies' strength in the Mediterranean.

Eisenhower was having none of it. In a telegram to General Marshall, he pointed out that the British plan 'seems to discount the fact that the Combined Chiefs of Staff have long ago decided to make Western Europe the base from which to conduct decisive operations against Germany. To authorize any departure from this sound decision seems to me ill-advised and potentially dangerous.' He recommended that Anvil (later renamed Operation Dragoon) should be undertaken 'at the earliest possible date'.[34] Marshall wrote afterwards that disagreements over Anvil had resulted in 'a bitter and unremitting fight with the British right up to the launching'.[35]

On 21 June Churchill called a staff conference, especially to hear the views of Smuts, who was on the point of leaving London for South Africa. With his own 'Springbok' troops now in Italy, Smuts endorsed the British plan whole-heartedly, being in favour 'of extending our right hand across the Balkans towards the Russians and the development of a threat to Austria from our bases in the Trieste-Venice area'. This plan, he said, 'might well result in the loss to Germany of the whole of the Balkans'.[36]

Acknowledging the new demands created by the Battle of Normandy, Churchill remained 'not at all attracted' by any Anvil-type operation on the French Riviera.[37] Surplus troops and equipment, he maintained, should be diverted to Trieste rather than used to mop up further resistance in France. Arriving home, Smuts sent Churchill a message saying that if Trieste could be captured by September, 'the cooperation between our and the Russian advance towards Austria and Germany would constitute as serious a threat to the enemy as Eisenhower's advance from the west, and the three combined are most likely to produce early enemy collapse'.[38]

Eisenhower remained unpersuaded, however. He did not think an advance on the region around Istria, Trieste and Ljubljana (in nearby Yugoslavia), en route to the Austrian border would have any positive effect until 1945. 'France is the decisive theatre,' he said.[39] And, despite a barrage of messages and personal appeals from Churchill to Roosevelt, the president could not be moved either.

On 24 June the dispute over strategy was brought to an emphatic end by a cable from Washington: the British proposal for the commitment of Mediterranean resources to large-scale operations in northern Italy and into the Balkans 'is unacceptable to the United States Chiefs of Staff'.[40] If the success of Overlord was to be fully exploited, the message continued, it should be by capturing another major French port.

There was no longer any doubt about who called the shots in Europe now. The prime minister's aide, John Colville, recorded wistfully: 'Up till Overlord, he [Churchill] saw himself as the supreme military authority to whom all military decisions were referred. Thereafter he became, by force of circumstances, little more than spectator.'[41]

Amid strong British disapproval, Anvil (now Dragoon) went ahead on 15 August 1944, when 150 000 American, British, Canadian and French troops landed at Nice, St Tropez and other smart resorts along the French coast. The Allies drove rapidly up to Lyon, in the centre of France, but were unable to cut off the strongest units of the German army, which escaped into the Vosges Mountains, on the border between eastern France and the Rhineland. The capture of the strategic ports of Toulon and Marseilles, however, provided the Allies with important supply hubs for future operations in France.

Churchill witnessed the Dragoon landings from the deck of a destroyer, HMS *Kimberley*, but thereafter showed scant interest in the operation, giving it his 'full support' but admitting that he had done his best 'to constrain or deflect it'.[42] He did not dissent from Smuts's opinion that Dragoon was a 'futile joy-ride',[43] an unwise distraction from more pressing engagements elsewhere in the Mediterranean.

From the Cape, Smuts continued to shower Churchill with messages of advice. He urged the prime minister not to be distracted by Dragoon when there were much bigger decisions looming: 'From now on it would be wise to keep a very close eye on all matters bearing on the future of Europe. This is the crucial issue on which the future of the world will depend. In its solution, your vision, experience and great influence may prove a main factor.' Churchill clearly agreed with these high-flown sentiments, as he included the passage verbatim in his war memoirs.[44]

*

Churchill's high regard for Smuts's opinions was evident from the way in which he brought South Africa's prime minister into the highly secretive Anglo-American discussions about the atomic bomb. In late 1943 the greatest physicist of the time, Danish Nobel Prizewinner Niels Bohr had managed to escape from Nazi-occupied Denmark and flee to Britain via Stockholm. He was immediately put to work on Tube Alloys, the code name for the British atomic project.

It had become apparent to Churchill and his advisers that the task of building the atom bomb was too great for a financially strapped and still vulnerable Britain, so it was decided that Tube Alloys' designs and personnel should be shipped across to the US, where the development of a potentially war-winning weapon would become a joint Anglo-American project. It did not take long for the security-conscious Americans to regard the British involvement as expendable.[45] Despite that, Bohr was one of the 'British' scientists accepted by the US to work on what had become the top-secret Manhattan Project.

Bohr was more than just a brilliant physicist: he was a philosopher with a broad international vision, and deeply concerned about the potentially harmful effects of nuclear weapons on the future of the planet – something that Roosevelt and Churchill had barely had time to consider. While in America, he warned Roosevelt about the dangers of nuclear proliferation and impressed upon a seemingly sympathetic president the need for stringent international safeguards. On his return to Britain, Bohr was sent on a similar mission to Churchill. The encounter was a disaster.

Churchill did not take well to the diffident, softly-spoken Dane's complex explanation of nuclear technology and concerns about its application, and had no time for the suggestion that atomic secrets should be shared with the Russians. Churchill restated his view that the atomic bomb was simply a bigger bomb than others then in existence. For him, it was a weapon to be used for strategic purposes, and one that he and his friend Roosevelt had under control. The prime minister insisted that keeping knowledge of the bomb to a handful of British and American scientists, and away from the emerging Russian superpower, was the most sensible way forward. With D-Day imminent and many other pressing issues on his mind, he asked Smuts to examine and advise him on Bohr's proposals.[46]

Smuts and Bohr, both like-minded in their concern for the future of humanity, quickly became friends. Smuts agreed with Bohr that the new discovery – whether used in war or for peaceful purposes – was the most important that science had ever made and supported the Dane's argument in favour of international controls. But on the question of whether the atomic secrets should be shared with the Russians or not, Smuts could give no conclusive answer. All he could say was that the problem was more America's than Britain's, but that a final decision needed to be made soon by the American president and the British prime minister jointly.[47]

As it turned out, the Americans declined to divulge details of the bomb to the Russians (who managed to obtain them anyway through their extensive spy network and subsequently designed their own nuclear weapon soon after World War II). Bohr went back to a liberated Denmark and continued to campaign for the rest of his life for the peaceful application of nuclear energy. He remembered Smuts with fondness, and sometimes turned to him for assistance and support. Shortly before Smuts died, Bohr wrote to him to express his concern about reports of his illness:

> I hope that you are now on [a] good way to recovery and that in years to come you will still be able to offer the world such human wisdom and leadership in world affairs as you have given in the past. I need not say how much your encouragement and sympathy in the difficult war years meant to me.[48]

CHAPTER 22

Aegean interlude

Great Britain will take the lead in a military sense and try to help the existing Royal Greek Government to establish itself in Athens upon as broad and united a basis as possible.

— CHURCHILL TO STALIN[1]

The Aegean region was an area of special interest to both Churchill and Smuts, not only because of its democratic heritage but also its strategic significance. Since 1936 Greece had been ruled by the authoritarian General Ioannis Metaxas, who, after years of civil upheaval, had seized power in a *coup d'état* approved by the Greek king, George II. Metaxas had been educated in Germany and was staunchly pro-German, whereas the king was pro-British – a matter of ongoing disagreement between them. Greece's security was ultimately dependent upon Britain, the dominant naval power in the Mediterranean. However, Mussolini, intent on rebuilding a Roman Empire, also had designs on the Aegean Sea.

When World War II broke out, Metaxas attempted to maintain Greece's neutrality, but Mussolini's expansionist aims led eventually to a Greco-Italian war. Metaxas's forces managed to drive the Italians out of Greece and back into Albania, whence they had come. A reluctant Hitler had to send troops to support his Fascist ally and, together, the Axis powers invaded Greece via Yugoslavia and Bulgaria in April 1941.

Shortly before that, Metaxas had died suddenly in suspicious circumstances. There were brief hopes of a return to more liberal parliamentary rule in Greece, but these were dashed when the king kept the ruling administration in place. By May 1941, despite support for the Greeks from British-led forces in the Mediterranean, the Germans had overrun much of the country, and the royal family and the government been forced to flee to Crete. There they stayed temporarily until the island fell in June, when they fled to Egypt to set up a government in exile. Churchill insisted that the new Cabinet should be moderate, which meant that only two of Metaxas's ministers were retained, but the exiled government was to exercise very little influence on the course of events on the Greek mainland.

In Athens the Axis powers had installed a puppet government that had no legitimacy and little public support. Into this vacuum stepped a variety of resistance movements, supporting ideologies ranging from royalist to communist. These partisans, all of whom despised the king, took the fight to the occupying Axis authorities and set up extensive spying networks. The largest group, the National Liberation Front (EAM, from the Greek), whose leaders were communists, were intent on eradicating all opposition, thereby sowing the seeds of civil war.

Churchill had never been particularly sympathetic towards the Greek king – or any other of the Mediterranean monarchs, such as King Peter of Yugoslavia or Victor Emmanuel III of Italy – but had taken the pragmatic view that if their regimes were on the side of Britain, like the Greeks, they should be given support.[2] However, Greece's King George, described by Churchill's private secretary, Jock Colville, as one of the worst advertisements for hereditary monarchy,[3] presented a particular difficulty. While the king had moved to London to keep out of harm's way, liberation movements on the mainland and the Greek armed forces in Cairo had rebelled against him and his exiled government. On 7 April Churchill suggested that he should go back to Egypt to prop up his tottering regime. The king did as he was told, returned to Cairo and appointed George Papandreou to head a new administration in exile.

On 11 June Churchill wrote to Roosevelt about the situation in Greece:

> The Greek King and Greek Government have placed themselves under our protection. They are at present domiciled in Egypt … Not only did we lose … 40 000 men in helping Greece [against Hitler], but a vast mass of shipping and warships, and by denuding Cyrenaica to help Greece we also lost the whole of Wavell's conquest … These were heavy blows to us

... Why can you and I not keep this in our own hands, considering how we see eye to eye on so much of it?[4]

Without saying so explicitly, what Churchill was proposing to the president was that Stalin should be kept out of any deliberations about Greece. The anti-imperialist Roosevelt cautiously agreed, saying, 'We must be careful to make it clear that we are not establishing any post-war spheres of influence.'[5]

*

After fleeing Crete in 1941, the king, his brother, Crown Prince Paul, and their families sought and were given refuge out of harm's way in South Africa. Smuts and his wife, Isie, were welcoming to the visitors, putting them up initially in various official residences. The king did not stay long, however, and returned via London to Egypt. His younger brother, Paul, did likewise, leaving behind his wife, Crown Princess Frederika, with their two small children. For the next two years, the prince returned regularly to South Africa to see his wife and children, as well as other members of his extended family.

Smuts was drawn to the Greek royals, and in particular to young Frederika, the granddaughter of the German emperor, Kaiser Wilhelm II, and whose four brothers were in the German army fighting for Hitler. A descendant also of Queen Victoria, Frederika was, at the time of her birth, thirty-fourth in line to the British throne. When she arrived in South Africa, she had not yet learnt to speak Greek and still conversed with her husband in German and English.

On 1 June 1942, Smuts became godfather to the Greek couple's third child, Princess Irene, and held a dinner party at his official residence, Groote Schuur, to celebrate. Afterwards, he wrote to Margaret Gillett, his English confidante:

> Through it all one could never forget that the pretty young mother was a granddaughter of the Kaiser. A shrewd, able and good woman in addition to being a German. It was clear that she was a real good German who hated Hitler and all his works and thoughts and longed for a peace which would finish Nazism but spare her people.[6]

The fast-growing friendship between the youthful Frederika and the septuagenarian Smuts was cemented by her reading of his book, *Holism and Evolution*, and her enjoyment of philosophy. The pair went on long walks together, discussing politics, science, religion and holism. Smuts's sympathy for the German people, suffering under the Hitler regime, made a profound impression on her.

Smuts revelled in his role as father confessor to the attractive young woman, dispensing advice on how she should prepare for her future role as queen of Greece, if and when the monarchy was restored after the war. He also suggested she should become fluent in Greek to make herself more acceptable to her people.[7]

Smuts's close relationship with Frederika played into the hands of his political opponents, as well as the chattering classes, who dined out on the gossip about the prime minister and 'his little Greek princess'. Smuts took no notice of the rumour-mongering and, fortunately for him, neither did Isie, who had become fond of 'Freddie' and her young family. But news of the relationship reached the ears of Churchill, who didn't trust any German while the war was on. After Frederika's return to Cairo to be at her husband's side, he appointed a British aide-de-camp – ostensibly to protect her, but also to find out whether she had used her friendship with Smuts to pass on any Allied secrets to her parents, who were still living in Germany.[8]

Smuts and Frederika continued to correspond with each other well after the war was over. As we shall see, South Africa's prime minister was instrumental in persuading delegates to the Paris conference in 1946 to restore the Greek king to his throne. However, as Smuts's official biographer points out, by devoting a disproportionate amount of his time to Greek affairs from 1942 onwards, he once again laid himself wide open to charges that he was more at ease with royalty and foreigners of high rank than with the people of South Africa.[9]

*

In early August 1944, Churchill ordered his Imperial General Staff to make plans for a British expedition to Greece when German rule over the country finally collapsed.[10] Determined to keep Greece out of the communist clutches, he aimed to ensure there was no political vacuum for the EAM and its military wing, ELAS, to exploit. The Americans kept well away. As Marshall later recalled, 'We were very much afraid that Mr Churchill's interest in matters near Athens and in Greece would finally get us involved in that fighting, and we were keeping out of it in every way we possibly could.'[11]

In October, the liberation of Greece began when British ground and naval forces took up positions on the mainland, on the heels of Hitler's scorched-earth withdrawal. From Egypt the government in exile returned to a country in ruins, its road and rail network destroyed and supplies of food exhausted.

Churchill, in the meantime, though not in the best of health again, had embarked on a round of flying visits to British bases across the Mediterranean, a journey to Quebec and back on board the *Queen Mary* to meet Roosevelt, and a flight to Moscow to confer with Stalin again. He recorded in his war memoirs:

> As everything in Eastern Europe became more tense, I felt the need of another personal meeting with Stalin. ... The Russian armies were now pressing heavily upon the Balkan scene, and Roumania [*sic*] and Bulgaria were in their power. As the victory of the Grand Alliance became only a matter of time, it was natural that Russian ambitions should grow. Communism raised its head behind the thundering Russian battlefront. Russia was the Deliverer, and Communism the gospel she brought.[12]

Before leaving for Moscow, he and Smuts engaged in a lengthy exchange of messages about preparations for the proposed new international peacekeeping organisation, the United Nations, and the developing crisis in Greece. The British prime minister recorded that Smuts's 'meditations from his farm in the veldt led him along the same paths of thought [as mine]'.[13] Smuts was concerned that the EAM-ELAS movement might be gaining control in Greece: 'I hope this may still be prevented ... and that our loyal Greek friends may be heartened by positive action on our part.'[14]

'I do not say this in any spirit of hostility to Russia,' he continued. 'It is upon close co-operation between the Big Three that our best hope rests for the near future ... But the more firmly Russia can establish herself in the saddle now, the farther she will ride in the future and the more precarious our holdfast will become.'[15]

In the Kremlin, Churchill took up with Stalin the situation in Poland, southern Europe and the Balkans. Britain had a 'particular interest' in Greece, he told the Soviet leader, whereas Romania 'was very much a Russian affair'.[16] He did not want to use the phrase 'dividing into spheres', however, as that might displease the Americans, but produced what he told Stalin was a 'naughty document' – a piece of paper on which he had written that in Romania the Russians should have a 90 per cent interest and 'the others' 10 per cent; whereas in Greece, Great Britain (in accord with the US) should have 90 per cent, and the others 10 per cent. 'I pushed this across to Stalin,' Churchill wrote. 'There was a slight pause. Then he took his blue pencil and made a large tick upon it, and passed it back to us. It was all settled in no more time than it takes to set down.'[17]

Upon returning from Moscow, Churchill put his 'percentages agreement' with Stalin to the test.[18] He watched with concern as the government in Athens found it impossible to demobilise the militant EAM-ELAS guerrillas.[19] With civil war imminent, he told Foreign Secretary Anthony Eden: 'It is important to let it be known that if there is a civil war in Greece, we shall be on the side of the Government we have set up in Athens, and that above all we shall not hesitate to shoot.'[20] He gave instructions that more British troops were to be rushed from Italy to Athens, where a communist-inspired general strike broke out on 2 December.

Two days earlier, on 30 November, Churchill had celebrated his seventieth birthday. Among the shoal of telegrams was one from Smuts, in Pretoria: 'My thoughts today are much with you my friend, the one in all the world to whom so many owe so much. May God continue to bless you with strength of body as he has blessed you with strength of soul.'[21]

In reply, Churchill declared, 'Of all the messages which reached me on my birthday, none was more movingly phrased or gave me greater encouragement than yours, my old and trusted friend.'[22]

On 3 December, twelve people were killed and sixty injured at a communist demonstration in Athens. Churchill decided that the battle for the Greek capital should take priority over the campaign in Italy. He ordered the British commander in Greece, General Ronald Scobie, to make any regulations he liked for control of the streets of Athens and to fire at any armed male who assailed British or Greek government authority. 'Do not ... hesitate to act as if you were in a conquered city ... We have to hold and dominate Athens. It would be a great thing for you to succeed in this without bloodshed, but also with bloodshed if necessary.'[23]

Scobie's crackdown in Athens caused ructions in the House of Commons. Labour members of the coalition government who regarded the EAM-ELAS as a legitimate left-wing movement demanded that the communist alliance be accommodated in the governance of Greece. Churchill's response was blunt:

> One must have respect for democracy and not use the word too lightly.
> The last thing which resembles democracy is mob law, with bands of
> gangsters, armed with deadly weapons forcing their way into great cities,
> seizing the police stations and key points of government, endeavouring to
> introduce a totalitarian regime with an iron hand ...[24]

He declared, in a memorable phrase, that 'democracy is no harlot, to be picked up in the street by a man with a tommy gun'[25] and, offering his own resignation, he demanded a vote of confidence in his handling of the situation in Greece. The House gave him its backing by 279 votes to 30.

Of much more concern to Churchill was the vehement condemnation of his actions in Greece from the US State Department, which had leaked his secret orders to Scobie to the news media. In the words of Andrew Roberts, 'there was much criticism in the American press about Limey attempts to impose a reactionary, monarchical regime on freedom-loving Greek republicans'.[26] Churchill was hurt by a wave of criticism from leading members of the Roosevelt administration, and a weak-kneed response from the president, who wrote:

> No one will understand better than yourself that I, both personally and
> as Head of State, am necessarily responsive to the state of public feeling.
> It is for these reasons that it has not been possible for this government to
> take a stand along with you in the present course of events in Greece.[27]

In a message to Roosevelt's adviser Harry Hopkins, Churchill was blunt: 'I consider we have a right to the President's support in the policy we are following. If it can be said in the streets of Athens that the United States are against us, then more British blood will be shed and much more Greek.'[28]

In a follow-up message, the prime minister said: 'It grieves me very much to see signs that we are drifting apart at a time when unity becomes ever more important, as danger recedes and faction arises.'[29] Stalin, he observed grimly, had adhered to the 'percentages' agreement.

Public opinion in the US was not only hostile to the Greek king and the Papandreou government, but also deeply suspicious of any attempt to install a regency in Greece, regarding it as a British stratagem to preserve the monarchy. The British ambassador in Athens and others had already concluded that the king was the chief obstacle in the way of a government of national unity that might include communists, and were proposing that the Archbishop of Athens should become regent and try to bring together the warring factions. Among those against the idea, besides the Americans, were the king and Churchill, who did not like the look of a prelate with a black beard and a pointy hat, who might well turn out to be a 'dictator from the Left'.[30]

Britain's travails in Greece led Smuts to write to Churchill:

> I am very distressed at the anxiety which the situation in Greece is causing you and the Cabinet ... We may, I fear, find that if private Partisan armies are kept alive, the peace [will degenerate] into civil convulsions and anarchy, not only in Greece but elsewhere in Europe. ... My own view, for what it is worth, is that after the suppression of the EAM, the Greek King should return to discharge his proper constitutional functions, and the onus of practically running Greece should no longer be borne by His Majesty's Government.[31]

On 12 December, Field Marshal Alexander arrived from the front line in Italy to assess for himself the situation in Athens, where a battle was raging for control of the streets. The situation was more serious than he thought. Alexander, a favourite of Churchill's, as well as Britain's Minister in the Mediterranean,

Harold Macmillan, and the ambassador, Reginald Leeper, were all in favour of appointing the archbishop as regent and the creation of a unity government. They urged the prime minister to act quickly, but Churchill remained uneasy. By appointing the archbishop, he argued, 'we should be punishing the King for obeying his constitutional oath and be ourselves setting up a dictator'.[32]

Asking about Archbishop Damaskinos of Athens, he wanted to know whether he was a 'clever scheming prelate, more interested in temporal power than celestial glory'. On being told that indeed he was, Churchill immediately warmed to him. 'Then he's our man,' he declared.[33]

After sending Smuts a telegram on 23 December expressing his concerns about a regency, Churchill reduced Clementine to tears[34] by deserting a family gathering at Chequers on Christmas Eve to travel to Athens. He wanted to see 'the situation on the spot and make the acquaintance of the Archbishop, around which so much was turning'.[35]

Arriving at Kalamaki Airport outside the capital, while still inside the freezing plane, Churchill plunged immediately into discussions with Macmillan, Alexander and Leeper. They decided to invite the Greek communists to a conference at which an all-party government would be set up, to be led by the archbishop, who made a favourable impression upon Churchill from the moment they met. Far from being pro-left, as Churchill had feared, Damaskinos was extremely critical of the communists. And he was obviously physically tough, having been a champion wrestler before entering the Orthodox Church. 'I was already convinced that he was the outstanding figure in the Greek turmoil,'[36] Churchill wrote later.

At the hurriedly summoned meeting of Greek leaders at the Foreign Ministry, Damaskinos agreed to preside over an all-party conference. It was 'intensely dramatic,' Churchill wrote to Clementine. 'All those haggard Greek faces round the table and the Archbishop with his enormous hat, making him, I should think, seven foot high.'

The British prime minister did not stay long at the meeting. To the sound of gunfire in the streets outside, he announced that it was for the Greeks to decide whether they remained a monarchy or became a republic. 'We do not intend to obstruct your deliberations.' Rising to his feet, he said, 'I should like to go now. We have begun the work. See that you finish it.'[37]

Back on the deck of the destroyer HMS *Ajax*, in which Churchill was accommodated during his stay, the captain asked whether or not he should return the spasmodic communist mortar fire landing close by. 'I have come to Greece on a mission of peace, Captain. I bear the olive branch between my teeth. But far be it from me to interfere with military necessity. "RETURN FIRE",' Churchill thundered.[38]

By the time the prime minister departed for home, via Naples, on 28 December, it had become clear that the communist leaders would not participate in any unity government in Greece.

On arriving in London, Churchill immediately gave the War Cabinet an account of his visit before calling in the Greek king for two long discussions that night. Faced with the choice of accepting a regency or having recognition of his government withdrawn, the king issued a proclamation at four o'clock the next morning: 'Being ourselves resolved not to return to Greece unless summoned by a free and fair expression of the national will ... we appoint you, Archbishop Damaskinos, to be our regent during this period of emergency ... and we require you to take all steps necessary to restore order and tranquillity throughout our kingdom.'[39]

Twenty-two hours after he had left Naples, a tired Churchill went to bed.[40]

Smuts was among those to congratulate Churchill and Eden on the success of their initiative in Greece, and to offer some 'wise advice':

> It is with deep interest and much anxiety that we have followed your Athens mission. It will have a profound and beneficial effect on world opinion. ... Now is the time, I suggest, to paint ELAS in its true colours. So that the world will see that Britain, as friend and ally, had no choice, a factual exposure should now be made of the bitter suffering inflicted on the Greek people, the dynamiting of property, the ruthless destruction and distortion, the rounding up and execution of innocent hostages, the coercion of the civilian population by terroristic methods in true Nazi style ... Following immediately on your courageous mission, a full and

accurate statement of the facts may lead to a wholesome reversal of public opinion.[41]

Churchill's headline-making Christmas mission to Athens turned out to be his last independent achievement in wartime policymaking.[42] It had not brought an end to the civilian conflict in Greece, which simmered on, nor did it establish a government of national unity, but it altered the balance of forces in the Aegean and raised the morale of British forces and advisers there immeasurably. It also sent the Americans and other doubters the clear signal that Churchill's Britain was not to be trifled with.

CHAPTER 23

Victory – and defeat

Democracy, with its promise of international peace, has no better guarantee
against war than the old dynastic rule of kings.

– SMUTS[1]

In late 1944, in a long message to his friend Smuts about the war's progress, Churchill added a paragraph in jesting vein:

> Meanwhile there approaches the shadow of the General Election which before many months have passed will break up the most capable government England [*sic*] has had or is likely to have. Generally we have a jolly year before us. Our financial future fills in any spaces in the horizon not already overcast with clouds. However, I am sure we shall master all these troubles as they come upon us, singly or in company, even though the tonic element of mortal danger is missing.[2]

The war in Europe had reached its terminal phase. The Allied leaders, Churchill and Stalin especially, were turning their thoughts to the post-war settlement. From his sickbed on New Year's Day 1945, Churchill greeted what he described as a 'new, disgusting year'.[3] Roosevelt had responded positively to his suggestion that they should meet in Malta before flying on to join Stalin at Yalta, in the Crimea, so he sent the president a jocular message: 'No more let us falter! From Malta to Yalta! Let nobody alter!'[4]

Despite Roosevelt's fast-failing health, Stalin had again declined, this time on medical grounds, to leave the borders of the Soviet Union for a 'big three' meeting, forcing the other two Allied leaders to make the long and arduous air journey. Churchill told Harry Hopkins, 'If we had spent ten years on research, we could not have found a worse place [than Yalta] in the world.'[5]

The British Prime Minister was in sombre mood: Stalin was being intransigent over Poland, Hitler's V-2 rockets were still falling on London and despite the failure of Hitler's counter-offensive against Montgomery's Allied army in the wooded Ardennes on the Belgium/Luxembourg border, an end to German resistance seemed a long way off.

On 29 January 1945, Churchill left London for Malta, where he met a frail Roosevelt, whose physical decline was all too apparent. It was obvious to Churchill that he would have to speak for America as well as Britain at Yalta, for by now the president was a desperately ill man. Yet, as Max Hastings notes, 'Human sympathy for Roosevelt was eclipsed by dismay about the implications of his incapacity to defend the interests of the West.'[6]

Two issues dominated the discussions at the conference: Poland and the establishment of the United Nations Organization, for which the planning had already begun at Dumbarton Oaks in Washington. Churchill also pressed for an occupation zone in Germany for the French, in case the Americans departed Europe after the war and left Britain to stand on its own against the might of the Soviet Union.[7]

Churchill fought his corner bravely at Yalta, but he knew he was arguing from a position of weakness. Stalin promised free elections in Poland after the war – a promise that 'Uncle Joe' had no intention of keeping. Once again, the Americans were not much help to the British: they were much more anxious to please Stalin, so as to win his support for the fight against the Japanese.[8] In what Churchill described as a 'momentous declaration', Roosevelt volunteered that American troops would be out of Europe within two years after the end of the war. This was intended to allay Stalin's suspicions that the Anglo-Americans were conspiring against him but it confirmed Churchill's belief that a strong France would be needed to counter Soviet expansionism.[9]

On his way back from Yalta, Churchill flew via Athens to see how Archbishop Damaskinos and his new Greek Government were faring. The city was in much better shape than it had been seven weeks earlier. Britain's prime minister was given a rapturous welcome, driving through the streets with the archbishop beside him to Constitution Square, where he addressed a crowd of over 40 000. 'I have never seen anything like the size of the crowd or so much enthusiasm,' he cabled his wife.

In his honour, the Acropolis was floodlit for the first time since the German occupation.[10] From Athens, Churchill flew to Cairo to bid farewell to Roosevelt, who was resting on a US warship after a meeting with King Ibn Saud in Saudi Arabia. It was to be the last time that president and prime minister were to see each other.

*

On 27 March 1945, the last of more than a thousand V-2 rockets landed on England, the launch site having been destroyed by the Allied armies earlier that day. For Churchill, the welcome news that the threat from the skies was over was tempered by news of the death, on the previous day, of his old friend and once close colleague, David Lloyd George.

Paying tribute in the House of Commons, Churchill said: 'There was no man so gifted, so eloquent, so forceful, who knew the life of the people so well.'[11] The prime minister could well have been speaking of himself when he said of Lloyd George: 'As a man of action, resource and creative energy, he stood, when at his zenith, without a rival.'[12] Some days later, Churchill attended the World War I leader's memorial service in Westminster Abbey, with Smuts beside him in his Field Marshal's uniform.

Smuts had arrived in early April, on his last and longest wartime visit to Britain, from where he was to continue to Europe, the US and Canada, once more accompanied by his son. He was as apprehensive as Churchill about the post-war pretensions of the Soviet Union. Before leaving South Africa, he had confided to Margaret Gillett:

> Without being a pessimist, I must confess that I feel deeply concerned about the future. ... Much as I think of the good in us, I have no confidence that we shall be wiser than in 1919 ... my faith in man does not extend to faith in Russia, with no check on her in Europe and Asia, and mistress of the continent of Europe. Such a position is too much a temptation even to the wisest, let alone an upstart power like Russia.[13]

Early on the morning of 13 April, while in his London hotel room, Smuts was given the shocking but not unexpected news of the death of Roosevelt during the night. Jannie describes how his father, who was shaving, was grey-faced as he put down his razor. 'God, how terrible,' he exclaimed. 'This is a knock-out blow.'[14] Even though he had never put Roosevelt on the same exalted plane as Churchill in either achievement or ability, Smuts had always liked and admired the American president for his struggle against isolationism and his humanitarian concerns.[15]

Churchill greeted the news of the president's death with the words 'I am much weakened in every way by his loss'.[16] To Harry Hopkins, he wrote:

> I feel with you that we have lost one of our greatest friends and one of the most valiant champions of the causes for which we fight. I feel a very painful personal loss, quite apart from the ties of public action which bound us so closely together. I had a true affection for Franklin.[17]

That afternoon, he moved the adjournment of the House of Commons as a tribute to Roosevelt, 'whose friendship,' he said, 'for the cause of freedom and for the causes of the weak and poor have won him immortal renown'.[18]

Yet, strangely – in a decision he came to regret – after ordering an aircraft to be made ready, the peripatetic British prime minister decided not to attend the funeral in Washington. Either he felt he could not afford to be away from London as the war neared its end or his personal relations with the president were not nearly as warm as most people imagined. As many post-war historians have concluded, although the two leaders had mostly got on well together, there was 'in reality no great measure of trust on either side. Both parties had entered into an alliance to benefit their own national interests.'[19]

*

On 18 April, General Eisenhower rang Churchill to tell him of how Allied troops had entered several Nazi concentration camps in Germany. The sights that met them defied description: they had found the emaciated bodies of thousands of Russian prisoners of war, Polish slave labourers and Jews.

The next day General Bedell Smith rang General Ismay to report scenes that were 'indescribably more horrible than those about which General Eisenhower spoke to you yesterday and of which photographs have appeared in the press today'.[20] The American described the newly liberated Buchenwald concentration camp as 'the acme of atrocity'.[21] Churchill immediately told the House of Commons of the discovery of 'these frightful crimes',[22] and sent an all-party team of MPs to Germany without delay to undertake a gruesome, on-the-spot investigation.

*

Like Churchill, Smuts was an ardent believer in the need for a new world organisation that would be more effective than the discredited League of Nations in preventing the outbreak of future war and promoting international peace. For this purpose, the nations of the world were to come together to put the finishing touches to work 'hammered into preliminary shape'[23] at Dumbarton Oaks in the US in September 1944 in preparation for a founding conference of the United Nations, to be held in San Francisco from April to June 1945. Although Smuts had played no part at Dumbarton Oaks, the rumour went around that he was to be president of the conference. He dismissed the notion as 'preposterous', however. 'Russia does not like me, France distrusts me, even in British circles there is divided opinion and South Africa is too small fry for such exaltation,' he said.[24]

Smuts had reservations about the proposed wording of the charter, which he found too impersonal and legalistic. At a meeting of Commonwealth prime ministers, convened primarily to discuss the charter, he proposed a formulation that would have more appeal for the common man, including phrases such as 'We the United Nations ... declare our faith in basic human rights ... We believe in the practice of tolerance ... We believe in the enlargement of freedom ... We believe in nations living in peace ...'[25] The Commonwealth prime ministers agreed that Smuts's wording would be 'a noble Preamble to the Charter' and proposed that it be put forward, in slightly amended form, to the UN conference.[26] In the charter adopted by the conference, 'basic' human rights subsequently became 'fundamental' human rights, and there

Smuts talking to Scottish-born new Zealand Prime Minister Peter Fraser and
Churchill during a dominion conference, 31 March 1945.

BOB LANDRY/THE LIFE PICTURE COLLECTION/GETTY IMAGES

were other minor changes to what had become known as 'the Smuts draft',
but the essence of his proposal was taken up in the preamble.

Ironically, Smuts's introduction of 'fundamental human rights' into the
charter gave the Indian government a powerful stick with which to beat him,
and South Africa, for his country's racial policies.* As Hancock writes, 'The

---

* As I explain in *Jan Smuts: Unafraid of Greatness* (Jonathan Ball, 2014, p 230), by 'human rights', Smuts meant protection
against invasion, freedom of religion, freedom of expression etc., but not political or racial equality. (He was well aware,
at the time, that he was giving his critics ammunition to use against him. Francis Williams, press secretary to Clement
Attlee, recounted how he had met Smuts at a reception in London and 'offered some rather empty compliments' about
a speech he had made. Williams recalled: 'He looked at me with the steady open-air stare which was one of his characteristics and said, "I know what you young liberals think when you hear me talking like that. You say: 'Why doesn't
he do better by the Africans in his own country, instead of talking to us about human rights?'" Well, my friend, some
day you'll appreciate what an avalanche I've been holding back.' (See Richard Toye, *Churchill's Empire: The World That
Made Him and The World He Made*. Macmillan, 2010, p 105.)

San Francisco Conference proved to be the last international gathering which Smuts attended as a world statesman still untarnished by the sins imputed to his country, and to himself as its prime minister.'[27]

At the prime ministers' conference, Smuts had warned that

> scientific discoveries have been made in this war which have not yet been embodied in war weapons, have not yet materialised in a munitions pro- gramme – discoveries which if any war were to take place in the future, would make this calamity seem small by comparison [and] might even mean the end of the human race.[28]

On arrival in San Francisco, he told the assembled media that the last great battle of the war 'is not being fought in Berlin, or anywhere else, but right here in San Francisco'.[29]

The founding UN conference was officially opened by President Truman on 25 April by means of a recorded message to the 3 300 delegates. (Smuts thought privately that the president ought to have been present in person on such an auspicious occasion.[30]) Described by Anthony Eden as 'the doyen of the Conference – quite unrivalled in intellectual attributes and unsurpassed in experience and authority',[31] South Africa's prime minister was one of the first speakers at the plenary session but then had to sit and watch in frustra- tion as the proceedings became bogged down in interminable haggling over principles and procedure.

*

In Europe, in the meantime, momentous events were unfolding. In Italy, Mussolini had given up the fight. Having been captured by partisans, he was summarily executed on 28 April and his body strung up head downwards in the main square of Milan. A couple of days later, on 1 May, Hitler also met his end, committing suicide by shooting himself in his bunker in Berlin. He had left instructions that Admiral Doenitz was to be his successor.

A week later, on 8 May 1945, Germany formally surrendered to the Allies and the war in Europe was over. In London, a triumphant but strangely subdued Churchill broadcast on radio to the people of Britain before driving to the House of Commons to speak to MPs and then to address a vast, exultant crowd gathered in Whitehall: 'This is *your* victory,' he said. 'Everyone, man or woman, has done their best. Neither the long years, nor the dangers, nor the fierce attacks of the enemy, have in any way weakened the independent resolve of the British nation. God bless you all!'[32]

An avalanche of congratulatory messages descended upon Churchill's head. From San Francisco, Eden declared: 'All my thoughts are with you on this day which is so essentially your day. It is you who have led, uplifted and inspired us through the worst days. Without you, this day could not have been.'[33]

Smuts also cabled his congratulations on the cessation of hostilities, lauding the exceptional contribution that Churchill had made. The prime minister wired back:

> Nothing in these past stirring days has brought me greater pleasure than your most kind message. Your presence beside me in the councils of the Empire and at the fronts in those long hard years has been to me a constant source of strength and inspiration for which I am most sincerely grateful. I pray that you may long remain with us a trusty friend and guide in war and peace.[34]

Yet apprehension for the future was foremost in Churchill's mind as he moved among the cheering throng of Londoners. The war against the Japanese was far from over, the atom bomb was ready for use, and with Hitler now dead, the 'bond of common danger' that had kept the Allies together had vanished.[35] At home, the foundations of national unity, upon which his wartime government had stood so successfully, were gone. And as far as he was concerned, 'the Soviet menace had already replaced the Nazi foe'.[36]

Churchill was also apprehensive about the general election that lay ahead and would have preferred to defer the poll until after the war against Japan was over. However, MPs of both main parties were keen on an early election – the Tories because they wanted to cash in on Churchill's achievements; Labour because they sensed that the leadership given in war was not what the nation wanted in peacetime. As it turned out, the broad mass of voters, especially the millions of returning servicemen, were unconcerned about the Soviet threat or the future of Empire; they wanted a pro-worker, pro-social-welfare government and were ready for a change.[37]

On his way home from the US to South Africa via London, Smuts found Churchill in 'an electioneering mood'.[38] The prime minister seemed confident of winning a majority of around a hundred in the House of Commons. On 23 May, he formally resigned as premier, and was invited by the king to form a caretaker Conservative government until the election on 5 July. Keeping a largely Tory Cabinet in place, he descended into the political arena to carry the fight to his deputy in the wartime coalition, Clement Attlee, and the 'socialists' whom he so disliked.

The British election campaign of 1945 was fought largely on the radio.[39] People had become used to clustering around the 'wireless' for news of the war, and each night they were able to tune into one of a carefully balanced set of party political broadcasts. Churchill made the first and last of the Conservatives' recordings. In the former, he made one of the worst mistakes of his political career, suggesting that socialism and totalitarianism were interwoven and that any Labour government would not tolerate dissent and fall back instead on 'some sort of Gestapo' to govern. When he had shown his wife his script beforehand, she had urged him to omit the odious reference to the Gestapo, but he had refused. It was to cost him dearly in the election.[40]

*

As the British people went to the polls, their prime minister's thoughts were mainly on the war in the Far East, which he feared might go on for another year at least and require more British troops to end it. He could not believe the country would entrust the hazards of the post-war world to someone like Attlee, whom he once described as 'a sheep in sheep's clothing',[41] rather than himself. However, as soon as the voting was over, and while the three-week-long count was in progress, Churchill took the precaution of inviting Attlee to accompany him to Potsdam in Germany for the last wartime meeting of the 'big three' nations. (In Parliament, a Labour MP wanted to know whether he would be taking 'the Gestapo' with him too.)[42]

The Potsdam conference, appropriately code-named (for Churchill) Terminal, was easily the longest of the three summits. Midway through it, he and Attlee flew home to London to await the election results, the PM having told Stalin privately that he expected the Conservatives to win by eighty votes.[43]

It was not to be. For the first time in history, Labour won more votes than the Conservatives, and with 393 seats in the new Parliament, had a 146-vote majority in the House of Commons. *The New York Times* described the Conservatives' defeat as 'one of the most stunning electoral surprises in the history of democracy'.[44] On the afternoon the results were declared, Churchill recorded a characteristically graceful concession speech for broadcast on the BBC. In it, he said:

> The decision of the British people has been recorded in the votes counted today. I have therefore laid down the charge which was placed upon me in darker times. I regret that I have not been permitted to finish the work against Japan. ... It only remains for me to express to the British people, for whom I have acted in these perilous years, my profound gratitude for the unflinching, unswerving support which they have given me during my task, and for the many expressions of kindness which they have shown towards their servant.[45]

A less than distressed Clementine remarked to her dismayed husband that the election result 'may be a blessing in disguise'.

'At the moment it seems quite effectively disguised,' was his reply.[46]

Under the terms of the constitution, Churchill would have been entitled to return to Potsdam and resign only once Parliament had reassembled, but he declined to do so. Attlee, accompanied by his new Foreign Secretary, the tough-minded trade-unionist Ernest Bevin, returned to Germany to do battle with Stalin. As the result of the election sank in, Churchill's physician, Lord Moran, remarked on the 'ingratitude' of voters. 'Oh no,' said his despondent patient, 'I wouldn't call it that. They've had a very hard time.'[47]

Later that night, while in his bath, a weary Churchill said to his aide, Captain Pim, 'They are perfectly entitled to vote as they pleased. This is democracy. This is what we've been fighting for.'[48]

CHAPTER 24

Dealing with Gandhi

*The incident … caused me much anxiety, because Mr Gandhi's death
would have produced a profound impression throughout
India, where his saintly qualities commanded
intense admiration.*

– CHURCHILL[1]

Throughout World War II, the future of India had been one of many
matters preying on Churchill's mind. The main obstacle in the way of
political progress, he stoutly maintained, was Gandhi, the enigmatic, ascetic
religious leader with whom he and Smuts had clashed over the years. Though
at one with Smuts on most matters of war and peace, and India's importance
to the empire, he disagreed with him about the Mahatma's motivations. To
Churchill, Gandhi was no saint, but a spiritual charlatan who was not a true
representative of the Indian people. Smuts, who had dealt with the Indian
leader at first hand, knew better.

'He is a man of God,' Lord Moran recounts Smuts telling Churchill
over lunch in Cairo. 'You and I are mundane people. Gandhi has appealed
to religious motives. You never have. That is where you have failed.' To
which Churchill jokingly responded: 'I have made more bishops than anyone since St Augustine.'[2] Yet Smuts was being serious. 'There is a pattern
in history, but it is not easy [for man] to follow,'[3] he said, having grasped a
truth he believed had eluded Churchill: Gandhi's exceptional spirituality,
Smuts had come to realise, had made him the single most powerful force in

Indian politics, even if he did not command the loyalty of all the people.*

Churchill's inflexible attitude to Indian self-determination was based partly on his appreciation of India's importance to the Allied war effort and partly on his fear of Britain losing control of the country. It was also premised on his conviction that India was much better off under the Raj than if the country were to become self-governing. He did not believe the Indian Congress Party, under the spell of Gandhi, represented most Indians, especially not the substantial Muslim minority. Britain's imposition of a wartime state of emergency, he thought, would demonstrate who was really in charge in India and show up the slenderness of Congress's hold over the dominant forces in Indian society.[4] Gandhi, for his part, had persuaded himself that World War II offered a heaven-sent opportunity to rid India once and for all of the British, even if it meant risking the possibility of the Japanese replacing the Raj. His search for spiritual truth led him to believe that passive resistance was the antidote to temporal power, no matter if it put the lives of the masses at risk. Liberty was God's supreme achievement, and, without it, life – even his own – was meaningless.[5] He once said he would far rather that India perished than won her freedom at the price of God's truth. This was all very well in theory, but as the historian of Empire, Lawrence James, notes drily, 'for a public figure who had gone to elaborate lengths to create an image of himself as a man of peace, Gandhi was cavalier with the lives of others'.[6]

It was not so much Gandhi's failed Quit India campaign as the devastating Bengal famine of 1942/43 that undermined more than anything else the confidence of Indians in imperial rule. A cyclone that ripped through Bengal in late 1942 had ruined the rice crop, leading to the deaths from starvation of several million people in one of the great human disasters of the century.

Totally focused on events in Europe, Churchill had declined at first to send emergency supplies of food to Bengal because transport ships were badly needed

---

* Lord Tedder was also present at the Cairo lunch and describes more amusingly the exchange between Smuts and Churchill: 'Gandhi,' Smuts declared, 'is inspired by sheer idealism. His appeal is essentially a spiritual one. And that is your weakness, Winston. It is by facing up to and overcoming fear that you have led the British people to great deeds of courage and endurance; but you have not been able to give them truly spiritual inspiration.' To which Churchill retorted, 'Field Marshal, I take the gravest exception to this dastardly attack upon my character. I would have you know that in this past year, I have appointed no less than six bishops. If that is not spiritual inspiration, what is? And with a grin to the rest of the lunch party, he asked, "How's that for an adequate answer to an unforgiveable attack on my character?"' (See Arthur Tedder, *With Prejudice: The War Memoirs of the Marshal of the Royal Air Force, Lord Tedder.* Cassell, 1966, p 324.)

by the Allied forces invading Italy. He was eventually persuaded by his Secretary of State and close friend, Leo Amery, to send a quarter of the relief required, defiantly insisting that there were also food shortages in liberated southern Europe and Greece, as well as India. Bengali maladministration compounded the famine, but Lord Wavell, the new British Viceroy to India, almost resigned over Whitehall's procrastination and inaction.[7] He described the food crisis as 'one of the worst disasters that had befallen any people living under British rule'.[8]

Born in India himself, the determined Wavell managed not only to obtain more emergency food supplies for Bengal and arrange their distribution by the army, but also to reorganise India's defences and put an end to the Quit India movement before it threatened Britain's hold on power or opened the door to a Japanese invasion. As he recorded in his diary, he had one great advantage over previous Viceroys: they had to decide whether and when to lock up Gandhi; when he arrived, he found Gandhi already locked up.[9]

The viceroy decided that a political solution in India could not wait until after the war was over. Without Gandhi's sanction, Congress would not move, and without Congress, no headway was possible. So Wavell flew to London to propose to the Cabinet's India Committee an all-party summit of Indian leaders who supported the 1935 constitution and the Allied war effort. He thought that even Gandhi might agree to attend. But, to the viceroy's disgust, he ran up against an unyielding Churchill, who furiously denounced Congress and swore that only over his 'dead body would any approach to Gandhi take place'.[10] It took Smuts to make Wavell understand Churchill's position: '[The PM] is not thinking beyond the end of the war – about India or anything else,' he said.[11]

In April 1944, after a year's preparation, the Japanese launched an attack on India. Aided by the Axis-supporting nationalist Subhas Chandra Bose's Indian National Army, Japanese troops attacked at Imphal and Kohima, two towns on the Indian side of its border with the then Burma. After several months of fierce fighting, India's mainly Hindu army, backed by British aircraft, drove the Japanese back into the Burmese jungle, in what was aptly described as the new army's 'finest hour'. It was thought that as many as 80 000 Japanese lost their lives in the worst defeat in the country's history. Although the short-lived battle for India had been won, an even more brutal fight over Burma was now to begin.

*

In a barb directed at President Roosevelt, Churchill once said memorably that he had not become the King's First Minister to preside over the liquidation of the British Empire.[12] During World War II, however, his dreams of a post-war empire stronger and more united than ever had begun to founder on the rock of American opposition to the pre-war colonial status quo. At the same time, Britain's dire financial situation and mounting war debts made imperial solidarity and support more imperative than ever. And despite the prime minister's efforts to keep the empire intact, the cracks were beginning to show. Attlee's Labour Party had already signalled its readiness to grant Indian self-rule soon after the war ended.

One month before D-Day in Europe, Wavell ordered Gandhi's release from his not uncomfortable detention. The Mahatma had contracted malaria – to add to his anaemia and high blood pressure – and his medical advisers warned that he might die at any minute.[13] Given his severe health problems, his doctors doubted whether he would ever be a force in active politics again.

Aware of the consequences should the Indian sage die in captivity, Churchill reluctantly agreed to Wavell's recommendation, but once Gandhi was free, he gave vent to his true feelings:

> He is a thoroughly evil force, hostile to us in every fibre, largely in the hands of the native vested interests and frozen to the idea of the hand spinning-wheel and inefficient cultivation methods for the overcrowded population of India. I look forward to the day when it may be possible to come to an understanding with the real forces that control India.[14]

Wavell did not think well of Gandhi either, considering him 'verbose, petty-minded and quite devoid of any constructive statesmanship ... [and] bent mainly on his own self-justification'.[15] But he recognised that the Mahatma was part of the solution to India's future and sought permission from Churchill to meet him in person. Permission was flatly denied, which made the viceroy realise there could be no real progress towards Indian self-rule as long as Churchill was prime minister.

To those close to Churchill, it had become obvious that the war was taking its toll. A visibly flagging and increasingly irrational prime minister had become prone to outbursts of fury, at summits as well as Cabinet meetings, whenever the future of the empire was mentioned. At Yalta, when a delegate raised the question of the trusteeship of 'former colonies', Churchill raged that he 'would not have the British Empire run by a crowd of bunglers'.[16] In public, however, he was more positive and upbeat, declaring in his victory broadcast on 13 May that 'the British Commonwealth and Empire stands more united and more powerful than at any time in its long romantic history'.[17]

He had begun to realise, however, that history was no longer on his side. As he confessed to Clementine:

> I have had for some time a feeling of despair about the British connection with India, and still more about what would happen if it is suddenly broken. Meanwhile we are holding on to this vast Empire from which we get nothing, amid the increasing criticism and abuses of the world and our own people.[18]

At the end of May 1945, before the outcome of the general election was known, Wavell's threat of resignation led to a meeting of the full British Cabinet to discuss the future of India. Churchill presided, and after delivering a fierce rant against the viceroy's plan for an all-party conference of Indian leaders, suddenly changed course and said he would support Wavell's draft as long as it was on a take-it-or-leave-it basis, and not subject to further negotiation. The viceroy was stunned. But the reason for Churchill's dramatic volte-face became apparent later: members of the India Committee had assured him that no agreement among Indian leaders was possible, so offering the impossible might delay independence indefinitely, and perhaps even for ever.[19]

Wavell convened a summit of leaders, held at the viceregal lodge at Simla on 25 June. At the very last minute, Gandhi decided to attend, representing himself only. He and an intensely curious Wavell met for the first time and had a cordial two-hour discussion, but after three weeks of negotiation, the talks foundered over Muslim demands for partition. Gandhi accepted the collapse of the summit with equanimity. Like Churchill, he had expected nothing else.

A few weeks later, Labour's unexpected election victory altered the equation: suddenly Churchill and the Conservatives were absolved from further

responsibility for India, and the country was granted independence by the
Attlee government in 1947.

There was a strange sequel to the Simla conference. After his release from
prison in 1944, Gandhi had written Churchill a letter:

> Dear Prime Minister, You are reported to have a desire to crush the sim-
> ple 'Naked Fakir', as you are said to have described me. I have been long
> trying to be a Fakir and that naked – a more difficult task. I therefore
> regard the expression as a compliment, however unintended. I approach
> you then as such and ask you to trust and use me for the sake of your
> people and mine and through them those of the world. Your sincere
> friend, M K Gandhi.[20]

It was Gandhi's way of reaching out to one of his longest-standing foes, and
would have been the only direct communication between them for almost
forty years. Unfortunately, the letter seems never to have reached Churchill,
who failed to reply. A year later, and before attending the Simla meeting, in
the hope of opening a dialogue with Churchill, Gandhi decided for some
reason to make the letter public, even though its contents were 'of a sacred
character and not meant for the public eye'.[21]

*

Smuts was able to understand and appreciate Gandhi's spiritual dimension,
but his views of the Mahatma as a politician were similar to those of Churchill
and Wavell. As he explained to his son:

> The attitude of Gandhi is anti-material and as the British personified the
> material world, he is automatically anti-British. Gandhi stressed the spir-
> itual value of things, the religion and soul of India. The position in India
> is very complex. Fundamentally it is a battle of religions – the Hindu and
> the Moslem. It was only the presence and power of Britain that kept India
> together. Remove it, and you will have the sects once more at each other's
> throats and India will once again split up into an infinity of small states.

> The views of Gandhi were aggravating matters and it would perhaps be a
> good thing if he could pass quietly away into the next world.[22]

Years earlier, Gandhi had given Smuts the politician and statesman unending
difficulties. Shortly before World War II had broken out, the government of
which Smuts was deputy leader had passed legislation designed to confine or
'peg' Indians to their existing residential areas and business premises in the
Transvaal. From India, Gandhi rebuked him: 'Why is the agreement of 1914
being violated with you as witness? Is there no help for Indians except to pass
through fire?'[23]

Two months later, Smuts became South Africa's prime minister again, declaring the Commonwealth (including India) to be his 'great cause'.[24] However,
some of his pro-war coalition partners thought differently. The Dominion Party
in Natal, where most of the rapidly growing Asian population in South Africa
was concentrated, viewed the encroachment of Indians onto white-owned land
with mounting apprehension, and complained that they had not been consulted. Yet Smuts depended on the Dominion Party's support if he were to
retain his precarious hold on power and take the country to war.

Throughout World War II, he remained aware that any further restrictions on Indians' rights would reawaken a twenty-five-year-long domestic
dispute which flared up intermittently and was sure to jeopardise South
Africa's relations within the Commonwealth. Nevertheless, he could not risk
losing control over the white electorate while the war against Hitler was in
progress.[25] To his temporary rescue came moderates in the leadership of the
Natal Indian Congress, who managed, informally, in the war's early stages, to
contain the influx of Indians into white areas. Caught in a cleft stick, Smuts
resorted to the time-honoured political tactic of appointing a judicial commission – in this case to investigate Indian penetration of European areas in
the Transvaal and Natal between 1927 and 1940.

In April 1944, armed with information from the Broome Commission
that the extent of Indian expansion had been exaggerated, Prime Minster
Smuts called a conference in Pretoria between members of his Cabinet and
representatives of the Natal Indian Congress. The outcome was the Pretoria
Agreement, which established procedural collaboration between whites and
Indians on matters of common concern, such as residential and trading

rights. Delighted with the outcome, Smuts sent a summary of the agreement to the viceroy and Secretary of State Amery, expressing the view that it might be as welcome to them as it was to him.[26]

With the Pretoria Agreement in his pocket, Smuts set off for the prime ministers' conference in London, before going on to San Francisco for negotiations over the UN Charter. No sooner had he left than the dominionites in Natal revolted, calling on Free State Afrikaner Nationalists, of all people, to come to their aid against the 'Asiatic hordes' threatening their way of life.[27] That put a swift end to the moderation of the Natal Indian Congress, whose leadership had to give way to a new pressure group, the Anti-Segregation Council. The council immediately drew up a ten-point programme based on the tenets of the Atlantic Charter, the essence of which could be summarised in two words: 'equality now'.[28]

By now the Pretoria Agreement was a dead duck. In a letter to Wavell, Smuts told the viceroy that he intended to introduce legislation to give the Indians limited representation in both Parliament and provincial councils. When he tried to do so, however, he ran into a gale of protests from Afrikaner Nationalists and Dominion Party MPs alike. Although Smuts eventually won the vote on Indian representation in Parliament, the Indians in Natal and the Transvaal rejected the measure as being 'too little too late' and began a Gandhi-style campaign of passive resistance. In India, Nehru's provisional government imposed an economic boycott on South Africa and recalled its High Commissioner. A dismayed Smuts told Wavell that the Pretoria Agreement had failed largely because of his enforced absences from South Africa.[29]

On 18 March 1946, Smuts received a cable from Gandhi: 'Your Asiatic policy needs overhauling. It ill becomes you.' He went on to propose a round-table conference of Union, British and Indian governments to consider South Africa's colour policies, signing off his message as 'Your and South Africa's sincere friend'.[30]

Smuts replied by saying he much appreciated Gandhi's interest and his 'kind message of friendship, which is warmly reciprocated'. However, Indian difficulties in Natal had become acute, he said, and had to be urgently dealt with 'to prevent deterioration from which Indians may be the greatest sufferers'. Explaining his proposed 'conferment of political status on Indians', Smuts commended his reforms to Gandhi, who knew 'how great are the difficulties in maintaining harmony among South Africans of all races'. He assured the Indian leader of 'the friendly spirit in which I am acting in a situation which may easily get out of control'.[31]

In mid-June 1946, India put South Africa's treatment of its Asiatic population on the agenda of the UN General Assembly. As Smuts had been warned by Indian negotiators in London twenty-three years earlier, South Africa's domestic policy had become an issue of foreign policy – and he was to be at the epicentre of a storm about to erupt in New York.

Writing to Isie from Paris, Smuts predicted that to divert attention from the inter-racial massacre of some half-million Muslim refugees in Calcutta and Bengal, Indian opposition to South Africa would sharpen. Nehru, he claimed, was thinking of sending Gandhi to the UN. 'The world will find it quite interesting to see Gandhi and me once more in conflict in our old age before a world court,' he said.[32] In a letter to his deputy, JH Hofmeyr, Smuts forecast 'heavy weather' at the UN. 'There is a growing widespread opinion adverse to us,' he wrote.[33]

His fears were well founded. There was no Gandhi in New York, but leading India's delegation was Nehru's sister, VL Pandit, whose virulent attacks on South Africa's racial policies for being in breach of the UN Charter were met with loud applause. In vain did Smuts point out that India's caste system and communal conflicts were also in breach of the charter. The framers of the charter, he argued, had never intended to make political equality a fundamental human right; South Africa had violated no one's fundamental human rights and, furthermore, there could be no invasion by the UN of any state's domestic jurisdiction.

In the new anti-racist, anti-imperialist post-war zeitgeist, these legalistic arguments fell on unreceptive ears. By a two-thirds majority, the General Assembly directed South Africa to bring its racial policies into line with the UN Charter. This was a humiliation for Smuts, who confessed to Isie: 'It is not particularly pleasant for me, at the end of my life and work, to become involved in this kind of conflict which leaves me little time for other things in which I am interested. But I have no choice and shall have to climb the greasy pole as best I may.'[34]

After the vote, Pandit told Smuts that before she had left India, Gandhi had said to her: 'I don't mind whether you come back having won your case or having suffered defeat. But you must come back as a friend of Field Marshal Smuts.' Smuts's grim rejoinder to her was that her winning the UN vote would put him out of power at the next election.

Reflecting much later on his relationship with Gandhi, Smuts remarked ruefully on the Mahatma's successful tactic of encouraging civil disobedience and receiving 'what he no doubt desired – a short period of rest and quiet in gaol'. Said Smuts:

> For him, everything went according to plan. For me – the defender of law and order – there was the usual trying situation, the odium of carrying out a law which had not strong public support, and finally the discomfiture when the law had to be repealed ... Nor was the personal touch wanting, for nothing in Gandhi's procedure is without a peculiar personal touch ... In gaol, he had prepared for me a very useful set of sandals which he presented to me when he was set free. I have worn these sandals every summer since then, even though I may feel that I am not worthy to stand in the shoes of so great a man[35] ... Smuts wore the sandals until 1939, when he sent a photograph of them to their maker as a token of affection and respect on Gandhi's 70th birthday.[36]

Smuts continued:

> It was in this spirit that we fought out our quarrels in South Africa. There was no hatred or personal ill-feeling, the spirit of humanity was never absent, and when the fight was over there was an atmosphere in which a decent peace could be concluded. Gandhi and I made a settlement which Parliament ratified, and which kept the peace between the races for many years.[37]

This was surely a case of absence making Smuts's heart grow fonder. Churchill, who never really knew Gandhi, would never have reached so mellow or generous a conclusion about India's troublesome holy man.

CHAPTER 25

Out to grass

It is with deep grief that I watch the clattering down of
the British Empire with all its glories and all the services
it has rendered to mankind.

— CHURCHILL[1]

Besides the unexpectedly rejected Churchill, no one was more surprised and dismayed by the outcome of the British election than Smuts. He fired off two 'heartfelt' telegrams of commiseration to his old friend, who declined to acknowledge them. As Churchill confessed to Lord Moran, he was miffed with Smuts for also sending a telegram to Attlee to congratulate him on his 'brilliant victory'. It was the word 'brilliant' that stuck in the throat, Moran's patient groused: 'If he had just congratulated him on his victory, it would have been different. Why brilliant? It wasn't brilliant at all.'[2]

Three days after the election, Smuts expressed his concern at the result in a letter to Margaret Gillett:

> I fear the dropping of the pilot may have a bad effect on the stormy seas
> ahead. ... [The British] have lost a leader who was not conservative, but
> a great human, with vast experience and a great breadth of sympathies ...
> I have publicly congratulated Attlee. Privately I have quoted to Churchill
> the lines from Mommsen on Hannibal's end. ... 'On those whom the
> Gods love, they lavish infinite joys and infinite sorrows.' What else could
> one say that is adequate to such a situation and such a fall after achieving
> the most colossal success in history ... One cannot forbear sympathising

deeply with Churchill. To be so decisively rejected in the very hour of victory by the people whom he saved by his courage and stupendous exertions is truly the unkindest cut of all.[3]

Two weeks later, he wrote to her again:

It is a dangerous world ... and the loss of a champion like Churchill cannot fail to be seriously felt in our dealings with colossi like the United States and USSR. Unfortunately [Churchill] had allowed himself to become Conservative leader without being himself a Conservative in conviction. And this is now the result of that initial mistake. So our mistakes catch us out in the end ...[4]

If there was any ice to be broken, it was achieved when Smuts delivered to Churchill, by air, some of the best South African brandy and sherry, together with an accompanying letter:

I have not written you before as I thought you would prefer not to be bothered with correspondence and would rather learn the taste of the grass to which the old warhorse has been put. But now may I express to you that the elections have been one of the major surprises of my life. Nothing I knew or had heard from the best sources had prepared me for this shock. But there it is, and what cannot be prevented had better be enjoyed. And so I hope you are making the best of the new life, as I know you will ... At this moment when all is at stake for Britain, and her future is at the mercy of vast, almost uncontrollable forces, she drops the one man who could have provided leadership and a measure of insurance for herself. No doubt the people were desirous of a change from the Conservative policies, but dropping the pilot in mid storm![5]

Smuts continued: 'I am full of troubles of my own. Perhaps the worst is the Indian question which, like most of our present world problems seems almost insoluble in the present temper. To you, it will appear small.'[6]

Another leader who couldn't make sense of Churchill's defeat was Stalin, who had never experienced a democratic impulse in his life. At Potsdam, he asked Attlee to explain what had happened in Britain. Labour supporters, the new PM pointed out, often acted in strange ways, cheering and applauding speakers at meetings but voting against them in the ballot box. The reverse had happened here. A distinction had to be made between Churchill the war leader and Churchill the Conservative Party leader. 'The people wanted a parliament based on a definite programme. Many people looked upon the Conservatives as a reactionary party which would not carry out a policy answering to peace requirements,'[7] Attlee explained.

Harry Truman was also sorry to see Churchill go, and did not think very highly of his Labour replacements. In a letter to his daughter, Margaret, he drew a contrast between Churchill, Attlee and Bevin:

> I did like old Churchill. He was as windy as old Langer [a Republican senator] but he knew his English language. And after he had talked half an hour, there'd be at least one gem of a sentence and two thoughts maybe, which could have been expressed in four minutes. But if we ever got him on record, which was seldom, he stayed put. Anyway, he is a likeable person, and these two are sourpusses.[8]

A letter that much amused the fallen British premier came from a friend stationed in a British embassy in the Balkans, who related the comment of an old lady in Zagreb, 'Poor Mr Churchill, I suppose that now he will be shot.' A now more cheerful Churchill, who had no intention of retiring from politics, responded by saying he'd not been shot, but sentenced to hard labour instead.[9]

The shock of the British election result was quickly overshadowed by a far more seismic event: the dropping of the atom bomb on Hiroshima on 6 August and on Nagasaki three days later. 'It was now for Japan to realise,' Churchill declared in a public statement, 'in the glare of the first atomic bomb which has smitten her what the consequences would be of an indefinite continuance of this terrible means of maintaining a rule of law in the world.'[10] On 15 August, the Japanese finally surrendered; World War II was at an end and Britain's six-year ordeal was over.

A day after Hiroshima, Churchill told Lord Camrose, publisher of *The Daily Telegraph*, that if he had still been in office, he could have persuaded the Americans to 'use this [atomic] power to restrain the Russians'. He would have had 'a showdown with Stalin and told him he had got to behave responsibly and decently in Europe and would have gone so far as to be brusque and angry with him if needs be'.[11]

Addressing Parliament as leader of the opposition a fortnight later, Churchill declared prophetically: 'The bomb brought peace, but only men can keep that peace, and henceforward they will keep it under penalties which threaten the survival, not only of civilisation, but of humanity itself.'[12]

Smuts reflected on the use of the atom bomb in a long letter to Margaret Gillett:

> I dare say this sudden collapse [of Japan] was largely due to the atomic bomb, the effect of which, both physical and psychological, must have been shattering. From that point of view its use has been justified. But it has been even more justified from the point of preventing war in the future … [People] would never have believed the warning about deadly weapons in future warfare unless there had been this actual display of them at the end of this war. We are now forewarned about what is coming if war is not ended for good. I knew all about it as I had been dealing with this matter for the last two years on my London visits. At last a discovery has been made which should put war out of court for good and all.[13]

After the war was over, although grumbling from time to time about the burdens of public office upon their ageing shoulders, neither Churchill nor Smuts thought their countries could do without them, and had no serious intention of leaving the national and international stage. Soon after Victory over Japan Day, Churchill took himself off to Lake Como, in Italy, and the French Riviera for long hours of sunshine and painting.* He wrote to

---

* A painting by Churchill of the Pyramids at Giza, circa 1946, which he gave to Smuts, went on sale in Churchill's old constituency of Epping in 2016. The highest price paid at auction for a Churchill painting to date is £1.5 million (see www.essex.news/paintings).

Clementine to say that he was feeling much better for not having seen any newspapers:

> This is the first time for very many years that I have been completely out of the world. The Japanese War being finished and complete peace and victory achieved, I feel a great sense of relief, which grows steadily, others having to face the hideous problems of the aftermath. On their shoulders and consciences weighs the responsibility for what is happening in Europe. It may all be a blessing in disguise.[14]

Churchill was deceiving no one but himself. He believed the threat of a war with the Soviet Union was real, and was certain that he was the man to prevent it. As he told the Canadian prime minister, Mackenzie King, the Russians were 'realist-lizards, all belonging to the crocodile family, who would be as pleasant to you as they could, although prepared to destroy you'. There was nothing to be gained, he asserted, 'by not letting the Russians know that we are not afraid of them'.[15]

In March 1946, invited by President Truman to speak at Fulton in his home state of Missouri, Churchill made full use of the opportunity to deliver one of the most powerful and best remembered of all his speeches. Choosing his words carefully, he declared his admiration for what Russia had achieved in the war and welcomed her 'to her rightful place among the leading nations of the world ... and her flag upon the seas'. However it was his duty to point out, that from Stettin in the Baltic to Trieste in the Adriatic, an 'Iron Curtain' had descended across the continent. Behind that curtain lay the ancient capitals of central and eastern Europe, each of them subject to a high and increasing measure of control from Moscow. As a result, the outcome of the war was not the liberated Europe which the US and UK had fought to build up. 'Nor is it one which contains the essential elements of permanent peace,' he said.[16]

Though widely denounced on both sides of the Atlantic for being a warmonger intent on forging a new military alliance against Russia, Churchill justified his stance by telling Attlee and Bevin on his return to London that 'some show of strength and resisting power is necessary for a good settlement with Russia', adding, presciently, 'I predict that this will be the prevailing opinion in the United States in the near future.'[17] Among those to react with fury to the speech was Stalin, who described it as 'calculated to sow the seeds of discord between the Allied Governments and make collaboration difficult'.[18]

Churchill's 'Iron Curtain' speech reverberated around the world. Before long, the term he coined had come to define international power relations post-World War II and to lay the foundation for the Truman doctrine of containing Soviet expansionism and the establishment of NATO. What is more, the border that Churchill had drawn across central and eastern Europe became the actual front line of Western defences against the advance of Marxism-Leninism throughout the ensuing fifty-year-long Cold War.

Smuts, whose concern about Russia was as great as Churchill's, warmly approved of the sentiments expressed at Fulton. Commenting on the speech in Parliament, he said, 'We are living in a very dangerous world. Peace cannot come automatically. It may take a generation or more. The world is going through the greatest revolution in history ...'[19]

He told Churchill: 'Your Fulton speech has been completely justified and has in fact become the policy of the West.'[20]

*

South Africa's now elderly prime minister paid two more visits to Britain and mainland Europe in 1946, the first to attend another Commonwealth prime ministers' conference, presided over by Attlee this time rather than Churchill, and the second to be at the long-postponed Peace Conference in Paris.

Smuts and Mackenzie King were both of the view that Churchill could only tarnish his reputation by soldiering on in domestic politics and encouraged him to retire, but he would not hear of it. At a dinner held by Attlee in honour of King, he rebuffed suggestions that he should devote himself to writing rather than politics. He had no intention of abandoning the fight, he declared, and planned to lead the Conservatives to victory at the next election. He told his close friend Lady Cranborne, wife of the leader of the opposition in the Lords, that nothing would induce him to retire.[21]

Smuts was the only one among the twenty-one delegates in attendance in Paris to have been present at the negotiations leading to the Treaty of Versailles in 1919. Once again, he held out little hope for a successful outcome to a post-war conference.[22] As he explained to an audience in Aberdeen, where he was given the Freedom of the City, the best that could be hoped for after Paris was a prolonged armistice until the world became more settled. In a broadcast on the BBC, he declared:

> Great events often unfold slowly, often take a long time to mature and come to pass … We must look upon world peace not as a mere accomplishment, or waiting just around the corner, but as a long-range task, calling for a new spirit among the nations and for mighty efforts to achieve it. Of that spirit there is little evidence at present.[23]

Still concerned with the events unfolding in Greece, and sharing Churchill's fears that the country might yet fall to the insurgent communists, Smuts invited Crown Prince Paul and Princess Frederika to visit him in Paris, where they stayed for several days before his plane took them back to Egypt. After the civil war in Greece between the American-supported royalists and the communists had ended in a victory for the former and following a referendum boycotted by the losers, King George II was allowed to return to his gutted and looted country, which he did in 1946. When he died suddenly a year later, Paul became King of Greece and Frederika his queen. The royal couple renamed a street in Athens after Smuts to acknowledge their debt to him.[24]

*

Besides India, the future of Palestine continued to trouble both Churchill and Smuts. The establishment of a Jewish national home in Palestine, in fulfilment of the Balfour Declaration of 1926, had always been one of Smuts's dearest causes.[†] Disregarding what to many were the disastrous consequences

---

[†] Smuts had always had a special regard for the Jewish people, whom he saw as similar to Afrikaners – God-fearing, hardworking and without their own homeland. Back in 1917, he had encouraged Lloyd George's Foreign Secretary Arthur Balfour to declare, in a letter to Zionist leaders, that Britain would support the establishment of a Jewish homeland in Palestine. In 1929, on a US lecture tour, he gave 26 addresses in 18 days in support of the League of Nations and the Jewish cause in Palestine. (See Richard Steyn, *Jan Smuts: Unafraid of Greatness*, Jonathan Ball, 2014, p 119.)

of the Balfour Declaration on British interests in the Middle East, in a letter to Leo Amery in 1948, Smuts lamented Britain's fumbling of its great redemptive cause in Israel. 'We can't scuttle from responsibility before history,' he told the imperial-minded British politician. 'Getting out of it anyhow' was, to him, the worst possible option.[25]

Churchill had also spoken out strongly against Labour's policy towards Israel. 'Had I had the opportunity,' he told the House of Commons, 'of guiding events after the war was won a year ago, I should have faithfully pursued the Zionist cause as I have defined it ... although this is not a popular moment to espouse it.'[26] Yet he also strongly deprecated Jewish terrorist attacks on British targets, reminding Jews that it had been Great Britain alone that had carried forward the Zionist cause: 'We have discharged a thankless, painful, costly, inconvenient task for more than a quarter of a century with a very great measure of success,' he said. Like Smuts, he cautioned against being in a hurry 'to turn aside from the large causes we have carried far'.[27]

In early January 1947, Churchill addressed the House on the question of Palestine, where forty-five British soldiers had already died at the hands of Jewish terrorists. Though deploring 'this series of detestable outrages',[28] he urged MPs not to turn their backs on a Jewish homeland. Stressing that Britain could no longer pay to keep its army in Palestine, he proposed – unless the United States agreed 'to take a half and half share of the bloodshed, odium, trouble, expense and worry'[29] – that responsibility for the mandate should henceforth be borne by the United Nations and not by 'poor, overburdened and heavily injured' Britain.[30]

Handing the mandate over to the UN, Churchill believed, was the only way in which Britain could honour its promise to create a national homeland for Jews, a pledge the country could no longer deliver on its own.[31]

Smuts echoed these by now discordant sentiments. He too viewed with concern Britain's enforced retreat as an imperial power, especially in countries in the eastern Mediterranean, which South African troops had shed blood to defend. He told the South African Senate: 'It is not that Britain is no longer a great Power. She is an invalid, having been incapacitated by the great effort she had to make in the war. You may be a strong man but nothing will keep you out of hospital if misfortune overtakes you.'[32]

On 14 February, the Labour Cabinet decided that Britain should hand over the Palestine mandate to the United Nations as soon as possible. With regard to India, only six days later, Attlee announced that power would be transferred into 'responsible Indian hands' by not later than June 1948 and that Lord Louis Mountbatten would succeed Wavell as viceroy. Churchill was dismayed. 'It is with deep grief that I watch the clattering down of the British Empire with all its glories and all the services it has rendered to mankind,' he said.[33]

*

Having now resigned himself to the inevitability of Indian self-rule, Churchill repeatedly emphasised the importance of accommodating India's Muslims in any future constitutional system. 'One cannot contemplate,' he declared in the House of Commons, 'that British troops should be used to crush Muslims in the interests of the caste Hindus.'[34] Although a supporter of the Muslims, and their leader, Mohammed Ali Jinnah, he was nonetheless surprised at some of the insulting things Muslims were saying about Britain, especially the allegation that they were being subjected to 'British slavery'.[35]

At the Conservative Party Conference in late 1946, Churchill had asserted that the interim government of India had been placed in the hands of men who had good reason to be bitterly hostile to the British connection, but who

> in no way represent the enormous mass of nearly 400 million of all races, states and peoples of India who have dwelt so long in peace with one another. I fear that calamity impends upon this sub-Continent, which is almost as big as Europe, more populous, and even more harshly divided. It seems that in quite a short time India will become separate, a foreign and a none too friendly country to the British Commonwealth ...[36]

Speaking again on India in the House of Commons later in 1946, Churchill observed that in the four months since Nehru and his Congress Party had been in government, more lives had been lost by violence than in the previous ninety years, during the reign of five sovereigns. 'This,' he said, 'is only a foretaste of what might come. It may be only the first few drops before the thunderstorm breaks upon us. These frightful slaughters over wide regions and in obscure uncounted villages have, in the main, fallen upon Muslim minorities.'[37]

In South Africa, Smuts had his own reasons for viewing self-government for India with foreboding. Although he had acknowledged as far back as the 1930s in correspondence with Amery – Britain's Colonial Secretary at the time – that self-rule was unavoidable, he was keenly aware of the implications of Indian independence for his own country, both internally and internationally. He had always been concerned that India might become, not a dominion, but a republic within the Commonwealth, which might boost the republican cause among Afrikaner Nationalists in South Africa.

Attlee's choice of Mountbatten, the man appointed by Churchill as Supreme Allied Commander in South East Asia in World War II, to bring down the curtain on the Raj by June 1948, no matter what, was astute. Mountbatten enjoyed one inestimable advantage over the outgoing viceroy, Wavell: Churchill liked him, as he did most people with connections to royalty. Yet giving the new viceroy only fourteen months to secure a working agreement with Nehru was outrageous. 'Is he to make a new effort to restore the situation, or is it merely "Operation Scuttle",' the Conservative leader wanted to know. 'One thing seems to me to be absolutely certain – the Government by the time limit has put an end to all prospects of Indian unity.'[38]

On 20 May, Attlee and Mountbatten met Churchill and other Tories to try to achieve an all-party consensus on the way forward with India. The plan was to partition the country into two states, the one Hindu, the other Muslim, and to grant them both dominion status within the Commonwealth and eventually full independence from the Crown if they so wished. Bowing to the inevitable, Churchill grudgingly accepted the Attlee–Mountbatten proposal.

At midnight on 14 August 1947, India and the new state of Pakistan[‡] became independent of Britain, the former as a union and the latter a dominion of

---

‡ At a function at Buckingham Palace, Churchill is alleged to have bowed to the monarch and his wife, and said, 'I believe this is the first time I have had the honour of being invited to luncheon by the King and Queen of Pakistan.' (See Dominique Enright, *The Wicked Wit of Winston Churchill*. Michael O'Mara, 2001, pp 129–130.)

the British Commonwealth. As Churchill had feared, the inter-communal violence between Hindus, Muslims and Sikhs, which had broken out earlier, intensified, spreading from the Punjab and Bengal across much of India and leaving more than 500 000 people dead. And, in one of the largest migrations in recorded history, some 12 million Indians moved in and out of the newly created nations of India and Pakistan.

In a thunderous speech to his constituency on 27 September, Churchill referred bitterly to the civil war raging in India, about which he had warned for so long:

> We are of course only at the beginning of these horrors and butcheries perpetrated upon one another, men women and children, with the ferocity of cannibals, by races gifted with capacities for the highest culture and who for generations dwelt side by side in general peace under the broad, tolerant and impartial rule of the British Crown and Parliament.

The chaos in India was 'one of the most melancholy tragedies that Asia had ever known,' he declaimed.[39]

From India, a chastened but defiant Gandhi responded to his old adversary by paying tribute to his war leadership but asking whether Churchill had ever considered the possibility that the blame lay 'with the builders of Empire, rather than those who had been subjected to it'.[40] The Mahatma made a plea to Churchill to put honour before party and 'work to make partition succeed, instead of rejoicing at its failure'.[41]

CHAPTER 26

Soldiering on

We do not want new orders. What the world wants is an old order
of 2 000 years ago – the order of the Man of Galilee.
— SMUTS[1]

Following his headline-making trip to the United States in mid-1946, Churchill returned to Britain to assemble a team of researchers to help with the writing of his war memoirs. There was much to divert him from the project at hand, however. In September, he spoke at the University of Zurich, where he surprised his audience with a call for a 'United States of Europe' as a means of ending centuries of animosity. The first step in the re-creation of a Europe now in the shadow of the atom bomb, he said, should be a partnership between France and Germany. There could be no revival of Europe 'without a spiritually great France and a spiritually great Germany', he declared.[2]

Nine months later, when introducing the Marshall Plan at a news conference, George C Marshall revealed that it was Churchill's proposal in Zurich that had made him realise that the countries of Europe should go about restoring their own economies, with financial help from the United States. Churchill was delighted with the American's endorsement. 'I feel greatly honoured,' he wrote, 'to have been the link in setting in train the Marshall Plan upon which all our Governments are united and all our hopes depend.'[3]

Churchill's awareness of the significance of the American link was corroborated when the Attlee government decided summarily to end Britain's role as protector of Greece and Turkey, leaving the US to fill the vacuum in the eastern Mediterranean. In March 1947 President Truman showed how much he had absorbed from Churchill's Fulton speech by introducing a bill in Congress that declared the US to be 'willing to help free people to maintain their institutions and their national integrity against aggressive movements that seek to impose upon them totalitarian regimes'.[4] The Truman Doctrine, as it became known, formed the basis of US foreign policy throughout the ensuing Cold War.

*

In South Africa, Smuts was preoccupied with planning for an official visit by King George VI and his family in early 1947 – an event that had a purpose beyond providing an opportunity for the royals to escape from the austerity of post-war Britain and relax in the sunshine after the strain of the war years. With the prospect of an election in the offing, Smuts hoped to garner support among English-speakers for his United Party. The king, on his part, wished to support Smuts in his domestic battle with DF Malan's pro-republican Nationalists and help keep South Africa within the Commonwealth.

Although the royal tour, which lasted two months and covered 10 000 miles, was hailed publicly as a huge success, its exhausting schedule did not allow the royal family much time for rest or relaxation. Travelling from one mayoral reception or welcoming tea party to another throughout the length and breadth of South Africa's countryside tested the endurance and patience of the royal party, and must have given the young Princess Elizabeth, who turned twenty-one on the visit, a foretaste of what lay in store for her as queen.

The unwell king, who confessed to finding the tour both 'exhilarating and tiring', and spent a week in bed at the end of it, wrote Smuts a farewell letter from HMS *Vanguard* on 2 May:

> Now that we are on our homeward voyage from our never to be forgotten
> visit to SA I feel I must write and tell you how sorry we were to leave Cape
> Town last week; we all wept as the *Vanguard* went out of Duncan Dock,

after our very pleasant stay with you. I am so glad that our long projected visit has been successfully accomplished and I thank you so much for all the help you gave in every way to make the visit both possible and such an interesting one. I regret that it was all too short ...[5]

Queen Elizabeth had confided to the king's mother, Queen Mary, however, that the tour was 'very strenuous as I feared it would be and doubly hard for Bertie who feels he should be at home',[6] where his subjects were having to endure food rationing and a bitterly cold winter of Arctic blizzards, snow and ice.[7]

On 20 November 1947, Smuts was an honoured guest at the wedding of Princess Elizabeth and Philip Mountbatten in Westminster Abbey. Cocking a defiant snook at the gossip-mongers, Smuts stopped over in Athens to collect Queen Frederika and take her with him to London. In the Abbey, he was seated in Attlee's pew between Churchill and Mackenzie King. Awed by the splendour of the ceremony, he likened it to a pageant from the Middle Ages, to which Churchill replied, 'It is *the* pageant of *all* ages.'[8] King recorded in his diary that Smuts had remarked in a parched voice, 'We shall not see the likes of this again. We shall soon be passing away.'[9]

*

Early in 1948 there came from India the shocking news of the assassination of Gandhi. Two Hindu fanatics had shot and killed the Mahatma as he strolled one evening with two young admirers in his garden in Delhi. The news electrified Indians everywhere. From around the world, condolences and tributes poured in to Delhi.

Albert Einstein said of Gandhi that 'in our time of utter moral decadence, he was the only statesman to stand for a higher human relationship in the political sphere'.[10] Smuts, who had often been critical of the sage, said: 'Gandhi was one of the great men of my time, and my acquaintance with him over a period of more than thirty years only deepened my high respect for him, however much we differed in our views and methods.'[11]

Writing to Leo Amery a few days after Gandhi's death, Smuts said:

Gandhi has played a very large part in the world and produced an effect on opinion which has in some respects surpassed that of any other contemporary of ours. And he has succeeded. And his success was due not only to his personality, but to strange methods, never resorted to by other leaders. Altogether he was a strange human phenomenon.[12]

There was one public figure, however, who made no comment at all about Gandhi's life and death: Winston Churchill. In his view, Gandhi was one more victim of the mass slaughter in India – for which Churchill believed Gandhi was partly responsible.[13]

*

On 23 May 1948, on the eve of his seventy-eighth birthday, Smuts made his final broadcast to the Commonwealth as South African prime minister. In a lengthy survey of world affairs, he drew attention to the Iron Curtain dividing the totalitarian world from the free peoples of the West: 'The Curtain stands for fear ... it is not a mere passive, inert fear; it is active, aggressive. It has already overwhelmed many small peoples in eastern Europe. It is the sort of fear which may mean great mischief, unless it is kept in check by wise precautions and active vigilance.'[14]

He ended with a graceful tribute to Mother Britain – the originator and leader of the most successful group of free countries [on earth]:

She has unrivalled experience of human affairs in all parts of the world, and has acquired a traditional technique for handling them. Her sense of justice and fair play and her balanced judgment must now more than ever be invaluable world assets in this time of unsettlement and unruffled tempers. A great human mission lies before her, perhaps greater than any in her glorious past.[15]

The following day, Smuts announced South Africa's de facto recognition of the State of Israel, an act of some boldness coming two days before a fiercely contested general election. He confessed afterwards that the decision had cost him many votes, but he never regretted it.

In Britain, the Labour government continued to withhold recognition of the new country, a stance that infuriated Churchill, who pointed out that nineteen nations, including the United States and the Soviet Union, had already recognised Israel 'and we who have played the directing part over so many years would surely be foolish in the last degree to be left maintaining a sort of sulky boycott'.[16] At the same time, he was critical of those whose Zionism had been converted into the narrow and aggressive nationalism that had claimed the lives of many non-Jewish victims in Israel, including his friend, Lord Moyne, the British envoy in Cairo.

The result of the South African general election of 1948 was as much of an unpleasant surprise to Smuts as unexpected defeat had been to Churchill in 1945. In a whites-only poll, DF Malan's pro-apartheid Nationalists won fewer votes but more parliamentary seats than the United Party, and became the new government. Smuts lost his seat in Standerton. The outcome shocked him 'more gravely than any event I have witnessed', his son, Jannie, recorded. 'He felt, like Churchill, that it was the unjust and ignominious sacking of an old war horse that had served well of its country.'[17]

Three days after the election, an angry and dejected Smuts went for a long walk in the bushveld with his son. Jannie urged his father to do 'as he had wisely counselled Mr Churchill' and to become

> an elder statesman and exercise your influence in the background, without getting involved in everyday active politics. Why not retire while you still have strength to do your writing which you owe to posterity? It's no use fighting all the weary old battles again … Let the young men carry on. Let them for once stand on their own feet and fend for themselves.[18]

Clementine Churchill had made a similar appeal to her husband in 1945. In both instances, the pleadings fell on deaf ears.

When a United Party senator came to persuade Smuts that his retirement might spell the end of the party, the old war horse perked up: 'I look forward with confidence to the eventual completion of the task for which fifty years

Smuts being installed as Chancellor of Cambridge University, June 1948.

INPRA

At the ceremony Churchill was the recipient of an honorary degree.

INPRA

has been too short a period,' he declared publicly: 'I hope to continue to take my part and do my duty as leader.'[19]

One of the factors contributing to Smuts's election defeat, in the eyes of his colleagues, was his eagerness to foreshorten the 1948 election campaign and postpone the annual budget debate, so that he could be in Britain by early June for his installation as chancellor of his alma mater, Cambridge University. Accepting nomination in January, after the death of the incumbent, Stanley Baldwin, Smuts expressed his gratitude for the recognition given 'to the whole Commonwealth ... I am naturally very proud and grateful for this high honour'.[20]

At his inauguration ceremony on 12 June, he made no mention of his electoral defeat, but reminisced touchingly about his arrival in Cambridge 'as a young son of the veld'[21] fifty-seven years earlier, and the comradeship he had experienced at the university. On returning to South Africa, he had been caught up in the Anglo-Boer War and found himself fighting the British people. Yet the war had not put out the light that Cambridge had kindled in him, and Boer and Briton had learnt to understand each other. This was due, he said, to men like Winston Churchill – who was also present that day to receive an honorary doctorate – and Prime Minister Henry Campbell-Bannerman, whose policy of reconciliation 'had rendered an immortal service to the British Empire, aye, to the cause of man everywhere'.[22] He told his listeners that his presence among them was a tribute to Campbell-Bannerman's wisdom, which was still needed because the world 'was so much more dangerous than the world of half a century ago'.[23]

Never one to let an opportunity to address an international audience go by, the new chancellor said he did not believe the world wanted or was in a position to fight another war, but the immediate problem was the 'Curtain', which divided the globe into two ideologically opposed halves, with one half practising aggression against the other. This new technique of aggression with its objective of 'conquest without war' was a new development in human history, he declared, to which the West had to discover an effective response.[24] The immediate task ahead, he concluded, was 'the salvaging of Europe, materially, politically and spiritually'.[25]

Although he felt tired on his arrival, Smuts regained his high spirits during his visit to Cambridge, telling his old friend Vice-Chancellor Charles Raven that he once again felt like 'a man and not a worm'.[26]

South Africa's Ambassador to the UK, Leif Egeland, recalled Smuts's buoyant mood at the lunch after the graduation ceremony. Proposing the wording of a toast to the graduands, he turned to Churchill and said playfully, 'Look at him. There he sits. They kicked him out.' Ignoring Churchill's glum look, Smuts went on: 'They kicked me out too. It's good for us old fogeys to be kicked out. But I call him Demogorgon [a scholar and pagan deity] – he marched with destiny; let us never forget it.'[27] According to Egeland, 'a gleam of appreciation came into Winston's eyes as he regained his good humour'.[28]

Smuts was delighted with his reception in Cambridge, and the attention paid by the media to his remarks about Russia's policy of 'aggression without war'. Writing to his friend, Daphne Moore, he said that the goodwill and sympathy all around him was 'not only touching but overwhelming'.[29] Churchill had rightly attracted more attention than the new chancellor. 'He is in a happy mood and full of fight – sad over the recession of Empire, but determined to call a halt to this process of defeatism,' said Smuts.[30]

Back in South Africa, anger and dismay at being ousted from government continued to roil the United Party. There was widespread criticism of JH Hofmeyr, Smuts's brilliant but liberal deputy and potential successor, for his role in the party's defeat, but the party leader did not escape unscathed either. His close colleague, Major Piet Van der Byl, the patrician Cabinet minister chosen to shepherd the royal family around South Africa, wrote later that 'with regard to Smuts, I strongly believe that no man over 75 should hold such a commanding position. A better age would perhaps be 70. Older men, who have great intellectual qualities and are fearless and powerful leaders, are apt when in command to resent criticism or obstruction and ignore advice.'[31]

This opinion was confirmed by Egeland, who recorded in his memoirs that if Smuts had been less of a committee of one, and had paid more attention to welding his Cabinet into a more effective team and preparing for his succession, 'the political story of South Africa might have been very different'.[32]

In Britain, where Churchill had gone from vowing to retire at the end of the war, to staying on for two years after the war, to offering (in 1948) to share the party leadership, his heir apparent, Anthony Eden, had come to a similar conclusion.[33]

CHAPTER 27

A disreputable transaction

There is only one duty, only one safe course, and that is to try to be right and not to fear to do or say what you believe to be right.

— CHURCHILL[1]

Although no longer prime minister of South Africa, Smuts continued to concern himself, as leader of the opposition, with international issues. In September 1948, he wrote to Churchill to say that he was having second thoughts about his recent declaration in Cambridge that no nations desired war:

> France is so broken by Communist infiltration and lack of leadership and some deeper decay that little can be expected from her, either in a great peace or a war crisis. Britain, our mainstay in the war, remains stricken by war exhaustion and financial dangers, which may come to a head should America cease to supply her dollar dope. The rest of Europe is ripe for the sickle.

Smuts asked rhetorically, 'What is to happen if Russia does make up her mind that this is her moment?'[2]

The wise course, he suggested, was 'boldly and openly to integrate Western Germany with the West, and instead of continuing to dismantle and cripple her, to put her on her feet again and make her part of our eastern defence wall, as she has been for centuries'. He urged Churchill to put their argument before General Marshall, in Paris, for 'if Stalin is going to play the game of

Hitler, something far more drastic will have to be called for … and in that case we should not for a moment hesitate to call in Germany to take her part in the struggle – and prepare for it in time'.[3]

Smuts also penned a long letter to Marshall stressing the strategic importance of Greece to the West, and urging him to couple the defence of Athens against the communists with the protection of Berlin. Marshall replied that Smuts's views on 'the firm induction of Germany into Western Europe' and the need to defend Greece coincided with his own.[4]

For Smuts, 1948 ended in a tragic fashion. On 11 October, his eldest son, Jacob 'Japie', a brilliant Cambridge graduate and mining engineer, died suddenly from cerebral malaria. It was a stunning blow for his father, who wrote in anguish to Margaret Gillett:

> The date was a mark of calamity in my history. On it fifty years ago, the Boer War was declared. On it at 12.30 this morning Japie passed away, after an illness of less than 24 hours. Japie was so much to us. Such a son, such a human, such a comrade – such a joy and pride of life. And some miserable invisible microbe has robbed us of him.[5]

His faith in the benign nature of the universe was tested once again only weeks later by the sudden death of his political right hand and intended successor, JH Hofmeyr, at the age of fifty-four. An intellectual prodigy, Hofmeyr had won a Rhodes scholarship at the age of fifteen, become principal of Witwatersrand University at the age of twenty-four and administrator of the Transvaal when only twenty-eight. With Smuts absent from South Africa for long periods during and after World War II, Hofmeyr had carried the administration of the government on his shoulders, besides being the liberal conscience of his party. Writing to Hofmeyr's mother, who blamed the administrative burden placed on her son for his untimely death, Smuts described him as one 'whose achievements in a comparatively brief life show no parallel in this land, and whose star at the end was still rising'.[6]

Towards the end of what for him had been a calamitous year, Smuts reviewed world affairs on the BBC Third Programme. In a talk entitled 'The Changing World Picture', he described the US as 'the answer of history' to the Soviet Union and expressed his approval of the historic movement towards greater political unity in Europe, advocated by the 'world's grand old man', Winston Churchill. 'That movement aims at a more ambitious union of European democracies, which in the long run will build up a ... United States of Europe which will form a powerful middle bloc ... between the two Great Powers of the USA and USSR.'[7]

*

In a New Year's message to members of his party, Churchill predicted that 1949 would be a 'year of destiny' for the Conservatives, who had become restive at their leader's frequent absences from the country as well as his pre-occupation with his war memoirs and lack of interest in domestic politics. Ever sensitive to what colleagues felt about him, Clementine Churchill wrote to her husband to say that she did not mind if he resigned from the leadership when things were good. But, she said, 'I can't bear you to be accepted mur-muringly and uneasily. ... Now and then I have felt chilled and discouraged by the deepening knowledge that you do only as much as will keep you in Power. But that much is not enough in these anxious times.'[8]

Churchill responded to her concern by shortening his forthcoming visit to America, where he expressed his gratitude to an audience in New York, on behalf of Britain and Western Europe, for all the US had done and continued to do. 'The Marshall Plan,' he said, 'was a turning point in the history of the world.'[9] Asking himself what had changed in the three years since his speech at Fulton, he said that no one but Stalin could have done more to change the international climate. 'He is the one.' He and his men in the Kremlin had deliberately united the free world against them because they feared the friendship of the West more than they did its hostility: 'They can't afford to allow free and friendly intercourse between their country, and those they control, and the rest of the world.' The Russian people, he said, 'must not see what goes on outside and the world must not see what goes on inside the Soviet Union'.[10] While Churchill was on his way home aboard the *Queen Mary*, Ernie Bevin, the British Foreign Secretary, put his signature to the agreement to set up the North Atlantic Treaty Organization.

Smuts strongly supported these measures by the US and UK to bolster and strengthen the Western Alliance, but was concerned at Churchill's acceptance of India as a republic within the Commonwealth. In April 1949 the dominion prime ministers met in London (with Malan in place of Smuts) and decided to admit India to the club as an independent republic. Smuts was disgusted. This violated every concept of the Commonwealth, he warned:

> You are either within the Commonwealth or out of it. If the Commonwealth concept is tampered with or destroyed, and it is still proposed to continue the Commonwealth system, there would have to be a new basis of agreement between the member states with a written constitution … Great care should be taken not to empty the Commonwealth of all substance.[11]

Churchill responded to Smuts in writing in May, saying that he was distressed to find himself taking a different line from him over India and the Crown:

> As Conservative leader, I found it my duty to look forward and to have a policy which would not place the Conservative Party in a position of permanent antagonism to the new Indian government. When I asked myself the question, 'Would I rather have them in even on these terms or let them go altogether, my heart gave me the answer, "I want them in."' Nehru has certainly shown magnanimity after sixteen years' imprisonment. The opposition to Communism affords a growing bond of unity.[12]

Smuts hastened to explain that had he been in Churchill's shoes, he would have done the same. He understood that the secession of India would have been a serious loss of face for Britain, primarily, but also for the Commonwealth. However, from South Africa's perspective, he had to take an anti-republican view:

> The campaign for the republic is coming and may be in full spate when I am no longer there to combat it. It will tear up South Africa … and it may succeed on the Indian model of a republic within the Commonwealth. But it will not stop there, as the fight since the First World War has been

for complete secession and Malan (who is at heart a moderate) will not be able to contain his republican forces, who are very powerful … Of course, as you say, the future overall menace may be Communism, and on that issue even the republicans will stand by the Commonwealth, as I imagine even India is likely to do.[13]

*

One of the last issues on which Churchill consulted Smuts illustrates the racial conservatism and prejudice that still lingered in parts of the British Commonwealth after World War II. Seretse Khama, young paramount chief-elect of the Bangwato people of Bechuanaland (now Botswana) wished to marry a white Englishwoman, Ruth Williams, in London in 1947. A British protectorate (upon which Rhodes had once had designs), Bechuanaland fell under the authority of the British High Commissioner in South Africa and its administrative capital, Mafeking, lay within the borders of the Union. As trustees of the Bechuana people, the British had never done much to develop the huge, arid territory, no doubt because they felt it was destined to become part of South Africa.

Khama's father, Sekgoma, the Kgosi (chief) of Bechuanaland's dominant Bangwato tribe, had died when his heir was four. The little boy's powerful uncle, Tshekedi Khama, became regent and the boy's guardian until he was old enough to assume his responsibilities as leader of the tribe. After graduating at Fort Hare University in South Africa, Seretse studied at Balliol College, Oxford, before moving to London in 1946 to become a barrister. There he met Ruth Williams, a clerk at Lloyd's underwriters, and a year later declared his intention of marrying her.

The announcement was met with fury in Britain, Bechuanaland and South Africa. Most angry of all was Tshekedi, who accused Seretse of turning his back on the tribe. Tshekedi called on the British for help, and heavy pressure was put on the young couple by the London Missionary Society, which had sent Seretse to Oxford. When the Bishop of London found himself too busy to wed the pair, they took themselves off to the Kensington Registry Office, where they married on 28 September 1948.

By now, a local matter which ought to have concerned only the Bangwato people had taken on an international dimension. Seretse and Ruth had become headline news in Britain and South Africa. But their travails had only just begun.[14] Under pressure from South Africa, whose new pro-apartheid government had banned interracial marriages and could not countenance a high-profile mixed-race couple just across the border, a well as the whites of Southern Rhodesia, Britain's Labour government refused to recognise Seretse's chieftainship.

In November 1949 Britain launched a formal inquiry into whether Seretse was 'a fit and proper person to discharge the functions of Chief'.[15] The day before the inquiry opened, the South African government announced that he and Ruth had been declared 'prohibited immigrants'.[16]

The inquiry found that Seretse had been properly elected by the tribe, but could not become chief because he was prohibited from South Africa and therefore could not discharge his duties in Mafeking on behalf of his people effectively. Moreover, friendship with South Africa and Southern Rhodesia was 'essential to the well-being of the tribe and the whole of the Bechuanaland Protectorate'.[17]

The Commonwealth Office was dismayed at the findings: if the inquiry's report were made public, it would undoubtedly cause indignation in Britain. The only solution was to persuade Seretse to give up the chieftainship of his own accord and go into a well-compensated exile. The Khamas were duly summoned to London for 'talks' with the British government.[18]

After Seretse had reacted with incredulity and anger to a suggestion that he should voluntarily abdicate and settle in the UK, the Cabinet took the decision to banish him from Bechuanaland and postpone any final decision about the chieftainship for five years. This startling news was given worldwide publicity by the Overseas Service of the BBC, forcing the Commonwealth Secretary, Patrick Gordon Walker, to make a statement in the House of Commons.

At this point, the leader of the opposition, Winston Churchill, sensing an opportunity to embarrass the government, entered the fray, leading to what *The Times* called 'a persistent and prolonged attack' on the Commonwealth Secretary.

Churchill did not question the decision to withhold the chieftainship from

Seretse, but demanded an assurance that the chief was being fairly treated 'as between man and man'. He especially wished to know whether Seretse had been enticed to Britain 'on false pretences' or warned that if he came to Britain he might not be allowed to return home.[19] He was not convinced by Gordon Walker's replies: 'It's a very disreputable transaction,'[20] Churchill growled.

Seretse's enforced exile was now being exploited by African nationalists in every British colony to illustrate the iniquity of the colour bar and the Foreign Office had become seriously concerned at the 'disastrous effect'[21] it was having on world opinion. Even the American Embassy in South Africa weighed in, reporting that the 'British action jeopardises their reputation for fair dealing with Natives' – conveniently overlooking the fact that mixed marriages were still banned in thirty-eight out of forty-eight states in the US.[22]

The South African High Commissioner in London, Leif Egeland, reported to Prime Minister Malan that the Conservatives were not about to bring down the government over the Seretse issue, but its leader, Churchill, was 'out of step' with his own party and troubled by the whole affair.[23] On 15 March 1950, Churchill sent an urgent message to Smuts in South Africa: 'Should be grateful for full information about your views Seretse by swiftest airmail. Feeling here very strong against Government muddle. – Winston'[24]

By now, Malan was suggesting that the British government had blundered so badly that the time had come for South Africa to take over the protectorate.[25] Yet Smuts thought it quite the wrong time to press South Africa's claim before the Privy Council. Responding to Churchill by telegram, he agreed that Seretse had probably been tricked into going to Britain, but could not see how the British government could change its decision without doing grave damage to the South African point of view. 'A form of passive resistance or boycott has already been started by the tribe against the government and any change now ... will be looked upon as a capitulation, which might seriously damage British authority and indeed all government in South Africa,'[26] he said.

Using arguments that showed how little his racial views had changed over the years, Smuts continued: 'Natives traditionally believe in authority and our whole Native system will collapse if weakness is shown in this regard.'[27]

To ignore (white) South African opinion over Seretse's undesirable marriage, he suggested, would harden Malan's claim to the protectorates and advance the case for a republic:

> I think it would be a mistake to exploit British feeling in favour of Seretse to an extent which may damage the relations of South Africa to the Commonwealth and the Commonwealth itself. I would therefore counsel caution in this matter, as it may raise an issue between South Africa and Britain which I am naturally most anxious to avoid.[28]

Churchill allowed himself to be persuaded by this advice, and ceased to raise the issue with Labour ministers from then on.[29]

Few of Churchill's or Smuts's biographers have given more than a passing mention to Seretse's 'disreputable' treatment at the hands of Britain and South Africa, perhaps because the episode was one from which nobody, bar Seretse, Ruth and the patient Bangwato tribe, emerged with any credit.* Observing that both political parties in Britain had behaved badly, *The Times* in London concluded that the fundamental mistake of the sorry affair had been the British government's attempt to disguise a decision taken for deeply-based imperial reasons as 'a concession to the wishes of the tribe'.[30]

---

* In 1956, after his party had not only affirmed but extended the ban on Seretse, and Churchill had finally left office, the Conservative government allowed Seretse to return home. In 1962 he founded the Bechuanaland Democratic Party, which swept aside all opposition to win the territory's first general election. A year later, he became Sir Seretse Khama, shortly before being elected as president of an independent Botswana. In 1980, at the early age of fifty-nine, he died of cancer and was survived by Lady Khama and three children, among them their son, Ian, the current president of Botswana.

CHAPTER 28

Last days

Jan Smuts commands in his majestic career the admiration of all.

— CHURCHILL[1]

B ritain's general election of 1950 was remarkable not so much for its result as for the extraordinary turnout of voters. Almost 84 per cent of those eligible to vote did so, the highest percentage since universal suffrage in the country began.[2] As Churchill often pointed out, since the end of the war the country may have been in poor shape financially and materially, but this was not reflected in voter disenchantment with the two major parties. Another surprising feature of British politics since 1945 had been that despite by-election opinion polls showing the Conservatives leading Labour, the Tories had not reduced the government's large parliamentary majority by a single seat.[3]

Early in the New Year, Churchill was at work on his war memoirs in Madeira – where he was intending to spend several weeks – when Attlee unexpectedly called a general election for 23 February. Writing to Clementine, he wondered what to say to 'our poor and puzzled people. I am much depressed about the country because for whoever wins, there will be nothing but bitterness and strife, like men fighting savagely on a small raft which is breaking up'.[4]

To the public, he was scarcely more upbeat, saying in one of his only two radio broadcasts:

It is my earnest hope that we may feel our way to some more exalted and august foundation for our safety than this grim and sombre balancing power of the bomb. We must not, however, cast away our only shield of safety unless we can find something surer and more likely to last.[5]

His election rhetoric reflected his favourite theme since the end of the war – the inability of socialist parties everywhere to mount an effective resistance to communist aggression. This was to become his consistent refrain when eventually he was returned to office and he emphasised the need for a summit with Russia 'to bridge the gulf between the two worlds, so that each can live their life, if not in friendship, at least without the hazards of the cold war'.[6]

The outcome of the 1950 election was a disappointment to Churchill, but not an unwelcome surprise this time. His Conservatives had reduced Labour's parliamentary majority to a mere six seats.[*] Writing to newspaper baron Lord Kemsley to thank him for his support during the campaign, he asserted confidently: 'One more heave before the year is out, and we may have a stable government in Britain.'[7]

From South Africa, a concerned Smuts wrote:

My dear Winston, I need not tell you how much my thoughts have been with you these last weeks and how sorry I am that you did not achieve a full measure of success. Still, your own stock stands very high and complete victory in the near future now appears a certainty. Both in Britain and abroad the continuance of the present government in power is awkward, but if there had to be a stalemate, it was better for the Labour government to carry on than for you to struggle under such a handicap … I trust your heavy labours have not imposed too heavy a strain on you. Your speeches have been magnificent and had all the old ring and appeal. The rest will follow in due course … Here the Nationalist government are continuing to lose ground all round, and I look forward to my victory following yours in Britain in due course.[8]

By this time, however, Smuts was far from well. The passage of years and the

---

[*] Churchill's Conservative Party won the 1951 election, and he became prime minister again. In April 1955, Churchill retired as prime minister and was succeeded by Sir Anthony Eden.

burden of work he imposed upon himself had exacted their toll. During the parliamentary session that began in January 1950, he suffered acute sciatic pain from a slipped disc, and displayed the first signs of serious heart trouble.[9] Writing to the Gilletts, he confessed, 'This old dog has other fleas enough and needs no sciatic fleas to keep him from brooding.'[10]

In March, depressed at the unfolding situation in Korea, he wrote to Leo Amery to say that Russia was in virtual occupation of the Far East, 'which other European Powers have evacuated. ... It is a fateful prospect, not only for the Far East, but for Europe and the whole world. I sometimes think we do not realise the significance of this moment in world history.'[11] The Korean War broke out three months later.

'People are intent on killing me quickly,'[12] he wrote to Isie from Cape Town, outlining the timetable of events two months later to mark his 80th birthday. Writing again to his wife on their 53rd wedding anniversary on 23 April, he conveyed his deep thankfulness for their long life together, which had been filled with tragedy and comedy, good and evil, but well worth living. He hoped that their life in the world to come 'would reveal a different pattern, provided I am not expected to wear a crown and twang a harp'.[13]

On the day before Smuts turned 80, more than 300 000 people lined the streets of Johannesburg in tribute as he drove to the City Hall to receive the Freedom of the City and inspect an honour guard of ex-servicemen. In an acceptance speech in which there was more than a hint of pathos, he said that he 'had served to the best of his ability, and with what strength God gave [him]'.[14]

The highlight of the banquet in his honour that night was a recorded tribute from Winston Churchill:

> Here is a man who raised the name of South Africa in peace and war to the highest respect among the freedom-loving nations of the world. Let us pray that this may not be swept or cast away in the demoralisation which so often follows the greatest human triumphs. Such a melancholy stroke will certainly not fall on South Africa if Smuts's life and strengths are prolonged and that is why we rejoice in his presence here tonight and

why I call upon you to drink to his health and wish him from the bottom
of my heart many, many happy returns of the day.[15]

In his speech of thanks, Smuts referred, as usual, to the international situation, repeating his plea that Germany should be treated as an equal by the
West, as it 'may also lead to that equilibrium of world power which will in the
long run be the real safeguard of world peace and security'.[16]

The following evening, at another birthday banquet, held in Pretoria,
Smuts made what turned out to be his last public appearance. Five days later,
he was stricken by a coronary thrombosis from which he was never to recover.
Churchill wrote to him in August to say 'with what joy Clemmie and I have
watched from afar, but every hour, your grand recovery. I look forward so
keenly to seeing you again. God protect you.'[17]

On the evening of 11 September 1950, after enjoying two long drives in the
countryside and a convivial family supper, Smuts died in his bedroom at
Doornkloof, as his daughters, Sylma and Louis, were helping him take off
his boots. On his bedside table was a well-thumbed copy of his favourite
novel, Emily Brontë's *Wuthering Heights*, in which the following lyrical passage had been marked:

> I lingered round then under that benign sky: watched the moths flutter-
> ing among the heath and harebells, listened to the soft wind breathing
> through the grass, and wondered how anyone could ever imagine unquiet
> slumbers for the sleepers in that quiet earth.[18]

Among the tributes to Smuts that flooded in from around the world was a
typically eloquent one from Her Majesty's leader of the opposition in the
House of Commons. An emotional Churchill said:

> In all the numerous fields in which he shone – warrior, statesman, phi-
> losopher, philanthropist – Jan Smuts commands in his majestic career
> the admiration of all. There is no personal tragedy in the close of so long
> and complete a life as this. But his friends who are left behind to face the

unending problems and perils of human existence feel an overpowering sense of impoverishment and irreparable loss. This sense is also a measure of the gratitude with which we, and lovers of freedom and civilisation in every land, salute his memory.[19]

A few weeks later, in the privacy of the Other Club, a society containing many of the great and good in London, of which he and Smuts had been long-standing members, Churchill reminisced about his friend of almost five decades:

> Jan Smuts used to love to come here. He planned to meet us during the visit to be paid after the celebrations of his eightieth birthday. Now he is dead. We must feel, in view of his manifold achievements and the place that he held in the world, that we have lost our greatest living member.
>
> I remember when we first met. I was wet and draggle-tailed. He was examining me on the part I had played in the affair of the armoured train – a difficult moment. At our next meeting at the Colonial Office, I was an under-secretary. The officials were alarmed at the prospect of a young and untried minister encountering this formidable and sinister man, a sort of compound of Molotov and Vyshinsky. Accordingly, a large screen was erected in the corner of the room, behind which Eddie Marsh [Churchill's private secretary] was installed – the idea being that if I said anything dangerous to the state, Eddie could deny that I had said it.
>
> We are right to mark his loss, breaking our rules and customs. Long may his name be honoured and cherished.[20]

Churchill allowed time to pass before composing a letter of condolence to Smuts's widow, Isie. A colleague recalled that he shut himself away in his bedroom to write it, and would not allow anyone near him. He wanted to do justice to the person whom he deemed to be the only equivalent statesman of his era, the last of his generation to whom he could talk as an equal.[21] Choosing his words carefully, Churchill wrote:

> Please accept my deepest sympathy in your sorrow and deprivation. I know how vain words are in such sadness and how much worse it is for

those who stay than for those who go. But there must be comfort in the proofs of admiration and gratitude which have been evoked all over the world for a warrior-statesman and philosopher who was probably more fitted to guide struggling and blundering humanity through its suffering and perils towards a better day than anyone who lived in any country during his epoch.[22]

Six years later, unveiling a statue to Smuts in Parliament Square, Westminster, in the midst of the Suez crisis and with Nasser in mind, Churchill declared: 'Today, among the many clamours and stresses of the world, we are beset by a narrow and sterile form of the vast and sometimes magnificent force of nationalism. To Smuts, great patriot though he was, this shallow creed would have been distasteful and alien. His own qualities transcended nationality.'[23]

CHAPTER 29

In retrospect

Nothing is more unfair than to judge a statesman of a past day
by the light of the present.[1]

By all accounts, Winston Churchill did not make close friends easily. He was too self-absorbed, too calculating, too intent on being the centre of attention to attract many people to him. He had little small talk, preferred listening to himself speak and lost interest in most conversations that were not centred on his interests and activities. He once admitted that he had very few friends. 'Why should I have more?' he asked. 'With my busy, selfish life … I fail too often in the little offices which keep friendships sweet and warm.'[2]

He was never short of company, however, surrounded always by admirers, political supporters, secretaries, research assistants as well as assorted hangers-on. Yet he had few long-lasting relationships and none of them with political intimates of an equivalent rank. His personal physician, Lord Moran, who from 1940 was constantly at his side, thought his patient's frequent inability to pick the right people was because he wasn't sufficiently interested in anyone else but himself.

Jan Smuts also had many devotees and followers, but few intimate friends. His closest relationships were with intelligent women, to whom he would confide his innermost thoughts and feelings. But his most intimate comrade during his early political and military career was the genial and outgoing Louis Botha, whose warmth of personality contrasted with that of his more reserved and introverted lieutenants, whose intellect daunted even members of his own family. Like Churchill, however, Smuts could be animated and even loquacious on subjects that held a particular interest for him. He was also more inclined to unburden himself to women than men.*

So, what was it that drew these two egocentric, self-driven, hard-working, singular characters to one another over a span of half a century? Historical circumstance, in the first place, but each must have seen in the other the human qualities they most admired. Both were supremely gifted and ambitious individuals, imbued with a belief that their lives had some special purpose. As a young subaltern in India, Churchill confided to his mother: 'I have faith in my star – that is I am intended to do something in this world.'[3] Throughout his life, he had an almost primordial sense that he was destined to play a role in the making of history.

As a devout young Calvinist, Smuts would not have viewed his own destiny in such ambitious terms. His more modest aim was to help bring together the two Teutonic peoples who had found themselves, by divine purpose, at the foot of Africa. By so doing, he might advance the cause of 'civilisation' in the remote part of the world into which he had been born. But in later life, much like Woodrow Wilson, he came to equate his own conscience with the conscience of mankind.[4]

Churchill and Smuts were both military men – Churchill a soldier by instinct and upbringing, Smuts out of necessity. Yet neither glorified war, believing that if wars had to be fought they should be redeemed by some higher good. It was in South Africa that Churchill came to appreciate the virtue of magnanimity in victory and regard for the welfare of the defeated, a lesson that Smuts learnt in Britain from Churchill's leader, Henry Campbell-Bannerman.

Both men were heedless of their personal safety, however dangerous the circumstances, and were much admired for their physical bravery under fire. In his young days in uniform, Churchill acted with conspicuous courage in India, the Sudan and South Africa. Smuts performed heroically on

---

* An inveterate letter writer who preferred to put his most intimate thoughts on paper, Smuts wrote some 23 000 letters to various female friends, mostly on matters political and spiritual, none of which contained any hint of impropriety. (See Piet Beukes, *The Romantic Smuts: Women and Love in his Life*. Human & Rousseau, 1992, p 9.)

commando in the Boer War and on more than one occasion confronted armed enemies and political rebels while unarmed himself. As politicians, both experienced at first hand the toughness of life in the field, acquiring the necessary strength of mind to take hard-headed, unpopular decisions in the broader interests of the men under them – a quality found in few political leaders of today.

Smuts's official biographer, Sir Keith Hancock, observed perceptively that although Smuts hated war, 'when it came, he smelt gunpowder'. His closest bond with Churchill, Hancock thought, was the exhilaration they both felt in the face of danger. Smuts loved the exuberant greetings that Churchill sent him when the fight was hottest. As Hancock puts it, 'They were on trek together, they were on commando together, they were shipmates together on an unsinkable ship.'[5] This goes some way to explaining the warmth of Churchill's feelings for the leader of a far-off country, whose contribution to World War II was not as great as that of the more advanced dominions.

What also attracted these two utterly different individuals to each other were their old-fashioned Victorian values and abiding belief in the civilising mission of the British Empire. In Churchill's view, the empire was a precious asset not only for Britain, but for the world as a whole.[6] Imperial Britain, he thought, was uniquely qualified to advance enlightenment and progress around the world, and more especially in its widely dispersed colonies. Smuts, a latecomer to the virtues of Empire but a proponent of Holism – the theory that mankind and its institutions are ever striving towards greater wholeness – came to view the imperial connection as the means by which his country could grow and prosper as part of the greatest empire the world had seen. He also believed that the empire's values were of benefit to mankind in general. To the end of his life, the interests and virtues of the Commonwealth were always in the forefront of his mind.

As party politicians, both were to pay a price for their imperial fervour. In Britain, Churchill was cast into the political wilderness for a time because of his intransigence over India; in South Africa, Smuts was regarded with hatred by much of the anti-British white population, and with indifference by the black majority. Many modern historians, with the benefit of hindsight, regard the pair as prime symbols of an anachronistic empire. Already on its deathbed in the wake of the worldwide nationalism emerging after World War I, it eventually expired on the granting of independence to India and Pakistan after World War II.[7]

*

Each man was keenly aware of the power of the spoken word, though their respective abilities as orators were never comparable. Churchill's early belief in oratory was revealed in an unpublished essay titled 'The Scaffolding of Rhetoric', quoted in his son Randolph's biography, which contains the following passage: 'Of all the talents bestowed upon men, none is more precious than the gift of oratory. He who enjoys it wields a power more durable than that of a great king.'[8] Churchill had made a study of Britain's great orators, including his father, Lord Randolph, and it was as a speechmaker of rare distinction – whose well-prepared, set-piece addresses were famous for their orotund, rhythmical and hypnotic cadences – that he carved out his career in politics. Smuts thought that Churchill spoke an English of an earlier age. As he told a fellow admirer, 'No one, except him, uses English like that any more.'[9]

As an orator, Smuts could not hold a candle to Churchill, but was nonetheless effective because of the sheer power of his personality. His parliamentary colleague BK Long, once a leader writer for *The Times*, described how Smuts, despite often being a 'stumbling, halting' speaker, managed to project his intellectual eminence whenever he spoke:

> He prints himself upon the instinct of the audience that he is a remarkable man. No one would call Smuts an orator, but lacking the gift of oratory altogether, his speeches achieve almost all the effects of great oratory. That is because he has, at a very high pitch, the ability to project his personality. Without it, eloquence is hollow.[10]

Churchill, like Smuts, had thought out his own personal philosophy to guide him through life. In Churchill's case, as Paul Addison explains, he was agnostic:

For orthodox religion, he substituted a secular belief in historical progress, with a strong emphasis on the civilising mission of Britain and the
British Empire. This was accompanied by a mystical faith, alternating
with cynicism and depression, in the workings of Providence. He was
inclined to believe that Providence had intervened on a number of occasions to save his life, and that he was being protected in order to fulfil his
destiny – whatever that was.[11]

While Churchill understood the real comfort that Christian faith could
offer to those under fire in combat, it was not for him: 'I therefore adapted
quite early in life to a system of believing whatever I wanted to believe.'[12]
Nevertheless, he loved the liturgical language of Anglicanism and, using his
phenomenal memory, would season his speeches with quotations from his
favourite hymns and the King James Bible.[13] His respect for Smuts may well
have been tinged with the mild envy that many agnostics feel for people of a
firmer faith.

Smuts, undoubtedly, was much more philosophically inclined. Abandoning
his Calvinistic orthodoxy at Cambridge under the influence of the American
poet, essayist and humanist Walt Whitman, he set out his thoughts on man's
place in the universe in his book on Holism. His belief in the harmonisa-
tion of the unit with the whole was the foundation of his political credo: it
persuaded him that he had to repudiate Afrikaner nationalism and neutrality
in order to make South Africa part of the worldwide British Empire, and it
underpinned his efforts to found the League of Nations and subsequently
the United Nations, so as to advance the cause of international peace. Once
he had published *Holism and Evolution*, however, Smuts seldom referred to
it privately or publicly again, modestly asserting that he 'had simply tried to
hammer out some rule of thought to carry my action along'.[14]

*

Their friendship was grounded in the mutual respect each developed over
the years for the qualities and judgement of the other. 'My faith in Smuts
is unbreakable,'[15] Churchill once said to Brendan Bracken, who had made

a dismissive remark about the South African premier. Smuts's reciprocal view of Churchill, often repeated to Lord Moran, was that he was simply 'indispensable'.[16]

Their admiration of each other's capabilities had begun during World War I, when Churchill came to appreciate Smuts's intellectual qualities, unusual organisational abilities and capacity for hard work. Having supported Churchill's appointment as Minister of Munitions in 1917, Smuts, in his capacity as Chairman of the War Priorities Committee, was no less impressed with Churchill's administrative abilities and effectiveness in that role.

The war historian Andrew Roberts describes the esteem in which Smuts was held in Britain as evidence of the soft spot Churchill's countrymen have always shown for defeated but brave former foes, citing examples stretching from Cetewayo of the Zulus to Napoleon and Rommel.[17] Affectionate admiration, however, does not adequately explain the high regard in which Smuts was held by Britain's leaders over many years. During World War I, for example, Lloyd George quickly came to appreciate Smuts's remarkable abilities, persuaded him to accept appointment to his War Cabinet and assigned him a number of tricky domestic and foreign tasks. In the War Cabinet, Smuts sat alongside men of the calibre of Lloyd George, Lords Curzon, Milner and Carson, Austen Chamberlain and Bonar Law – unprecedented for someone not a member of either of the Houses of Parliament. King George V, who consulted Smuts throughout his last years, made him a privy counsellor and the first of his newly created Companions of Honour.[18] The politically well-connected British businessman FS Oliver thought Smuts superior to anyone else in the War Cabinet 'for pure intellect, the ability to go into the heart of a subject as well as the rarer quality of being able to state clearly what he has seen'.[19]

Britain's military establishment in World War II, most of whom had not met Smuts before, were no less captivated. Lord Alanbrooke quickly developed a high regard for Smuts, describing him as 'a wonderful statesman'.[20] Lord Tedder, Britain's Chief of Air Staff and Eisenhower's deputy during Operation Overlord, went even further, describing Smuts as 'incomparably the greatest man I ever met, possessing Churchill's versatility and vision without his vices'.[21] General Mark Clark, the American commander of the Allied army in Italy, thought Smuts one of the most remarkable men he met during the war: 'Smuts's personality was of the magnetic kind, but in addition he impressed me as a "can do" man – the sort of leader who always had an aggressive and optimistic outlook in tackling a job or problem'.[22]

Yet the person who held the highest opinion of all for Smuts was Churchill himself. Over a well-lubricated lunch with Eden and Tedder in 1942, he said he imagined that Smuts was like Socrates must have been.[23] Paul H Courtenay, a senior editor of *Finest Hour* and former chairman of the International Churchill Society (UK), confirms that if there was one man whom Churchill regarded not only as an equal, but in many ways superior to himself, it was Jan Smuts.[24]

Some modern historians, of whom Roy Jenkins is a prime example, take a less exalted and more sceptical view of the Churchill–Smuts relationship. In his biography of Churchill published in 2001, Jenkins describes Smuts, among dominion leaders, as being 'almost excessively house trained', pointing out that much of the wise advice he dispensed was vitiated by the fact that it was usually exactly what Churchill wanted to hear.[25] Jenkins argues that Churchill was always good at getting on with erstwhile foes, with Botha and Smuts being two obvious examples.[26]

It's most unlikely, it must be said, that Churchill's opinion of Smuts was based on sycophancy. As much of a committee of one as Smuts ('all I want,' Churchill would say to colleagues, 'is compliance with my wishes after reasonable discussion'[27]), Britain's leader in wartime would quite often disregard his friend's advice, most notably in denying air support to France after the retreat from Dunkirk and in his dealings with India. And it would have taken more than flattery for Churchill to value Smuts as 'one of the most enlightened, courageous and noble-minded men of the twentieth century'.[28] Even Jenkins might find it hard to quibble with the veteran British diplomat Brian Urquhart's more recent verdict that Smuts was 'one of history's most remarkable *éminences grises*'.[29]

Smuts's appreciation for Churchill's leadership qualities ran equally deep. As he told Churchill's physician, Sir Charles Wilson (Lord Moran), in Cairo in 1942, Smuts believed in the supremacy of men of ideas: 'Winston ... has ideas. If he goes, there is no-one to take his place. Men of action live on the surface of things, they do not create.'[30] In a speech he gave at the Guildhall on 19 October 1943, Smuts described Churchill as 'the greatest leader [the British] have ever had'.[31] To Churchill's bodyguard, Inspector Walter Thompson, he once said 'take great care of Mr Churchill, he is one of the greatest men the world has ever known'.[32]

Smuts was constantly concerned that Churchill's poor state of health might render him incapable of bearing up under the strain of World War II. After Churchill had returned from visiting Stalin in Moscow in 1942, Smuts sent Moran a personal coded message from Pretoria: 'Please continue your efforts for the Prime Minister's health. I feel convinced he cannot continue at the present pace without breaking down. Great national responsibility rests upon you for Leader's health.'[33]

In Tunis in 1943, after the Tehran conference, Moran was sufficiently worried about his patient's state of exhaustion, and his determination to visit the front line in Italy while still under the weather, that he wrote to Smuts urging him to intervene, recording in his diary:

> He [Smuts] is the only man who has any influence with the PM; indeed he is the only ally I have in pressing counsels of common sense on the PM. Smuts sees so clearly that Winston is irreplaceable that he may make an effort to persuade him to be sensible, but I doubt whether even Smuts can alter his plans.[34]

*

History has treated Churchill and Smuts quite differently. Despite the best efforts of a few revisionist historians, Churchill's reputation has grown rather than diminished since his death in 1965 at the grand age of ninety. Smuts, on the other hand, has been largely forgotten.

Churchill's boast that history would be kind to him because he intended to write it himself – as he did voluminously and brilliantly – is only part of the reason why his legend has grown. Organisations such as the International Churchill Society, which aims to perpetuate his memory, have sprung up in many parts of the English-speaking world. Biographies, both laudatory and critical, have streamed off the printing presses, and politicians on both sides of the Atlantic continue to invoke his example as the epitome of bravery and bloody-minded resolution.

In race-conscious South Africa, by contrast, Smuts's legacy has been deliberately ignored for more than half a century. To the Afrikaner Nationalists who succeeded him, he was not segregationist enough to preserve white supremacy; to the ANC, which came to power in 1994, there was little difference between him and the architects of apartheid. Neither has been inclined, for their own self-serving reasons, to preserve Smuts's heritage: his type of heroism does not fit their respective historical narratives.

In the wider world too, Smuts has received less than his due from Clio, the muse of history. In the view of an American diplomat and scholar, Gregory Garland, historiography has left Smuts behind because 'he represents the wrong Africa for today's world'.[35] Yet, by letting the racism ingrained in his people and the Western world determine our judgement of him today, Garland says, 'we undervalue the accomplishments of perhaps the most effective internationalist ever'.[36]

Contrasting how America overlooks the white-supremacist beliefs of its own icons – from Washington to Lincoln and Woodrow Wilson to the Roosevelts – because their achievements so greatly outweighed their shortcomings, Garland points out that their views [and prejudices] were no different from those of Smuts, 'whose ghost must be jealous of American tolerance for imperfection in its heroes'.[37] The same could be said of Churchill, in Britain, whose intermittent outbursts of racism have not been allowed to undermine his stellar accomplishments.

America's equivalent of Smuts as an internationalist, Garland observes, was Senator J William Fulbright, a standard bearer of American cultural diplomacy, who also believed that the best interests of his country lay in strong global institutions, underpinned by a strong European heritage. Yet Fulbright's 'secular canonisation' has grown over the years, says Garland, notwithstanding his segregationist past and opposition to civil-rights legislation until the Voting Rights Act of 1965. The moral choices of Smuts and Fulbright were the very ones that most of their contemporaries made. 'As did Washington and Lincoln, they accepted the racial hierarchy as a given that could not and should not be changed.'[38]

At the same time, Garland concludes, Smuts and Fulbright

> left to posterity remarkable legacies as architects of the modern international system – all the more remarkable considering their provincial origins. They both believed that a commonality of the world's most talented would forestall the inhumane elements of their societies. Their imaginations fell short only in their utter inability to imagine a world in which white men did not dominate.[39]

*

Their views on race have meant that neither Churchill nor Smuts is remembered with much affection in the India or South Africa of today. Segregation, once the way of life in both countries, is now regarded as uniquely evil, and Gandhi, who fought for most of his life to end the colour bar in the empire and Commonwealth, is the figure venerated in both countries as a hero. As Arthur Herman observes, what Gandhi had started in India was 'not the extraordinary dream of a living saint, or a seditious fakir, but part of a historically inevitable process'.[40] The shift of perspective he initiated brought 'an end to the imperial ideal'.[41]

Some modern historians even place the blame for apartheid on the shoulders of Churchill and Smuts. It was Churchill, they argue, as Undersecretary for the Colonies in 1906, who accepted the agreement reached at Vereeniging that the question of the 'native franchise' would be resolved after, rather than before, independence for the Boers and the establishment of the Union. This was the doing of Smuts, however, and not Churchill, who could hardly renege on the commitment of his colonial predecessor. As Churchill told Parliament, 'We must be bound by the interpretation which the other party places on it and it is undoubted that the Boers would regard it as a breach of that treaty if the franchise were in the first place extended to any persons who are not white.'[42]

Yet it must be said that by not extending and incorporating the Cape's non-racial franchise into the Act of Union, as the Cape leader John X Merriman had urged, British Liberals and the Boers, Churchill and Smuts included, passed up an opportunity to draw moderate, 'civilised' and patriotic men (and later women) of colour into the political polity of South Africa. In so doing, they helped to embed the structure of race in a society that still struggles to come to terms with its past more than a century later. For that, Smuts, one of the negotiators at Vereeniging and the architect of the Union, was primarily to blame.

One must remember, though, as the distinguished Africanist Kenneth Ingham points out, that Smuts and company's attitude was far from reactionary in those days. To people in technologically advanced Western Europe, and their kinsmen in Africa, 'it seemed inconceivable that Africans could, in the foreseeable future, deserve parity of esteem or equal rights with Europeans'.[43] Smuts's desire to bring about white unity in South Africa was so great that he was reluctant to endanger it by taking account of African needs.[44]

One should also remember that Smuts managed, through a mixture of pragmatism and compromise, to hold together and build a South African nation riven by every sort of racial, ethnic, religious and linguistic division. If that meant taking the world as he saw it, rather than as he would have wished it to be, the price was one he was prepared to pay. He laid the groundwork for economic expansion and growth in a country that was to become Africa's leading economy for almost a century. Against the wishes of many of his fellow Afrikaners, he took South Africa into two world wars on the side of Britain, and by so doing established the country as a regional power that continues to this day to make its presence felt – for good or ill – in the international arena.

*

Like Gandhi, who set his face against the partition of Hindus and Muslims, and had to witness the birth of Pakistan, neither Churchill nor Smuts saw his hopes for the future of Empire realised. All three had to come to terms with the non-fulfilment of their most cherished ideals. As the winds of change blew through Africa and Asia after World War II, and the Union Jack was hauled down from imperial flagpoles, the voices of the decolonised could be heard at the United Nations, arguing over the application of the newly created doctrine of universal human rights in their own countries.

A decade after Smuts died, the elderly Churchill had still not come to terms with the passing of Empire. Remarking on the movement towards self-government in Africa in the 1950s, he declared that it was 'crazy' to give the vote to 'naked savages'[45] and flatly refused to be hectored by colonialism's critics. As he had once told Eisenhower, colonialism had been and remained a desirable and beneficial process of 'bringing forward backward races and opening up jungles. ... I was brought up to feel proud of much we had done,' he insisted.[46]

Yet the fading Churchill had failed to realise, according to Lawrence James, that Britain's former colonial possessions had become highly desirable and sought-after acquisitions in the Cold War that had broken out between East and West. The upshot was 'the creation of independent, often impoverished states, which by various methods (chiefly bribery) could be lured into the Russian or American camps'.[47] This was a development that neither he – nor Smuts, for that matter – could easily have foreseen.

*

Today, the empire 'that spread its wings wider than Rome'[48] – and for which Churchill and Smuts had fought so hard – has been replaced by the less exalted Commonwealth, an organisation of independent states committed to the upholding of standards of good governance among its members. And Churchill's beloved Britain has changed in ways he could scarcely have dreamed of. As Geoffrey Best elegantly puts it: 'So violently have the continuities of British culture and politics been ruptured since the 1960s, so totally have the conditions of international relations been transformed since 1945, that it is impossible to imagine another Churchill as national leader or imagine circumstances that could make such a leader necessary.'[49]

The same may be said of Smuts, whose driven intensity, outdated racial views and general high-mindedness seem almost quaint today. Yet great men, we are reminded, come in all kinds and colours, and are not the same thing as saints.[50] Churchill and Smuts were far from being saintly but they were both, in their own way, among the greatest figures of their century – living refutation of the theory that men of their calibre are at the mercy of historical forces rather than the makers of history themselves.

As Isaiah Berlin wrote memorably of Churchill, he was 'a mythical hero who belongs to legend as much as to reality, the largest human being of our time ...'[51] Smuts's contribution to the affairs of the last century is in no way comparable to Churchill's, but his enduring value to the great Englishman was as a confidant and counsellor, always ready to lend a sympathetic ear, whose judgement was valued and respected, and who reinforced many of the decisions that bore upon the progress of World War II.

Winston Churchill will always be celebrated as one of history's towering figures, the saviour of his nation and upholder of Western democratic values. And Jan Smuts – as the photograph on the desk at Chartwell reminds us – was his most enduring, trusted friend.

Notes

PROLOGUE

1 Lawrence Malkin, quoted in John Ramsden, *Man of the Century: Winston Churchill and his Legend Since 1945*. Columbia University Press, 2002, p 527.
2 John Keegan, *Churchill*. Phoenix, 2002, p 171.
3 See Arthur Herman, *Gandhi and Churchill: The Epic Rivalry that Destroyed an Empire and Forged our Age*. Hutchinson, 2008, p 698.

CHAPTER I: A STUDY IN CONTRASTS

1 Winston Churchill, *My Early Life, 1874–1904*. Scribner, 1996, p 119.
2 WK Hancock, *Smuts: The Sanguine Years 1870–1919*. Cambridge University Press, 1962, p 28.
3 Ashley Jackson, *Churchill*. Quercus, 2013, p 15.
4 Carlo D'Este, *Warlord: A Life of Winston Churchill at War, 1874–1945*. Harper Perennial, 2009, p 6.
5 See Arthur Herman, *Gandhi and Churchill: The Epic Rivalry that Destroyed an Empire and Forged our Age*. Hutchinson, 2008, p 46.
6 Carlo D'Este, *Warlord: A Life of Winston Churchill at War, 1874–1945*. Harper Perennial, 2009, p 36.
7 John Keegan, *Churchill*. Phoenix, 2002, p 20.
8 See Arthur Herman, *Gandhi and Churchill: The Epic Rivalry that Destroyed an Empire and Forged our Age*. Hutchinson, 2008, p 46.

9 Ibid.

10 Eric Bolsmann, *Winston Churchill: The Making of a Hero in the South African War.* Galago, 2008, p 27.

11 William Manchester, *The Last Lion: Winston Spencer Churchill – Visions of Glory, 1874–1932.* Michael Joseph, 1983, p 166.

12 Carlo D'Este, *Warlord: A Life of Winston Churchill at War, 1874–1945.* Harper Perennial, 2009, p 32.

13 FS Crafford, *Jan Smuts: A Biography.* Howard Timmins, 1945, p 5.

14 Ashley Jackson, *Churchill.* Quercus, 2013, p 26.

15 William Manchester, *The Last Lion: Winston Spencer Churchill – Visions of Glory, 1874–1932.* Michael Joseph, 1983, p 44.

16 Geoffrey Best, *Churchill: A Study in Greatness.* Penguin, 2004, p 1.

17 Carlo D'Este, *Warlord: A Life of Winston Churchill at War, 1874–1945.* Harper Perennial, 2009, p 11.

18 Carlo D'Este, *Warlord: A Life of Winston Churchill at War, 1874–1945.* Harper Perennial, 2009, p 27.

19 Richard J Evans, *The Victorians: Empire & Race.* Lecture at Museum of London, 11 April 2011.

20 Ibid.

21 Lawrence James, *Churchill and Empire: A Portrait of an Imperialist.* Pegasus Books, 2015, p 181.

22 Ibid.

23 WK Hancock, *Smuts: The Sanguine Years 1870–1919.* Cambridge University Press, 1962, p 57.

24 Geoffrey Best, *Churchill: A Study in Greatness.* Penguin, 2004, p 143.

25 Richard Holmes, *In the Footsteps of Churchill: A Study in Character.* Basic Books, 2006, p 22.

26 Sarah Gertrude Millin, *General Smuts.* Faber and Faber, 1936, p 8.

27 William Manchester, *The Last Lion: Winston Spencer Churchill – Visions of Glory, 1874–1932.* Michael Joseph, 1983, p 35.

28 Roy Jenkins, *Churchill.* Macmillan, 2001, p 789.

29 John Ramsden, *Man of the Century: Winston Churchill and his Legend Since 1945.* Columbia University Press, 2002, p 304.

30 Gregory Garland, The Strange Disappearance of Jan Christian Smuts and What it can Teach Americans. *American Diplomacy,* 21 June 2010, p 12.

CHAPTER 2: THE YOUNG THRUSTER

1 See www.bbcamerica.com/anglophenia/churchill.

2 William Manchester, *The Last Lion: Winston Spencer Churchill – Visions of Glory, 1874–1932.* Michael Joseph, 1983, p 309.

3 Quoted by Carlo D'Este, *Warlord: A Life of Winston Churchill at War, 1874–1945.* Harper Perennial, 2009, p 28.

4 Ibid., p 16.

5 William Manchester, *The Last Lion: Winston Spencer Churchill – Visions of Glory, 1874–1932*. Michael Joseph, 1983, p 184.

6 John Keegan, *Churchill*. Phoenix, 2002, p 27.

7 Winston Churchill, *My Early Life, 1874–1904*. Scribner, 1996, p 52.

8 Ibid., p 82.

9 Quoted by Carlo D'Este, *Warlord: A Life of Winston Churchill at War, 1874–1945*. Harper Perennial, 2009, p 46.

10 John Keegan, *Churchill*. Phoenix, 2002, p 35.

11 Winston Churchill, *My Early Life, 1874–1904*. Scribner, 1996, p 118.

12 *The Times, Great Lives: A Century in Obituaries*, HarperCollins, 2005, p 223.

13 William Manchester, *The Last Lion: Winston Spencer Churchill – Visions of Glory, 1874–1932*. Michael Joseph, 1983, p 254.

14 Randolph Churchill, *Winston S Churchill: The Official Biography*, companion vol. I. Heinemann, 1967, p 856.

15 William Manchester, *The Last Lion: Winston Spencer Churchill – Visions of Glory, 1874–1932*. Michael Joseph, 1983, p 260.

16 Roy Jenkins, *Churchill*. Macmillan, 2001, p 31.

17 Ibid., p 35.

18 William Manchester, *The Last Lion: Winston Spencer Churchill – Visions of Glory, 1874–1932*. Michael Joseph, 1983, p 263.

19 Ashley Jackson, *Churchill*. Quercus, 2011, p 68.

20 William Manchester, *The Last Lion: Winston Spencer Churchill – Visions of Glory, 1874–1932*. Michael Joseph, 1983, p 282.

21 Quoted by Carlo D'Este, *Warlord: A Life of Winston Churchill at War, 1874–1945*. Harper Perennial, 2009, p 105.

22 William Manchester, *The Last Lion: Winston Spencer Churchill – Visions of Glory, 1874–1932*. Michael Joseph, 1983, p 283.

23 Ibid., p 288.

24 Roy Jenkins, *Churchill*. Macmillan, 2001, p 47.

25 William Manchester, *The Last Lion: Winston Spencer Churchill – Visions of Glory, 1874–1932*. Michael Joseph, 1983, p 291.

CHAPTER 3: A CHANCE ENCOUNTER

1 See www.azquotes.com.

2 Sarah Gertrude Millin, *General Smuts*. Faber and Faber, 1936, p 51.

3 WK Hancock, *Smuts: The Sanguine Years 1870–1919*. Cambridge University Press, 1962, p 52.

4 JC Smuts, *Jan Christian Smuts*. Cassell, 1952, p 31.

5 WK Hancock, *Smuts: The Sanguine Years 1870–1919*. Cambridge University Press, 1962, p 77.

6 Ibid., p 90.

7 Ibid., p 84.

8 Sarah Gertrude Millin, *General Smuts*. Faber and Faber, 1936, p 113.

9 Ibid., p 116.

10 Ibid., p 114.

11 JC Smuts, *Jan Christian Smuts*. Cassell, 1952, p 51.

12 Carlo D'Este, *Warlord: A Life of Winston Churchill at War, 1874–1945*. Harper Perennial, 2009, pp 110–111.

13 William Manchester, *The Last Lion: Winston Spencer Churchill – Visions of Glory, 1874–1932*. Michael Joseph, 1983, p 292.

14 Carlo D'Este, *Warlord: A Life of Winston Churchill at War, 1874–1945*. Harper Perennial, 2009, p 132.

15 William Manchester, *The Last Lion: Winston Spencer Churchill – Visions of Glory, 1874–1932*. Michael Joseph, 1983, p 293.

16 Winston Churchill, *My Early Life, 1874–1904*. Scribner, 1996, p 240.

17 Ibid.

18 Peter Clarke, *Mr Churchill's Profession: Statesman, Orator, Writer*. Bloomsbury, 2013, p 156.

19 Carlo D'Este, *Warlord: A Life of Winston Churchill at War, 1874–1945*. Harper Perennial, 2009, p 114.

20 Ibid., p 114.

21 Ibid., p 118.

22 Winston Churchill, *My Early Life, 1874–1904*. Scribner, 1996, pp 52, 250.

23 Martin Gilbert, *Churchill: A Life*. Owl, 1991, p 111.

24 Ibid., p 113.

25 Roy Jenkins, *Churchill*. Macmillan, 2001, p 53.

26 William Manchester, *The Last Lion: Winston Spencer Churchill – Visions of Glory, 1874–1932*. Michael Joseph, 1983, p 301.

27 Carlo D'Este, *Warlord: A Life of Winston Churchill at War, 1874–1945*. Harper Perennial, 2009, p 123.

28 Martin Gilbert, *Churchill: A Life*. Owl, 1991, p 113.

29 Carlo D'Este, *Warlord: A Life of Winston Churchill at War, 1874–1945*. Harper Perennial, 2009, p 123.

30 Winston Churchill, *My Early Life, 1874–1904*. Scribner, 1996, p 265.

31 William Manchester, *The Last Lion: Winston Spencer Churchill – Visions of Glory, 1874–1932*. Michael Joseph, 1983, p 303.

32 Ibid., p 304.

33 Martin Gilbert, *Churchill: A Life*. Owl, 1991, p 115.

34 Ibid., p 116.

35 Roy Jenkins, *Churchill*. Macmillan, 2001, p 56.

36 Ibid.

CHAPTER 4: A RELUCTANT PEACE

1 Churchill, 13 May 1901. Cited in Richard Langworth, *Churchill By Himself: The Definitive Collection of Quotations*. Rosetta Books, 2008.

2 Ashley Jackson, *Churchill*. Quercus, 2011, p 80.

3 Carlo D'Este, *Warlord: A Life of Winston Churchill at War, 1874–1945*. Harper Perennial, 2009, p 128.

4 Winston Churchill, *My Early Life, 1874–1904*. Scribner, 1996, p 309.

5 Norman Rose, *Churchill: An Unruly Life*. Tauris Parke, 2009, p 49.

6 Carlo D'Este, *Warlord: A Life of Winston Churchill at War, 1874–1945*. Harper Perennial, 2009, p 134.

7 William Manchester, *The Last Lion: Winston Spencer Churchill – Visions of Glory, 1874–1932*. Michael Joseph, 1983, p 316.

8 Ibid.

9 Ibid.

10 Ibid., p 317.

11 Roy Jenkins, *Churchill*. Macmillan 2001, p 63.

12 Carlo D'Este, *Warlord: A Life of Winston Churchill at War, 1874–1945*. Harper Perennial, 2009, p 137.

13 Ibid., p 138.

14 William Manchester, *The Last Lion: Winston Spencer Churchill – Visions of Glory, 1874–1932*. Michael Joseph, 1983, p 328.

15 Frank Welsh, *A History of South Africa*. HarperCollins, 1998, p 338.

16 Antony Lentin, *Jan Smuts: Man of Courage and Vision*. Jonathan Ball, 2010, p 13.

17 WK Hancock, *Smuts: The Sanguine Years 1870–1919*. Cambridge University Press, 1962, p 159.

18 Martin Plaut, *Promise and Despair: The First Struggle for a Non-Racial South Africa*. Jacana, 2016, p 34.

19 Ibid.

20 Ibid., p 55.

21 Ibid., p 57.

22 William Manchester, *The Last Lion: Winston Spencer Churchill – Visions of Glory, 1874–1932*. Michael Joseph, 1983, p 330.

23 Ibid., p 343.

24 Roy Jenkins, *Churchill: A Biography*. Macmillan, 2001, p 72.

25 Ibid.

26 William Manchester, *The Last Lion: Winston Spencer Churchill – Visions of Glory, 1874–1932*. Michael Joseph, 1983, p 356.

27 Ashley Jackson, *Churchill*. Quercus, 2011, p 90.

CHAPTER 5: RECONSTRUCTING SOUTH AFRICA

1 See www.azquotes.com.

2 Ashley Jackson, *Churchill*. Quercus, 2011, p 93.

3 William Manchester, *The Last Lion: Winston Spencer Churchill – Visions of Glory, 1874–1932*. Michael Joseph 1983, p 364.

4 Geoffrey Best, *Churchill: A Study in Greatness*. Penguin, 2004, p 24.

5 Roy Jenkins, *Churchill*. Macmillan, 2001, 109.

6 WK Hancock, *Smuts: The Sanguine Years 1870–1919*. Cambridge University Press, 1962, p 207.

7 Sarah Gertrude Millin, *General Smuts*. Faber and Faber, 1936, p 213.

8 WK Hancock and J van der Poel (eds), *Selections from the Smuts Papers*, Vol II, p 227, Cambridge University Press, 1966.

9 WK Hancock, *Smuts: The Sanguine Years 1870–1919*. Cambridge University Press, 1962, p 213.

10 Ibid., p 215.

11 Sarah Gertrude Millin, *General Smuts*. Faber and Faber, 1936, p 213.

12 Trewhella Cameron, *Jan Smuts: An Illustrated Biography*. Human & Rousseau, 1994, p 51.

13 Ockert Geyser, *Jan Smuts and his International Contemporaries*. Covos Day, 2001, p 96.

14 WK Hancock and J van der Poel (eds), *Selections from the Smuts Papers*, Vol 2, pp 272–3. Cambridge University Press, 1966.

15 William Manchester, *The Last Lion: Winston Spencer Churchill – Visions of Glory, 1874–1932*. Michael Joseph, 1983, p 383.

16 Ashley Jackson, *Churchill*. Quercus, 2011, p 97.

17 Roy Jenkins, *Churchill*. Macmillan, 2001, p 111.

18 Martin Gilbert, *Churchill: A Life*. Owl, 1991, pp 177–178.

19 Roy Jenkins, *Churchill*. Macmillan, 2001, p 118.

20 William Manchester, *The Last Lion: Winston Spencer Churchill – Visions of Glory, 1874–1932*. Michael Joseph, 1983, p 387.

21 Ibid.

22 Roy Jenkins, *Churchill*. Macmillan, 2001, p 119; William Manchester, *The Last Lion: Winston Spencer Churchill – Visions of Glory, 1874–1932*. Michael Joseph, 1983, p 387.

23 William Manchester, *The Last Lion: Winston Spencer Churchill – Visions of Glory, 1874–1932*. Michael Joseph, 1983, p 388.

24 Ibid.

25 Roy Jenkins, *Churchill*. Macmillan, 2001, p 120.

26 Ibid., p 121.

27 Ibid., p 120.

28 Sarah Gertrude Millin, *General Smuts*. Faber and Faber, 1936, p 215.

29 Piet Beukes, *The Holistic Smuts: A Study in Personality*. Human & Rousseau, 1989, p 144.

30 Trewhella Cameron and SB Spies, *An Illustrated History of South Africa*. Southern/Human & Rousseau, 1988, p 225.

31 Bernard Friedman, *Smuts: A Reappraisal*. Hugh Keartland, 1975, p 63.

32 Martin Plaut, *Promise and Despair: The First Struggle for a Non-Racial South Africa*. Jacana, 2016, p 6.

CHAPTER 6: A TROUBLESOME SAINT

1 See www.bbcamerica.com/anglophenia.

2 Arthur Herman, *Gandhi & Churchill: The Epic Rivalry that Destroyed an Empire and Forged Our Age*. Hutchinson, 2008, p 73.

3 WK Hancock, *Smuts: The Sanguine Years 1870–1919*. Cambridge University Press, 1962, p 326.

4 Ibid., p 324

5 Robert Payne, *The Life and Death of Mahatma Gandhi*. The Bodley Head, 1969, p 101.

6 Ibid., p 102.

7 Arthur Herman, *Gandhi & Churchill: The Epic Rivalry that Destroyed an Empire and Forged Our Age*. Hutchinson, 2008, p 91.

8 Ibid., p 111.

9 Ibid.

10 Ibid., p 114.

11 WK Hancock, *Smuts: The Sanguine Years 1870–1919*. Cambridge University Press, 1962, p 328.

12 Robert Payne, *The Life and Death of Mahatma Gandhi*. The Bodley Head, 1969, p 123.

13 Ibid.

14 WK Hancock, *Smuts: The Sanguine Years 1870–1919*. Cambridge University Press, 1962, p 329.

15 Arthur Herman, *Gandhi & Churchill: The Epic Rivalry that Destroyed an Empire and Forged Our Age*. Hutchinson, 2008, p 140.

16 Ibid., p 146.

17 Ibid., p 147.

18 Ibid.

19 Robert Payne, *The Life and Death of Mahatma Gandhi*. The Bodley Head, 1969, p 168.

20 Arthur Herman, *Gandhi & Churchill: The Epic Rivalry that Destroyed an Empire and Forged Our Age*. Hutchinson, 2008, p 150.

21 Robert Payne, *The Life and Death of Mahatma Gandhi*. The Bodley Head, 1969, p 168.

22 Arthur Herman, *Gandhi & Churchill: The Epic Rivalry that Destroyed an Empire and Forged Our Age*. Hutchinson, 2008, p 150.

23 Ibid., p 151.

24 Ibid.

25 Ibid., p 151.

26 WK Hancock, *Smuts: The Sanguine Years 1870–1919*. Cambridge University Press, 1962, p 330.

27 Ibid., p 332.

28 Ibid., p 333.
29 Arthur Herman, *Gandhi & Churchill: The Epic Rivalry that Destroyed an Empire and Forged Our Age*. Hutchinson, 2008, p 157.
30 Ibid., p 158.
31 WK Hancock, *Smuts: The Sanguine Years 1870–1919*. Cambridge University Press, 1962, p 338.
32 Robert Payne, *The Life and Death of Mahatma Gandhi*. The Bodley Head, 1969, p 191.
33 Ibid., p 195,
34 WK Hancock, *Smuts: The Sanguine Years 1870–1919*. Cambridge University Press, 1962, p 339.
35 Martin Meredith, *Diamonds, Gold and War*. Simon & Schuster, 2007, p 518.
36 Martin Plaut, *Promise and Despair: The First Struggle for a Non-Racial South Africa*. Jacana, 2016, p 128.
37 Martin Meredith, *Diamonds, Gold and War*. Simon & Schuster, 2007, p 519.
38 Martin Plaut, *Promise and Despair: The First Struggle for a Non-Racial South Africa*. Jacana, 2016, pp 101–102.
39 Arthur Herman, *Gandhi & Churchill: The Epic Rivalry that Destroyed an Empire and Forged Our Age*. Hutchinson, 2008, p 151.
40 Ibid., p 175.
41 WK Hancock, *Smuts: The Sanguine Years 1870–1919*. Cambridge University Press, 1962, p 340.
42 Arthur Herman, *Gandhi & Churchill: The Epic Rivalry that Destroyed an Empire and Forged Our Age*. Hutchinson, 2008, p 179.
43 WK Hancock, *Smuts: The Sanguine Years 1870–1919*. Cambridge University Press, 1962, p 341.
44 Arthur Herman, *Gandhi & Churchill: The Epic Rivalry that Destroyed an Empire and Forged Our Age*. Hutchinson, 2008, p 188.
45 WK Hancock, *Smuts: The Sanguine Years 1870–1919*. Cambridge University Press, 1962, p 345.
46 Ibid., p 343.
47 WK Hancock and J van der Poel (eds), *Selections from the Smuts Papers*, Vol III, p 190. Cambridge University Press, 1966.
48 Arthur Herman, *Gandhi & Churchill: The Epic Rivalry that Destroyed an Empire and Forged Our Age*. Hutchinson, 2008, p 197.
49 WK Hancock, *Smuts: The Sanguine Years 1870–1919*. Cambridge University Press, 1962, p 346.

CHAPTER 7: HONOURING AN UNDERTAKING

1 JC Smuts, *Jan Christian Smuts*. Cassell, 1952, p 180.
2 WK Hancock, *Smuts: The Sanguine Years 1870–1919*. Cambridge University Press, 1962, p 378.

3 Gerald L'Ange, *Urgent Imperial Service: South African Forces in South West Africa 1914–1915*. Ashanti, 1991, p 30.
4 FS Crafford, *Jan Smuts: A Biography*. Howard Timmins, 1945, p 115.
5 Ibid., p 121.
6 Antony Lentin, *Jan Smuts: Man of Courage and Vision*. Jonathan Ball, 2010, p 32.
7 Ibid., p 33.
8 Geoffrey Best, *Churchill: A Study in Greatness*. Penguin, 2004, p 27.
9 *Brief Lives: Twentieth Century Pen Portraits from the Dictionary of National Biography*. Oxford University Press, 2000, p 112.
10 Geoffrey Best, *Churchill: A Study in Greatness*. Penguin, 2004, p 28.
11 *Brief Lives: Twentieth Century Pen Portraits from the Dictionary of National Biography*. Oxford University Press, 2000, p 111.
12 David Lough, *No More Champagne: Churchill and His Money*. Head of Zeus, 2015, p 98.
13 Carlo D'Este, *Warlord: A Life of Winston Churchill at War*. Harper Perennial, 2009, p 185.
14 Roy Jenkins, *Churchill*. Macmillan, 2001, p 256.
15 Ashley Jackson, *Churchill*. Quercus, 2011, p 145.
16 Ibid., p 150.
17 Martin Gilbert, *Churchill: A Life*. Owl, 1991, p 320.
18 Geoffrey Best, *Churchill: A Study in Greatness*. Penguin, 2004, p 77.
19 William Manchester, *The Last Lion: Winston Spencer Churchill – Visions of Glory 1874–1932*. Michael Joseph, 1983, p 614.
20 Ashley Jackson, *Churchill*. Quercus, 2011, p 161.
21 Richard Toye, *Lloyd George & Churchill: Rivals for Greatness*. Macmillan, 2007, p 180.

CHAPTER 8: IN THE WAR CABINET

1 This aphorism was not coined by Churchill, but one that he heartily agreed with. See Geoffrey Best, *Churchill: A Study in Greatness*. Penguin, 2004, p 83.
2 JC Smuts, *Jan Christian Smuts*. Cassell, 1952, p 180.
3 Ibid.
4 Ibid., p 181.
5 Antony Lentin, *Jan Smuts: Man of Courage and Vision*. Jonathan Ball, 2010, p 42.
6 JC Smuts, *Jan Christian Smuts*. Cassell, 1952, p 186.
7 WK Hancock, *Smuts: The Sanguine Years 1870–1919*. Cambridge University Press, 1962, p 438.
8 WK Hancock and J van der Poel (eds), *Selections from the Smuts Papers*, Vol III, p 633. Cambridge University Press, 1966.
9 William Manchester, *The Last Lion: Winston Spencer Churchill – Visions of Glory 1874–1932*. Michael Joseph, 1983, p 444.
10 Ibid., p 449.
11 WK Hancock, *Smuts: The Sanguine Years 1870–1919*. Cambridge University Press, 1962, p 439.

12 Ibid., p 440.

13 Ibid., p 438.

14 Richard Toye, *Churchill's Empire: The World That Made Him and the World He Made*. Macmillan, 2010, p 135.

15 JC Smuts, *Jan Christian Smuts*. Cassell, 1952, p 204.

16 WS Churchill, *The Great War*, Volume 3. George Newnes, 1935 p 1026.

17 Carlo D'Este, *Warlord: A Life of Winston Churchill at War*. Harper Perennial, 2009, p 291.

18 *The Times, Great Lives: A Century in Obituaries*. HarperCollins, 2005, p 229.

19 Carlo D'Este, *Warlord: A Life of Winston Churchill at War*. Harper Perennial, 2009, p 291.

20 David Lough, *No More Champagne: Churchill and His Money*. Head of Zeus, 2015, p 116.

21 Carlo D'Este, *Warlord: A Life of Winston Churchill at War*. Harper Perennial, 2009, p 296.

22 Ibid.

23 Ashley Jackson, *Churchill*. Quercus, 2011, p 169.

24 William Manchester, *The Last Lion: Winston Spencer Churchill – Visions of Glory 1874–1932*. Michael Joseph, 1983, p 670.

25 Ibid., p 671.

26 Ibid., p 673.

27 Geoffrey Best, *Churchill: A Study in Greatness*. Penguin, 2004, p 94.

28 WK Hancock, *Smuts: The Sanguine Years 1870–1919*. Cambridge University Press, 1962, p 471.

29 JC Smuts, *Jan Christian Smuts*. Cassell, 1952, p 209.

30 WK Hancock, *Smuts: The Sanguine Years 1870–1919*. Cambridge University Press, 1962, p 478.

31 Kenneth Ingham, *Jan Christian Smuts: The Conscience of a South African*. Weidenfeld & Nicolson/Jonathan Ball, 1986, p 101.

32 WK Hancock, *Smuts: The Sanguine Years 1870–1919*. Cambridge University Press, 1962, p 500.

33 FS Crafford, *Jan Smuts: A Biography*. Howard Timmins, 1945, p 160.

34 Ibid.

35 William Manchester, *The Last Lion: Winston Spencer Churchill – Visions of Glory 1874–1932*. Michael Joseph, 1983, p 669.

36 Richard Holmes, *In the Footsteps of Churchill: A Study in Character*. Basic Books, 2006, p 133.

37 John Keegan, *Churchill*. Phoenix, 2002, p 90.

38 WK Hancock and J van der Poel (eds), *Selections from the Smuts Papers*, Vol V, pp 16–17. Cambridge University Press, 1973.

39 WK Hancock, *Smuts: The Sanguine Years 1870–1919*. Cambridge University Press, 1962, p 557.

CHAPTER 9: OUT OF FAVOUR

1 See www.bbcamerica.com/anglophenia.

2 WK Hancock, *Smuts: The Fields of Force, 1919–1950*. Cambridge University Press, 1968, p 38.

3 Geoffrey Best, *Churchill: A Study in Greatness*. Penguin, 2004, p 93.

4 Richard Toye, *Lloyd George and Churchill: Rivals for Greatness*. Macmillan, 2007, p 207.

5 John Keegan, *Churchill*. Phoenix, 2002, p 89.

6 Boris Johnson, *The Churchill Factor: How One Man Made History*. Hodder & Stoughton, 2014, p 211.

7 WK Hancock, *Smuts: The Fields of Force, 1919–1950*. Cambridge University Press, 1968, p 41.

8 Trewhella Cameron, *Jan Smuts: An Illustrated Biography*. Human & Rousseau, 1994, p 90.

9 Sarah Gertrude Millin, *General Smuts*. Faber & Faber, 1936, p 247.

10 Ibid.

11 Paper delivered at King-Hall Naval History Conference, 2009.

12 Ockert Geyser, *Jan Smuts and his International Contemporaries*. Covos Day, 2001, p 99.

13 WK Hancock, *Smuts: The Fields of Force, 1919–1950*. Cambridge University Press, 1968, p 152.

14 Ibid., p 154.

15 William Manchester, *The Last Lion: Winston Spencer Churchill – Visions of Glory 1874–1932*. Michael Joseph, 1983, p 745.

16 Ockert Geyser, *Jan Smuts and his International Contemporaries*. Covos Day, 2001, p 93.

17 William Manchester, *The Last Lion: Winston Spencer Churchill – Visions of Glory 1874–1932*. Michael Joseph, 1983, p 755.

18 Ashley Jackson, *Churchill*. Quercus, 2011, p 183.

19 Ibid., p 198.

20 Ibid., p 232.

21 WS Churchill, *The Great War*. George Newnes, 1935, p 1370.

22 WK Hancock and J van der Poel (eds), *Selections from the Smuts Papers*, Vol V, p 180. Cambridge University Press, 1973.

23 Ockert Geyser, *Jan Smuts and his International Contemporaries*. Covos Day, 2001, p 101.

24 Martin Gilbert, *Churchill: A Life*. Owl, 1991, p 459.

25 Ashley Jackson, *Churchill*. Quercus, 2011, p 183.

26 William Manchester, *The Last Lion: Winston Spencer Churchill – Visions of Glory 1874–1932*. Michael Joseph, 1983, p 783.

27 Martin Gilbert, *Churchill: A Life*. Owl, 1991, p 464.

28 Ibid., p 465; Ashley Jackson, *Churchill*. Quercus, 2011, p 185.

29 William Manchester, *The Last Lion: Winston Spencer Churchill – Visions of Glory 1874–1932*. Michael Joseph, 1983, p 785.

30 Ibid.

CHAPTER 10: OUTSIDE INTERESTS

1 See www.azquotes.com.
2 FS Crafford, *Jan Smuts: A Biography*. Howard Timmins, 1945, p 229.
3 WK Hancock, *Smuts: The Fields of Force, 1919–1950*. Cambridge University Press, 1968, p 137.
4 FS Crafford, *Jan Smuts: A Biography*. Howard Timmins, 1945, p 229.
5 WK Hancock, *Smuts: The Fields of Force, 1919–1950*. Cambridge University Press, 1968, p 137.
6 Ibid., p 138.
7 Ibid., p 139.
8 Ibid., p 149.
9 Ibid.
10 Geoffrey Best, *Churchill: A Study in Greatness*. Penguin, 2004, p 117.
11 Ibid., p 123.
12 *Brief Lives: Twentieth Century Pen Portraits from the Dictionary of National Biography*, ed. Colin Matthew. Oxford University Press, 1997, p 127.
13 William Manchester, *The Last Lion: Winston Spencer Churchill – Visions of Glory 1874–1932*. Michael Joseph, 1983, p 804.
14 John Keegan, *Churchill*. Phoenix, 2002, p 99.
15 Trewhella Cameron, *Jan Smuts: An Illustrated Biography*. Human & Rousseau, 1994, p 97.
16 WK Hancock, *Smuts: The Fields of Force, 1919–1950*. Cambridge University Press, 1968, p 176.
17 JC Smuts, *Jan Christian Smuts*. Cassell, 1952, p 288.
18 WK Hancock, *Smuts: The Fields of Force, 1919–1950*. Cambridge University Press, 1968, p 189.
19 Trewhella Cameron, *Jan Smuts: An Illustrated Biography*. Human & Rousseau, 1994, p 99.
20 WK Hancock, *Smuts: The Fields of Force, 1919–1950*. Cambridge University Press, 1968, pp 193–195.
21 WK Hancock and J van der Poel (eds), *Selections from the Smuts Papers*, Vol V, p 343. Cambridge University Press, 1973.
22 *Brief Lives: Twentieth Century Pen Portraits from the Dictionary of National Biography*, ed. Colin Matthew. Oxford University Press, 1997, p 121.
23 The Churchill Archive, Churchill College, Cambridge, 2/69.
24 Ibid., 1/256/77.
25 Ashley Jackson, *Churchill*. Quercus, 2011, p 206 *et seq*.
26 *The Times, Great Lives: A Century in Obituaries*. HarperCollins, 2005, p 231.
27 Lawrence James, *Churchill and Empire: Portrait of an Imperialist*. Phoenix, 2014, p 189.
28 Geoffrey Best, *Churchill: A Study in Greatness*. Penguin, 2004, p 135.
29 Ibid., p 127.
30 Lawrence James, *Churchill and Empire: Portrait of an Imperialist*. Phoenix, 2014, p 192.
31 Ibid.

32 Geoffrey Best, *Churchill: A Study in Greatness*. Penguin, 2004, p 149.

33 John Keegan, *Churchill*. Phoenix, 2002, p 104.

34 Ashley Jackson, *Churchill*. Quercus, 2011, p 219.

35 Deborah Cadbury, *Princes at War: The British Royal Family's Private Battle in the Second World War*. Bloomsbury, 2015, p 13.

36 John Keegan, *Churchill*. Phoenix, 2002, p 112.

37 Geoffrey Best, *Churchill: A Study in Greatness*. Penguin, 2004, p 157.

38 Martin Gilbert, *Churchill: A Life*. Owl, 1991, p 624.

39 WK Hancock and J van der Poel (eds), *Selections from the Smuts Papers*, Vol VI, p 191. Cambridge University Press, 1973.

CHAPTER 11: ON THE BACK FOOT

1   See www.bbcamerica.com/anglophenia.

2   TRH Davenport, *South Africa: A Modern History*. Macmillan, 1977, p 298.

3   WK Hancock, *Smuts: The Fields of Force, 1919–1950*. Cambridge University Press, 1968, p 322.

4   Ibid., p 331.

5   JC Smuts, *Jan Christian Smuts*. Cassell, 1952, p 381.

6   WK Hancock, *Smuts: The Fields of Force, 1919–1950*. Cambridge University Press, 1968, p 332.

7   JC Smuts, *Jan Christian Smuts*. Cassell, 1952, p 383.

8   Ibid.

9   Martin Gilbert, *Churchill: A Life*. Owl, 1991, p 623.

10 Ashley Jackson, *Churchill*. Quercus, 2011, p 237.

11 Richard Toye, *Lloyd George and Churchill: Rivals for Greatness*. Macmillan, 2007, p 342.

12 Martin Gilbert, *Churchill: A Life*. Owl, 1991, p 635.

13 WS Churchill, *The Second World War: Volume I The Gathering Storm*. Cassell, 1948, p 601.

14 Walter Reid, *Churchill 1940–1945: Under Friendly Fire*. Birlinn, 2012, p 13.

15 Martin Gilbert, *Churchill: A Life*. Owl, 1991, p 646.

16 Ibid.

17 WK Hancock and J van der Poel (eds), *Selections from the Smuts Papers*, Vol V, p 343. Cambridge University Press, 1973.

18 Martin Gilbert, *Churchill: A Life*. Owl, 1991, p 655.

19 Martin Gilbert, *Finest Hour: Winston S Churchill, 1939–45*. Heinemann, 1983, p 468.

20 WK Hancock, *Smuts: The Fields of Force, 1919–1950*. Cambridge University Press, 1968, p 241.

21 Ibid.

22 Ibid., p 341.

23 WS Churchill, *The Second World War: Volume II Their Finest Hour*. Cassell, 1949, p 129.

24 WK Hancock, *Smuts: The Fields of Force, 1919–1950*. Cambridge University Press, 1968, p 349.

25 Carlo D'Este, *Warlord: A Life of Winston Churchill at War*. Harper Perennial, 2009, p 482.

26 Lawrence James, *Churchill and Empire: Portrait of an Imperialist*. Phoenix, 2014, p 242.

27 WK Hancock, *Smuts: The Fields of Force, 1919–1950*. Cambridge University Press, 1968, p 350.

28 Ibid.

29 Martin Gilbert, *Churchill: A Life*. Owl, 1991, p 666.

30 Ibid., p 667.

31 Walter Reid, *Churchill 1940–1945: Under Friendly Fire*. Birlinn, 2012, p 21.

32 Ibid., p 58.

33 WS Churchill, *The Second World War: Volume II Their Finest Hour*. Cassell, 1949, p 281.

34 Martin Gilbert, *Churchill: A Life*. Owl, 1991, p 664.

35 Ashley Jackson, *Churchill*. Quercus, 2011, p 269.

36 Max Hastings, *Finest Years: Churchill as Warlord 1940–45*. Harper Press, 2009, p 80.

37 Ibid., p 97.

38 *Brief Lives: Twentieth Century Pen Portraits from the Dictionary of National Biography*, ed. Colin Matthew. Oxford University Press, 1997, p 132.

39 Martin Gilbert, *Churchill: A Life*. Owl, 1991, p 671.

CHAPTER 12: MEDDLING IN AFRICA

1   See www.quotationspage.com/quotes/Sir_Winston_Churchill.

2   Michael Carver, in John Keegan (ed.), *Churchill's Generals*. Orion, 1991, p 148.

3   Carlo D'Este, *Warlord: A Life of Winston Churchill at War*. Harper Perennial, 2009, p 483.

4   Ashley Jackson, *Churchill*. Quercus, 2011, p 280.

5   Carlo D'Este, *Warlord: A Life of Winston Churchill at War*. Harper Perennial, 2009, p 485.

6   Ian Beckett, in John Keegan (ed.), *Churchill's Generals*. Orion, 1991, p 70.

7   Ibid.

8   JC Smuts, *Jan Christian Smuts*. Cassell, 1952, p 395.

9   WK Hancock, *Smuts: The Fields of Force, 1919–1950*. Cambridge University Press, 1968, p 355.

10 Martin Gilbert, *Finest Hour: Winston S Churchill, 1939–45*. Heinemann, 1983, p 606.

11 WS Churchill, *The Second World War: Volume II Their Finest Hour*. Cassell, 1949, p 375.

12 Ibid., p 378.

13 Ibid., p 377.

14 According to Richard Langworth, authoritative compiler of Churchill's quotes, no attribution for this remark can be found.

15 WK Hancock, *Smuts: The Fields of Force, 1919–1950*. Cambridge University Press, 1968, p 357.

16 Ibid.

17 Max Hastings, *Finest Years: Churchill as Warlord 1940–45*. Harper Press, 2009, p 235.

18 WS Churchill, *The Second World War: Volume II Their Finest Hour*. Cassell, 1949, p 431.

19 Martin Gilbert, *Finest Hour: Winston S Churchill, 1939–45*. Heinemann, 1983, p 805.

20 Ibid.

21 WS Churchill, *The Second World War: Volume II Their Finest Hour*. Cassell, 1949, p 422.

22 Ibid., p 437.

23 Ibid., p 436.

24 Walter Reid, *Churchill 1940–1945: Under Friendly Fire*. Birlinn, 2012, p 61.

25 William Manchester and Paul Reid, *The Last Lion: Winston Spencer Churchill 1940–1965*. Bantam, 2012, p 183.

26 Walter Reid, *Churchill 1940–1945: Under Friendly Fire*. Birlinn, 2012, p 62.

27 WK Hancock, *Smuts: The Fields of Force, 1919–1950*. Cambridge University Press, 1968, pp 355–356.

28 Carlo D'Este, *Warlord: A Life of Winston Churchill at War*. Harper Perennial, 2009, p 492.

29 Ibid., p 491.

30 Ibid., p 493.

31 Ibid., p 492.

32 Martin Gilbert, *Finest Hour: Winston S Churchill, 1939–45*. Heinemann, 1983, p 906.

33 WS Churchill, *The Second World War: Volume II Their Finest Hour*. Cassell, 1949, p 481.

34 Max Hastings, *Finest Years: Churchill as Warlord 1940–45*. Harper Press, 2009, p 121.

35 Nigel Cawthorne, *Turning the Tide: Decisive Battles of the Second World War*. Arcturus, 2002, p 41.

36 Carlo D'Este, *Warlord: A Life of Winston Churchill at War*. Harper Perennial, 2009, p 509.

37 Ibid., p 508.

38 WS Churchill, *The Second World War: Volume II Their Finest Hour*. Cassell, 1949, p 542.

39 Carlo D'Este, *Warlord: A Life of Winston Churchill at War*. Harper Perennial, 2009, p 510.

CHAPTER 13: YEAR OF DESTINY

1 Richard M Langworth, *Churchill by Himself*, Rosetta Books, 2008, p 190.

2 WK Hancock, *Smuts: The Fields of Force, 1919–1950*. Cambridge University Press, 1968, p 357.

3 Walter Reid, *Churchill 1940–1945: Under Friendly Fire*. Birlinn, 2012, p 79.

4 Max Hastings, *Finest Years: Churchill as Warlord 1940–45*. Harper Press, 2009, p 130.

5 Ibid., p 134.

6 Carlo D'Este, *Warlord: A Life of Winston Churchill at War*. Harper Perennial, 2009, p 518.

7 Martin Gilbert, *Finest Hour: Winston S Churchill, 1939–45*. Heinemann, 1983, p 1113.

8 JC Smuts, *Jan Christian Smuts*. Cassell, 1952, p 408.

9 WS Churchill, *The Second World War: Volume III The Grand Alliance*. Cassell, 1950, p 85.
10 Ibid., p 93.
11 Ibid., p 94.
12 Ibid., p 97.
13 Max Hastings, *Finest Years: Churchill as Warlord 1940–45*. Harper Press, 2009, p 136.
14 WS Churchill, *The Second World War: Volume III The Grand Alliance*. Cassell, 1950, p 95.
15 Max Hastings, *Finest Years: Churchill as Warlord 1940–45*. Harper Press, 2009, p 151.
16 WS Churchill, *The Second World War: Volume III The Grand Alliance*. Cassell, 1950,
    p 331.
17 WK Hancock, *Smuts: The Fields of Force, 1919–1950*. Cambridge University Press, 1968,
    p 361.
18 Ibid.
19 Max Hastings, *Finest Years: Churchill as Warlord 1940–45*. Harper Press, 2009, p 171.
20 Ibid., p 176.
21 Ibid., p 185.
22 John Keegan, *Churchill*. Phoenix, 2002, p 138.
23 Jack Fishman, *My Darling Clementine*. Star 1974, p 200.
24 Ashley Jackson, *Churchill*. Quercus, 2011, p 272.
25 See https://historynewsnetwork.org/article/1712.
26 WS Churchill, *The Second World War: Volume III The Grand Alliance*. Cassell, 1950,
    p 113.
27 Max Hastings, *Finest Years: Churchill as Warlord 1940–45*. Harper Press, 2009, p 194.
28 Walter Reid, *Churchill 1940–1945: Under Friendly Fire*. Birlinn, 2012, p 164.
29 John Keegan, *Churchill*. Phoenix, 2002, p 139.
30 JC Smuts, *Jan Christian Smuts*. Cassell, 1952, p 415.
31 Ibid.
32 Ibid., p 419.
33 WS Churchill, *The Second World War: Volume III The Grand Alliance*. Cassell, 1950,
    p 679.
34 CHAR, The Churchill Archive, Churchill College, Cambridge, 20/38.
35 WK Hancock, *Smuts: The Fields of Force, 1919–1950*. Cambridge University Press, 1968,
    p 363.
36 Ibid., p 363.
37 WS Churchill, *The Second World War: Volume III The Grand Alliance*. Cassell, 1950,
    p 539.
38 Max Hastings, *Finest Years: Churchill as Warlord 1940–45*. Harper Press, 2009, p 213.
39 Ibid., p 214.
40 WS Churchill, *The Second World War: Volume III The Grand Alliance*. Cassell, 1950,
    p 562.
41 Martin Gilbert, *Churchill: A Life*. Owl, 1991, p 715.
42 Carlo D'Este, *Warlord: A Life of Winston Churchill at War*. Harper Perennial, 2009,
    p 559.

CHAPTER 14: MADAGASCAR

1 WS Churchill, *The Second World War: Volume IV The Hinge of Fate*. Cassell, 1951, p 197.
2 Martin Gilbert, *Road To Victory: Winston S Churchill, 1941–1945*. Heinemann, 1986, p 77.
3 WS Churchill, *The Second World War: Volume IV The Hinge of Fate*. Cassell, 1951, p 198.
4 Ibid., p 199.
5 Ibid,. p 200.
6 Ibid.
7 Ibid., p 202.
8 Ibid.
9 Ibid., p 203.
10 Ibid., p 205.
11 Ibid., p 204.
12 Ibid., pp 209–210.
13 Ibid.
14 Ibid., p 211.
15 Colin Smith, *England's Last War Against France: Fighting Vichy 1940–1942*. Phoenix, 2010, p 339.
16 William Manchester and Paul Reid, *The Last Lion: Winston Spencer Churchill 1940–1965*. Bantam, 2012, p 584.
17 Martin Gilbert, *Road To Victory: Winston S Churchill, 1941–1945*. Heinemann, 1986, p 100.
18 WS Churchill, *The Second World War: Volume IV The Hinge of Fate*. Cassell, 1951, p 212.
19 Ibid.

CHAPTER 15: TROUBLE IN THE EAST

1 Prime Minister Winston Churchill's Broadcast on the State of the War, 15 February 1942, http://www.ibiblio.org/pha/policy/1942/420215a.html.
2 WK Hancock, *Smuts: The Fields of Force, 1919–1950*. Cambridge University Press, 1968, p 364.
3 Ibid.
4 Walter Reid, *Churchill 1940–1945: Under Friendly Fire*. Birlinn, 2012, p 171.
5 Ibid.
6 WK Hancock, *Smuts: The Fields of Force, 1919–1950*. Cambridge University Press, 1968, p 365.
7 Ibid., p 367.
8 Ibid., p 373
9 Deborah Cadbury, *Princes at War: The British Royal Family's Private Battle in the Second World War*. Bloomsbury, 2015, p 247.
10 Carlo D'Este, *Warlord: A Life of Winston Churchill at War*. Harper Perennial, 2009, p 568.

11 Max Hastings, *Finest Years: Churchill as Warlord 1940–45*. Harper Press, 2009, p 239.

12 Carlo D'Este, *Warlord: A Life of Winston Churchill at War*. Harper Perennial, 2009, p 557.

13 Ibid., p 570.

14 Martin Gilbert, *Road To Victory: Winston S Churchill, 1941–1945*. Heinemann, 1986, p 56.

15 WK Hancock, *Smuts: The Fields of Force, 1919–1950*. Cambridge University Press, 1968, p 365.

16 Ashley Jackson, *Churchill*. Quercus, 2011, p 295.

17 Carlo D'Este, *Warlord: A Life of Winston Churchill at War*. Harper Perennial, 2009, p 570.

18 CHAR, The Churchill Archive, Churchill College, Cambridge, 20/63/69–73.

19 Ibid.

20 Deborah Cadbury, *Princes at War: The British Royal Family's Private Battle in the Second World War*. Bloomsbury, 2015, p 212.

21 Arthur Herman, *Gandhi and Churchill: The Epic Rivalry that Destroyed an Empire and Forged Our Age*. Hutchinson, 2008, p 482.

22 Ibid.

23 Geoffrey Best, *Churchill: A Study in Greatness*. Penguin, 2004, p 133.

24 Martin Gilbert, *Road To Victory: Winston S Churchill, 1941–1945*. Heinemann, 1986, p 343.

25 Ibid.

26 Ibid., p 343.

27 Ibid., p 350.

28 Ibid.

29 Ibid.

30 Ibid.

31 Arthur Herman, *Gandhi and Churchill: The Epic Rivalry that Destroyed an Empire and Forged Our Age*. Hutchinson, 2008, p 482.

32 Ibid., p 484.

33 Lawrence James, *Churchill and Empire: Portrait of an Imperialist*. Phoenix, 2014, p 295.

34 Ibid.

35 Arthur Herman, *Gandhi and Churchill: The Epic Rivalry that Destroyed an Empire and Forged Our Age*. Hutchinson, 2008, p 487.

36 Ibid., p 490.

37 Roy Jenkins, *Churchill*. Macmillan, 2001, p 688.

38 Ashley Jackson, *Churchill*. Quercus, 2011, p 298.

39 Arthur Herman, *Gandhi and Churchill: The Epic Rivalry that Destroyed an Empire and Forged Our Age*. Hutchinson, 2008, p 489.

40 WS Churchill, *The Second World War: Volume IV The Hinge of Fate*. Cassell, 1951, p 196.

41 Arthur Herman, *Gandhi and Churchill: The Epic Rivalry that Destroyed an Empire and Forged Our Age*. Hutchinson, 2008, p 491.

42 WS Churchill, *The Second World War: Volume IV The Hinge of Fate*. Cassell, 1951, p 196.

43 Ibid.
44 Ibid., p 182.

CHAPTER 16: CHANGING COMMANDERS

1 WK Hancock, *Smuts: The Fields of Force, 1919–1950*. Cambridge University Press, 1968, p 379.
2 See Wikipedia, Siege of Malta (World War II), https://en.wikipedia.org/wiki/Siege_of_Malta_(World_War_II).
3 Ibid.
4 Carlo D'Este, *Warlord: A Life of Winston Churchill at War*. Harper Perennial, 2009, p 250.
5 Ibid., p 574.
6 Walter Reid, *Churchill 1940–1945: Under Friendly Fire*. Birlinn, 2012, p 106.
7 Ibid., p 110.
8 WS Churchill, *The Second World War: Volume IV The Hinge of Fate*. Cassell, 1951, p 344.
9 WK Hancock, *Smuts: The Fields of Force, 1919–1950*. Cambridge University Press, 1968, p 375.
10 Carlo D'Este, *Warlord: A Life of Winston Churchill at War*. Harper Perennial, 2009, p 580.
11 WK Hancock, *Smuts: The Fields of Force, 1919–1950*. Cambridge University Press, 1968, p 375.
12 WS Churchill, *The Second World War: Volume IV The Hinge of Fate*. Cassell, 1951, pp 385–386.
13 Ibid., p 386.
14 Max Hastings, *Finest Years: Churchill as Warlord 1940–45*. Harper Press, 2009, pp 283–284.
15 Ibid., p 312.
16 WK Hancock, *Smuts: The Fields of Force, 1919–1950*. Cambridge University Press, 1968, p 378.
17 Richard Holmes, *In the Footsteps of Churchill: A Study in Character*. Basic Books, 2006, p 228.
18 Ibid.
19 Ashley Jackson, *Churchill*. Quercus, 2011, p 301.
20 Carlo D'Este, *Warlord: A Life of Winston Churchill at War*. Harper Perennial, 2009, p 581.
21 Ibid., p 579.
22 WK Hancock, *Smuts: The Fields of Force, 1919–1950*. Cambridge University Press, 1968, p 376.
23 Ibid., p 377.
24 Martin Gilbert, *Road To Victory: Winston S Churchill, 1941–1945*. Heinemann, 1986, p 159.

25 Ibid., p 160.
26 Field Marshal Lord Alanbrooke, *War Diaries 1939–1945*. University of California Press, 2001, p 289.
27 Ibid., p 290.
28 Ibid,. p 293.
29 Ibid., p 293.
30 Carlo D'Este, *Warlord: A Life of Winston Churchill at War*. Harper Perennial, 2009, p 586.
31 John Keegan, *Churchill*. Phoenix, 2002, p 145.
32 Martin Gilbert, *Road To Victory: Winston S Churchill, 1941–1945*. Heinemann, 1986, p 168.
33 JC Smuts, *Jan Christian Smuts*. Cassell, 1952, p 420.
34 Lord Moran, *Churchill At War 1940–45*. Robinson, 2002, p 62.
35 Field Marshal Lord Alanbrooke, *War Diaries 1939–1945*. University of California Press, 2001, p 312.

CHAPTER 17: THE TIDE TURNS

1 WK Hancock, *Smuts: The Fields of Force, 1919–1950*. Cambridge University Press, 1968, p 380.
2 WS Churchill, *The Second World War: Volume IV The Hinge of Fate*. Cassell, 1951, p 429.
3 Walter Reid, *Churchill 1940–1945: Under Friendly Fire*. Birlinn, 2012, p 200.
4 Max Hastings, *Finest Years: Churchill as Warlord 1940–45*. Harper Press, 2009, p 324.
5 Ibid.
6 Ibid.
7 Walter Reid, *Churchill 1940–1945: Under Friendly Fire*. Birlinn, 2012, p 201.
8 WS Churchill, *The Second World War: Volume IV The Hinge of Fate*. Cassell, 1951, p 433.
9 Max Hastings, *Finest Years: Churchill as Warlord 1940–45*. Harper Press, 2009, p 328.
10 Walter Reid, *Churchill 1940–1945: Under Friendly Fire*. Birlinn, 2012, p 231.
11 Carlo D'Este, *Warlord: A Life of Winston Churchill at War*. Harper Perennial, 2009, p 592.
12 WS Churchill, *The Second World War: Volume IV The Hinge of Fate*. Cassell, 1951, p 452.
13 WK Hancock, *Smuts: The Fields of Force, 1919–1950*. Cambridge University Press, 1968, p 379.
14 WS Churchill, *His Complete Speeches 1897–1963*, Vol. 6, No. 688–87. Chelsea House Publishers/RR Bowker, 1974.
15 Harold Nicolson, *Diaries and Letters*, Vol. II, 1939–1945. Collins, 1967, p 251.
16 Richard Toye, *Churchill's Empire: The World that Made Him and the World He Made*. Macmillan, 2010, p 229.
17 Deborah Cadbury, *Princes at War: The British Royal Family's Private Battle in the Second World War*. Bloomsbury, 2015, p 270.
18 Andrew Roberts, *Masters and Commanders: The Military Geniuses Who Led the West to*

Victory in World War II. Penguin, 2009, p 294.

19 Carlo D'Este, *Warlord: A Life of Winston Churchill at War*. Harper Perennial, 2009, p 602.

20 Max Hastings, *Finest Years: Churchill as Warlord 1940–45*. Harper Press, 2009, p 339.

21 Roy Jenkins, *Churchill*. Macmillan, 2001, p 704.

22 Max Hastings, *Finest Years: Churchill as Warlord 1940–45*. Harper Press, 2009, p 340.

23 Carlo D'Este, *Warlord: A Life of Winston Churchill at War*. Harper Perennial, 2009, p 610.

24 Ibid.

25 Ibid., p 614.

26 Max Hastings, *Finest Years: Churchill as Warlord 1940–45*. Harper Press, 2009, p 353.

27 John Keegan, *Churchill*. Phoenix, 2002, p 147.

28 Carlo D'Este, *Warlord: A Life of Winston Churchill at War*. Harper Perennial, 2009, p 617.

29 WK Hancock, *Smuts: The Fields of Force, 1919–1950*. Cambridge University Press, 1968, p 380.

30 Ibid., p 381.

CHAPTER 18: A DEMANDING MAN

1 Dominique Enright, *The Wicked Wit of Winston Churchill*. Michael O'Mara, 2001, p 83.

2 John Colville, *Footprints in Time: Memories*. Michael Russell, 1984, pp 127–128.

3 WS Churchill, *The Second World War: Volume I The Gathering Storm*. Cassell, 1948, p 375.

4 Carlo D'Este, *Warlord: A Life of Winston Churchill at War*. Harper Perennial, 2009, p 385.

5 Field Marshal Lord Alanbrooke, *War Diaries 1939–1945*. University of California Press, 2001, p 223.

6 Carlo D'Este, *Warlord: A Life of Winston Churchill at War*. Harper Perennial, 2009, pp 385–386.

7 Walter Reid, *Churchill 1940–1945: Under Friendly Fire*. Birlinn, 2012, p 330.

8 Boris Johnson, *The Churchill Factor: How One Man Made History*. Hodder & Stoughton, 2014, p 141.

9 William Manchester and Paul Reid, *The Last Lion: Winston Spencer Churchill 1940–1965*. Bantam, 2012, p 9.

10 Martin Gilbert, *Churchill: A Life*. Owl, 1991, p 825.

11 William Manchester and Paul Reid, *The Last Lion: Winston Spencer Churchill 1940–1965*. Bantam, 2012, p 10.

12 Geoffrey Best, *Churchill: A Study in Greatness*. Penguin, 2004, p 196.

13 Ibid.

14 Lord Moran, *Churchill At War 1940–45*. Robinson, 2002, p 8.

15 William Manchester and Paul Reid, *The Last Lion: Winston Spencer Churchill 1940–1965*. Bantam, 2012, p 16.

16 Field Marshal Lord Alanbrooke, *War Diaries 1939–1945*. University of California Press, 2001, p 194.

17 Walter Reid, *Churchill 1940–1945: Under Friendly Fire*. Birlinn, 2012, p 107.

18 Quoted in Richard Holmes, *In the Footsteps of Churchill: A Study in Character*. Basic Books, 2006, p 295.

19 JC Smuts, *Jan Christian Smuts*. Cassell, 1952, p 432.

20 Ibid.

21 Edmund Murray, *Churchill's Bodyguard*. Star, 1988, p 93.

22 John Colville, *The Fringes of Power: Downing Street Diaries*, Vol. 2. Sceptre, 1985, p 59.

23 Harold Macmillan, *War Diaries: The Mediterranean 1943–1945*. Papermac, 1985, p 247.

24 Lord Moran, *Churchill At War 1940–45*. Robinson, 2002, p 180.

25 Geoffrey Best, *Churchill: A Study in Greatness*. Penguin, 2004, p 179.

26 Max Hastings, *Finest Years: Churchill as Warlord 1940–45*. Harper Press, 2009, p 393.

27 Earl Mountbatten, quoted in Zelda Friedlander (ed.), *Jan Smuts Remembered*. Wingate, 1970, pp 13–14.

28 Ibid.

CHAPTER 19: A MEETING OF MINDS

1 WK Hancock, *Smuts: The Fields of Force, 1919–1950*. Cambridge University Press, 1968, pp 413–414.

2 Ibid., p 412.

3 Ibid., p 413.

4 Ibid.

5 Carlo D'Este, *Warlord: A Life of Winston Churchill at War*. Harper Perennial, 2009, p 622.

6 Martin Gilbert, *Road To Victory: Winston S Churchill, 1941–1945*. Heinemann, 1986, p 442.

7 Ibid., p 443.

8 Ibid.

9 Ibid.

10 Max Hastings, *Finest Years: Churchill as Warlord 1940–45*. Harper Press, 2009, p 389.

11 John Keegan, *Churchill*. Phoenix, 2002, p 149.

12 Ibid.

13 Max Hastings, *Finest Years: Churchill as Warlord 1940–45*. Harper Press, 2009, p 393.

14 Martin Gilbert, *Churchill: A Life*. Owl, 1991, p 793.

15 Max Hastings, *Finest Years: Churchill as Warlord 1940–45*. Harper Press, 2009, p 390.

16 WS Churchill, *The Second World War: Volume V Closing the Ring*. Cassell, 1952, pp 112–115.

17 Ibid.

18 Ibid.

19 Ibid., p 116.

20 Ibid.
21 WK Hancock, *Smuts: The Fields of Force, 1919–1950*. Cambridge University Press, 1968, p 415.
22 WS Churchill, *The Second World War: Volume V Closing the Ring*. Cassell, 1952, p 132.
23 Robert Rhodes James, *A Spirit Undaunted: The Political Role of George VI*. Abacus, 1998, p 252.
24 Roy Jenkins, *Churchill*. Phoenix, 2002, p 718.
25 Martin Gilbert, *Road To Victory: Winston S Churchill, 1941–1945*. Heinemann, 1986, p 531.
26 Roy Jenkins, *Churchill*. Phoenix, 2002, p 719.
27 JC Smuts, *Jan Christian Smuts*. Cassell, 1952, p 433.
28 Ibid., p 434.
29 Ibid., p 435.
30 Ibid., p 445.
31 Ibid., p 447.
32 Ibid., p 448.

CHAPTER 20: DOUBTS SET IN

1 Walter Reid, *Chuchill 1940–45: Under Friendly Fire*, Birlinn, 2012, p 282.
2 Carlo D'Este, *Warlord: A Life of Winston Churchill at War*. Harper Perennial, 2009, p 623.
3 Ashley Jackson, *Churchill*. Quercus, 2011, p 319.
4 Michael Burleigh, *Small Wars, Far Away Places: The Genesis of the Modern World 1945–65*. Macmillan, 2013, p 82.
5 Martin Gilbert, *Road To Victory: Winston S Churchill, 1941–1945*. Heinemann, 1986, p 534.
6 Ibid.
7 Ibid.
8 Ibid., p 435.
9 Carlo D'Este, *Warlord: A Life of Winston Churchill at War*. Harper Perennial, 2009, p 628.
10 Ibid., p 629.
11 Max Hastings, *Finest Years: Churchill as Warlord 1940–45*. Harper Press, 2009, p 401.
12 Carlo D'Este, *Warlord: A Life of Winston Churchill at War*. Harper Perennial, 2009, p 632.
13 Ibid., p 630.
14 Max Hastings, *Finest Years: Churchill as Warlord 1940–45*. Harper Press, 2009, p 429.
15 Ibid., 421.
16 Carlo D'Este, *Warlord: A Life of Winston Churchill at War*. Harper Perennial, 2009, p 630.
17 Ibid.

18 David Friedmann, *Unpublished Memoirs*, Vol II, Ch 7, p 2.
19 Ibid., p 3.
20 WK Hancock and J van der Poel (eds), *Selections from the Smuts Papers*, Vol VI, p 454. Cambridge University Press, 1973.
21 Ibid.
22 David Friedmann, *Unpublished Memoirs*, Vol II, Ch 7, p 1.
23 Ibid., p 3
24 Laurence Rees, *World War Two: Behind Closed Doors – Stalin, the Nazis and the West*. BBC Books, 2008, p 217.
25 Max Hastings, *Finest Years: Churchill as Warlord 1940–45*. Harper Press, 2009, p 432.
26 Walter Reid, *Churchill 1940–1945: Under Friendly Fire*. Birlinn, 2012, p 279.
27 Carlo D'Este, *Warlord: A Life of Winston Churchill at War*. Harper Perennial, 2009, p 632.
28 Max Hastings, *Finest Years: Churchill as Warlord 1940–45*. Harper Press, 2009, p 437.
29 Carlo D'Este, *Warlord: A Life of Winston Churchill at War*. Harper Perennial, 2009, p 649.
30 Ibid., p 655.
31 Ashley Jackson, *Churchill*. Quercus, 2011, p 319.
32 See www.militaryhistory.about.com/od/worldwarii.
33 WS Churchill, *The Second World War: Volume V Closing the Ring*. Cassell, 1952, pp 436–437.

CHAPTER 21: OVERLORD – AND BEYOND

1 WS Churchill, *The Second World War: Volume VI Triumph and Tragedy*. Cassell, 1954, p 5.
2 WS Churchill, *The Second World War: Volume V Closing the Ring*. Cassell, 1952, p 514.
3 Walter Reid, *Churchill 1940–1945: Under Friendly Fire*. Birlinn, 2012, p 304.
4 Ibid., p 290.
5 John Keegan, *Churchill*. Phoenix, 2002, p 151.
6 JC Smuts, *Jan Christian Smuts*. Cassell, 1952, p 450.
7 Martin Gilbert, *Road To Victory: Winston S Churchill, 1941–1945*. Heinemann, 1986, p 763.
8 Max Hastings, *Finest Years: Churchill as Warlord 1940–45*. Harper Press, 2009, p 479.
9 Martin Gilbert, *Road To Victory: Winston S Churchill, 1941–1945*. Heinemann, 1986, p 765.
10 Jackson, *Churchill*. Quercus, 2011, p 318.
11 Martin Gilbert, *Road To Victory: Winston S Churchill, 1941–1945*. Heinemann, 1986, p 765.
12 Ibid., p 767.
13 Ibid.
14 Ibid., p 765.
15 Ibid., p 767.

16 Ibid.

17 JC Smuts, *Jan Christian Smuts*. Cassell, 1952, p 451.

18 Martin Gilbert, *Road To Victory: Winston S Churchill, 1941–1945*. Heinemann, 1986, p 771.

19 Ibid., p 773.

20 JC Smuts, *Jan Christian Smuts*. Cassell, 1952, p 451.

21 Ibid., p 453.

22 WS Churchill, *The Second World War: Volume V Closing the Ring*. Cassell, 1952, p 527.

23 WS Churchill, *The Second World War: Volume VI Triumph and Tragedy*. Cassell, 1954, p 5.

24 JC Smuts, *Jan Christian Smuts*. Cassell, 1952, p 456.

25 WS Churchill, *The Second World War: Volume VI Triumph and Tragedy*. Cassell, 1954, p 552.

26 John Charnley, *Churchill: The End of Glory – A Political Biography*. Faber and Faber 2011, p 569.

27 Nicholas Rankin, *Churchill's Wizards: The British Genius for Deception 1914–1945*. Faber and Faber 2009, pp 580–581.

28 Adrian Fort, *Prof: The Life of Frederick Lindemann*. Jonathan Cape 2002, p 290.

29 Max Hastings, *Finest Years: Churchill as Warlord 1940–45*. Harper Press, 2009, p 489.

30 WS Churchill, *The Second World War: Volume VI Triumph and Tragedy*. Cassell, 1954, p 34.

31 Ibid., p 35.

32 Ibid., p 47.

33 WK Hancock, *Smuts: The Fields of Force, 1919–1950*. Cambridge University Press, 1968, p 417.

34 Martin Gilbert, *Road To Victory: Winston S Churchill, 1941–1945*. Heinemann, 1986, p 815.

35 Andrew Roberts, *Masters and Commanders: How Four Titans Won the War in the West 1941–1945*. Harper Perennial, 2010, p 457.

36 Martin Gilbert, *Road To Victory: Winston S Churchill, 1941–1945*. Heinemann, 1986, p 816.

37 Ibid., p 817.

38 Ibid., p 818.

39 Ibid., p 819.

40 Ibid.

41 Max Hastings, *Finest Years: Churchill as Warlord 1940–45*. Harper Press, 2009, p 496.

42 WS Churchill, *The Second World War: Volume VI Triumph and Tragedy*. Cassell, 1954, p 90.

43 WK Hancock, *Smuts: The Fields of Force, 1919–1950*. Cambridge University Press, 1968, p 417.

44 WS Churchill, *The Second World War: Volume VI Triumph and Tragedy*. Cassell, 1954, p 90.

45 WK Hancock, *Smuts: The Fields of Force, 1919–1950*. Cambridge University Press, 1968, p 434.

46 Ibid., p 436.

47 Ibid.

48 Ibid.

CHAPTER 22: AEGEAN INTERLUDE

1 WS Churchill, *The Second World War: Volume VI Triumph and Tragedy*. Cassell, 1954, p 204.

2 Roy Jenkins, *Churchill*. Macmillan, 2001, pp 735–736.

3 William Manchester and Paul Reid, *The Last Lion: Winston Spencer Churchill 1940–1965*. Bantam, 2012, p 776.

4 WS Churchill, *The Second World War: Volume VI Triumph and Tragedy*. Cassell, 1954, p 67.

5 Ibid.

6 WK Hancock, *Smuts: The Fields of Force, 1919–1950*. Cambridge University Press, 1968, p 403.

7 Piet Beukes, *The Romantic Smuts: Women and Love in his Life*. Human & Rousseau, 1992, p 114.

8 Ibid., p 118.

9 WK Hancock, *Smuts: The Fields of Force, 1919–1950*. Cambridge University Press, 1968, p 407.

10 WS Churchill, *The Second World War: Volume VI Triumph and Tragedy*. Cassell, 1954, p 247.

11 Andrew Roberts, *Masters and Commanders: How Four Titans Won the War in the West 1941–1945*. Harper Perennial, 2010, p 528.

12 WS Churchill, *The Second World War: Volume VI Triumph and Tragedy*. Cassell, 1954, p 181.

13 Ibid., p 182.

14 Ibid., p 184.

15 Ibid., p 185.

16 Ibid., p 198.

17 Ibid.

18 Martin Gilbert, *Churchill: A Life*. Owl, 1991, p 804.

19 Ibid., p 806.

20 WS Churchill, *The Second World War: Volume VI Triumph and Tragedy*. Cassell, 1954, p 252.

21 Martin Gilbert, *Road To Victory: Winston S Churchill, 1941–1945*. Heinemann, 1986, p 1079.

22 Ibid., p 1081.

23 Ibid., p 1086.

24 Ibid., p 1090.

25 Ibid., p 1091.

26 Andrew Roberts, *Masters and Commanders: How Four Titans Won the War in the West*

1941–1945. Harper Perennial, 2010, p 528.

27 Roy Jenkins, *Churchill*. Macmillan, 2001, p 768.

28 Martin Gilbert, *Churchill and America*. Free Press, 2005, p 321.

29 Ibid.

30 Roy Jenkins, *Churchill*. Macmillan, 2001, p 768.

31 WS Churchill, *The Second World War: Volume VI Triumph and Tragedy*. Cassell, 1954, p 263.

32 Ibid., p 268.

33 From *Brief Lives, Twentieth Century Pen Portraits from the Dictionary of National Biography*, ed. Colin Matthew. Oxford University Press, 1997, p 143.

34 Walter Reid, *Churchill 1940–1945: Under Friendly Fire*. Birlinn, 2012, p 326.

35 WS Churchill, *The Second World War: Volume VI Triumph and Tragedy*. Cassell, 1954, p 270.

36 Ibid., p 274.

37 Ibid., p 276.

38 Martin Gilbert, *Road To Victory: Winston S Churchill, 1941–1945*. Heinemann, 1986, p 1126.

39 WS Churchill, *The Second World War: Volume VI Triumph and Tragedy*. Cassell, 1954, pp 279–280.

40 Martin Gilbert, *Road To Victory: Winston S Churchill, 1941–1945*. Heinemann, 1986, p 1135.

41 WS Churchill, *The Second World War: Volume VI Triumph and Tragedy*. Cassell, 1954, p 282.

42 John Keegan, *Churchill*. Phoenix, 2002, p 155.

CHAPTER 23: VICTORY – AND DEFEAT

1 See www.azquotes.com.

2 Martin Gilbert, *Road To Victory: Winston S Churchill, 1941–1945*. Heinemann, 1986, p 1082.

3 Roy Jenkins, *Churchill*. Macmillan, 2001, p 773.

4 Ibid.

5 Martin Gilbert, *Churchill: A Life*. Owl, 1991, p 814.

6 Max Hastings, *Finest Years: Churchill as Warlord 1940–45*. Harper Press, 2009, p 547.

7 Ashley Jackson, *Churchill*. Quercus, 2011, p 327.

8 Ibid.

9 William Manchester and Paul Reid, *The Last Lion: Winston Spencer Churchill 1940–1965*. Bantam, 2012, p 902.

10 Martin Gilbert, *Road To Victory: Winston S Churchill, 1941–1945*. Heinemann, 1986, p 1221.

11 Ibid., p 1270.

12 Ibid.

13 WK Hancock and J van der Poel (eds), *Selections from the Smuts Papers*, Vol VI, p 257. Cambridge University Press, 1973.

14 JC Smuts, *Jan Christian Smuts*. Cassell, 1952, p 469.

15 Ibid., p 470.

16 Martin Gilbert, *Road To Victory: Winston S Churchill, 1941–1945*. Heinemann, 1986, p 1291.

17 Ibid., p 1292.

18 Ibid., p 1293.

19 Walter Reid, *Churchill 1940–1945: Under Friendly Fire*. Birlinn, 2012, p 143.

20 Martin Gilbert, *Road To Victory: Winston S Churchill, 1941–1945*. Heinemann, 1986, p 1304.

21 Ibid., p 1305.

22 Ibid.

23 WK Hancock, *Smuts: The Fields of Force, 1919–1950*. Cambridge University Press, 1968, p 428.

24 Ibid.

25 Ibid., p 432.

26 Ibid.

27 Ibid., p 433.

28 JC Smuts, *Jan Christian Smuts*. Cassell, 1952, p 471.

29 Ibid., p 470.

30 Ibid., p 471.

31 Ibid., p 472.

32 Ashley Jackson, *Churchill*. Quercus, 2011, p 331.

33 Ibid.

34 JC Smuts, *Jan Christian Smuts*. Cassell, 1952, pp 479–480.

35 WS Churchill, *The Second World War: Volume VI Triumph and Tragedy*. Cassell, 1954, p 495.

36 Ibid.

37 John Keegan, *Churchill*. Phoenix, 2002, p 159.

38 JC Smuts, *Jan Christian Smuts*. Cassell, 1952, p 484.

39 Roy Jenkins, *Churchill*. Macmillan, 2001, p 791.

40 Ibid., p 792.

41 See www.insults.net.

42 Martin Gilbert, *Churchill: A Life*. Owl, 1991, p 848.

43 Ibid., p 852.

44 William Manchester and Paul Reid, *The Last Lion: Winston Spencer Churchill 1940–1965*. Bantam, 2012, p 950.

45 Ibid., p 951.

46 Martin Gilbert, *Churchill: A Life*. Owl, 1991, p 855.

47 Ashley Jackson, *Churchill*. Quercus, 2011, p 334.

48 Martin Gilbert, *Churchill: A Life*. Owl, 1991, p 856.

CHAPTER 24: DEALING WITH GANDHI

1 WS Churchill, *The Second World War: Volume IV The Hinge of Fate*. Cassell, 1951, p 661.

2 Arthur Herman, *Gandhi and Churchill: The Epic Rivalry that Destroyed an Empire and Forged Our Age*. Hutchinson, 2008, p 506.

3 Lord Moran, *Churchill At War 1940–45*. Robinson, 2002, p 61.

4 Lawrence James, *Churchill and Empire: Portrait of an Imperialist*. Phoenix, 2014, pp 290–291.

5 Arthur Herman, *Gandhi and Churchill: The Epic Rivalry that Destroyed an Empire and Forged Our Age*. Hutchinson, 2008, p 507.

6 Lawrence James, *Churchill and Empire: Portrait of an Imperialist*. Phoenix, 2014, p 292.

7 Ibid., p 305.

8 Arthur Herman, *Gandhi and Churchill: The Epic Rivalry that Destroyed an Empire and Forged Our Age*. Hutchinson, 2008, pp 514–515.

9 Ibid., p 515.

10 Ibid., p 516.

11 Ibid.

12 Walter Reid, *Churchill 1940–1945: Under Friendly Fire*. Birlinn, 2012, p 215.

13 Arthur Herman, *Gandhi and Churchill: The Epic Rivalry that Destroyed an Empire and Forged Our Age*. Hutchinson, 2008, p 524.

14 Ibid., p 525.

15 Ibid., p 527.

16 Ibid., p 531.

17 WS Churchill, *The Second World War: Volume VI Triumph and Tragedy*. Cassell, 1954, p 666.

18 Arthur Herman, *Gandhi and Churchill: The Epic Rivalry that Destroyed an Empire and Forged Our Age*. Hutchinson, 2008, p 532.

19 Ibid., p 536.

20 Ibid., p 538.

21 Ibid., p 539.

22 JC Smuts, *Jan Christian Smuts*. Cassell, 1952, p 507.

23 WK Hancock, *Smuts: The Fields of Force, 1919–1950*. Cambridge University Press, 1968, p 457.

24 Ibid.

25 Ibid., p 459.

26 WK Hancock, *Smuts: The Fields of Force, 1919–1950*. Cambridge University Press, 1968, pp 462–463.

27 Ibid., p 464.

28 Ibid., p 465.

29 Ibid., p 463.

30 WK Hancock and J van der Poel (eds), *Selections from the Smuts Papers*, Vol VII, p 50. Cambridge University Press, 1973.

31 Ibid.

32 WK Hancock and J van der Poel (eds), *Selections from the Smuts Papers*, Vol VII, p 68. Cambridge University Press, 1973.

33 Ibid., Vol VII, p 103.

34 Ibid.

35 Robert Payne, *The Life and Death of Mahatma Gandhi*. The Bodley Head, 1969, p 272.

36 Ibid.

37 Ibid.

CHAPTER 25: OUT TO GRASS

1   Churchill, 'Europe Unite' speech, 6 March 1947.

2   John Ramsden, *Man of the Century: Winston Churchill and His Legend Since 1945*. HarperCollins, 2003, p 78.

3   WK Hancock and J van der Poel (eds), *Selections from the Smuts Papers*, Vol VI, p 546. Cambridge University Press, 1973.

4   Ibid., Vol VII, p 550.

5   Ibid., Vol V, p 21.

6   Ibid.

7   Martin Gilbert, *Never Despair: Winston S Churchill, 1945–65*. Heinemann, 1988, p 115.

8   Ibid.

9   Ibid., p 118.

10 Ibid., p 119.

11 Martin Gilbert, *Churchill and America*. Free Press, 2005, p 362.

12 Richard Holmes, *In the Footsteps of Churchill: A Study in Character*. Basic Books, 2006, pp 281–282.

13 WK Hancock and J van der Poel (eds), *Selections from the Smuts Papers*, Vol VI, p 551. Cambridge University Press, 1973.

14 Martin Gilbert, *Churchill: A Life*. Owl, 1991, p 858.

15 Ibid., p 861.

16 John Keegan, *Churchill*. Phoenix, 2002, p 165.

17 Martin Gilbert, *Churchill: A Life*. Owl, 1991, p 868.

18 Ibid.

19 JC Smuts, *Jan Christian Smuts*. Cassell, 1952, p 489.

20 WK Hancock and J van der Poel (eds), *Selections from the Smuts Papers*, Vol VII, p 263. Cambridge University Press, 1973.

21 Barbara Leaming, *Churchill Defiant: Fighting On 1945–1955*. Harper, 2010, p 81.

22 JC Smuts, *Jan Christian Smuts*. Cassell, 1952, p 495.

23 Ibid., p 496.

24 Piet Beukes, *The Romantic Smuts: Women and Love in his Life*. Human & Rousseau, 1992, p 119.

25 WK Hancock, *Smuts: The Fields of Force, 1919–1950*. Cambridge University Press, 1968, p 447.

26 Martin Gilbert, *Never Despair: Winston S Churchill, 1945–65*. Heinemann, 1988, p 250.
27 Ibid., p 251.
28 Ibid., p 295.
29 Ibid., p 297.
30 Ibid.
31 William Manchester and Paul Reid, *The Last Lion: Winston Spencer Churchill 1940–1965*. Bantam, 2012, 1983, p 979.
32 JC Smuts, *Jan Christian Smuts*. Cassell, 1952, p 504.
33 Martin Gilbert, *Never Despair: Winston S Churchill, 1945–65*. Heinemann, 1988, p 301.
34 Ibid., p 248.
35 Ibid.
36 Ibid., p 276.
37 Ibid., p 294.
38 Ibid., p 299.
39 Ibid., p 354.
40 Arthur Herman, *Gandhi and Churchill: The Epic Rivalry that Destroyed an Empire and Forged Our Age*. Hutchinson, 2008, p 577.
41 Ibid.

CHAPTER 26: SOLDIERING ON

1 Antony Lentin, *Jan Smuts: Man of Vision and Courage*. Jonathan Ball, 2010, p 144.
2 Martin Gilbert, *Churchill: A Life*. Owl, 1991, p 372.
3 Martin Gilbert, *Churchill and America*. Free Press, 2005, p 381.
4 Ibid.
5 Ockert Geyser, *Jan Smuts and his International Contemporaries*. Covos Day, 2001, p 180.
6 Deborah Cadbury, *Princes at War: The British Royal Family's Private Battle in the Second World War*. Bloomsbury, 2015, p 339.
7 Robert Rhodes James, *A Spirit Undaunted: The Political Role of George VI*. Abacus, 1998, p 292.
8 Jeremy Lawrence, *Harry Lawrence*. David Philip, 1978, p 214.
9 Barbara Leaming, *Churchill Defiant: Fighting On 1945–1955*. Harper, 2010, p 98.
10 Arthur Herman, *Gandhi and Churchill: The Epic Rivalry that Destroyed an Empire and Forged Our Age*. Hutchinson, 2008, p 588.
11 JC Smuts, *Jan Christian Smuts*. Cassell, 1952, p 507.
12 WK Hancock and J van der Poel (eds), *Selections from the Smuts Papers*, Vol VII, p 180. Cambridge University Press, 1973.
13 Arthur Herman, *Gandhi and Churchill: The Epic Rivalry that Destroyed an Empire and Forged Our Age*. Hutchinson, 2008, pp 588–589.
14 WK Hancock and J van der Poel (eds), *Selections from the Smuts Papers*, Vol VII, p 203. Cambridge University Press, 1973.
15 Ibid.

16 Martin Gilbert, *Never Despair: Winston S Churchill, 1945–65*. Heinemann, 1988, p 449.
17 JC Smuts, *Jan Christian Smuts*. Cassell, 1952, p 511.
18 Ibid.
19 Ibid., p 512.
20 Ibid., p 513.
21 WK Hancock, *Smuts: The Fields of Force, 1919–1950*. Cambridge University Press, 1968,
     p 517.
22 Ibid., p 518.
23 Ibid.
24 Ibid.
25 Ibid.
26 Trewhella Cameron, *Jan Smuts: An Illustrated Biography*. Human & Rousseau, 1994,
     p 178.
27 Zelda Friedlander, *Jan Smuts Remembered*. Howard Timmins, 1970, p 31.
28 Ibid.
29 WK Hancock and J van der Poel (eds), *Selections from the Smuts Papers*, Vol VII, p 209.
     Cambridge University Press, 1973.
30 Ibid.
31 Piet van der Byl, *The Shadows Lengthen*. Howard Timmins, 1973, p 63.
32 Leif Egeland, *Bridges of Understanding*. Human & Rousseau, 1977, pp 196–197.
33 Barbara Leaming, *Churchill Defiant: Fighting On 1945–1955*. Harper, 2010, p 82.

CHAPTER 27: A DISREPUTABLE TRANSACTION

1 See www.churchillcentral.com/quotes.
2 WK Hancock and J van der Poel (eds), *Selections from the Smuts Papers*, Vol VII, p 248.
    Cambridge University Press, 1973.
3 Ibid.
4 WK Hancock and J van der Poel (eds), *Selections from the Smuts Papers*, Vol VII, p 260.
    Cambridge University Press, 1973.
5 WK Hancock, *Smuts: The Fields of Force, 1919–1950*. Cambridge University Press, 1968,
    p 509.
6 Trewhella Cameron, *Jan Smuts: An Illustrated Biography*. Human & Rousseau, 1994,
    p 180.
7 JC Smuts, *Jan Christian Smuts*. Cassell, 1952, p 519.
8 Martin Gilbert, *Never Despair: Winston S Churchill, 1945–65*. Heinemann, 1988, p 462.
9 Ibid., p 463.
10 Ibid.
11 JC Smuts, *Jan Christian Smuts*. Cassell, 1952, p 520.
12 WK Hancock and J van der Poel (eds), *Selections from the Smuts Papers*, Vol VII, p 298.
     Cambridge University Press, 1973.
13 Ibid., Vol VII, p 299.

14 Susan Williams, *Colour Bar: The Triumph of Seretse Khama and his Nation*. Penguin, 2007, p 65.

15 Ibid., p 94.

16 Michael Dutfield, *A Marriage of Inconvenience: The Persecution of Seretse and Ruth Khama*. Unwin Hyman, 1990, p 124.

17 Ibid., p 132.

18 Ibid., p 138.

19 Ibid.

20 Susan Williams, *Colour Bar: The Triumph of Seretse Khama and his Nation*. Penguin, 2007, p 134.

21 Ibid., p 145.

22 Ibid.

23 Ibid., p 148.

24 Ibid.

25 JC Smuts, *Jan Christian Smuts*. Cassell, 1952, p 519.

26 Susan Williams, *Colour Bar: The Triumph of Seretse Khama and his Nation*. Penguin, 2007, p 148.

27 WK Hancock and J van der Poel (eds), *Selections from the Smuts Papers*, Vol VII, pp 348–9. Cambridge University Press, 1973.

28 Ibid.

29 Susan Williams, *Colour Bar: The Triumph of Seretse Khama and his Nation*. Penguin, 2007, p 149.

30 Ibid., p 285.

CHAPTER 28: LAST DAYS

1 WS Churchill, Speech in House of Commons, 13 September 1950.

2 Roy Jenkins, *Churchill*. Macmillan, 2001, p 827.

3 Ibid., p 828.

4 Martin Gilbert, *Never Despair: Winston S Churchill, 1945–65*. Heinemann, 1988, p 502.

5 Ibid., p 510.

6 Roy Jenkins, *Churchill*. Macmillan, 2001, p 830.

7 Martin Gilbert, *Never Despair: Winston S Churchill, 1945–65*. Heinemann, 1988, p 514.

8 WK Hancock and J van der Poel (eds), *Selections from the Smuts Papers*, Vol VII, p 346. Cambridge University Press, 1973.

9 Trewhella Cameron, *Jan Smuts: An Illustrated Biography*. Human & Rousseau, 1994, p 185.

10 WK Hancock, *Smuts: The Fields of Force, 1919–1950*. Cambridge University Press, 1968, p 527.

11 WK Hancock and J van der Poel (eds), *Selections from the Smuts Papers*, Vol VII, p 347. Cambridge University Press, 1973.

12 Ibid., Vol VII, p 345.

13 WK Hancock, *Smuts: The Fields of Force, 1919–1950*, Cambridge University Press, 1968, p 527.

14 JC Smuts, *Jan Christian Smuts*. Cassell, 1952, p 523.

15 Ibid., pp 523–524.

16 Ibid.

17 WK Hancock and J van der Poel (eds), *Selections from the Smuts Papers*, Vol VII, p 363. Cambridge University Press, 1973.

18 John van Hoogstraaten, news report in *The Star*, 15 February 1950.

19 WS Churchill, Speech in House of Commons, 13 September 1950.

20 Martin Gilbert, *Never Despair: Winston S Churchill, 1945–65*. Heinemann, 1988, p 565.

21 Ibid.

22 Ibid.

23 Ibid., p 1221.

CHAPTER 29: IN RETROSPECT

1 JE Ritchie, *The Life and Times of Viscount Palmerston*. London Printing and Publishing Company, 1866–1867, p 185.

2 Norman Rose, *Churchill: The Unruly Giant*. Free Press, 1995, p 195.

3 Richard Holmes, *In the Footsteps of Churchill: A Study in Character*. Basic Books, 2006, p 47.

4 Kenneth Ingham, *Jan Christian Smuts: The Conscience of a South African*. Weidenfeld & Nicolson/Jonathan Ball, 1986, p 7.

5 WK Hancock, *Smuts: The Fields of Force, 1919–1950*. Cambridge University Press, 1968, p 356.

6 Lawrence James, *Churchill and Empire: Portrait of an Imperialist*. Phoenix, 2014, p 1.

7 Carlo D'Este, *Warlord: A Life of Winston Churchill at War*. Harper Perennial, 2009, p 27.

8 Richard Holmes, *In the Footsteps of Churchill: A Study in Character*. Basic Books, 2006, p 40.

9 BK Long, *In Smuts's Camp*. Oxford University Press, 1945, p 90.

10 Ibid., p 93.

11 Geoffrey Best, *Churchill: A Study in Greatness*, Penguin, 2004, p 10.

12 William Manchester and Paul Reid, *The Last Lion: Winston Spencer Churchill 1940–1965*. Bantam, 2012, p 783.

13 John Ramsden, *Man of the Century: Winston Churchill and His Legend Since 1945*. HarperCollins, 2003, p 145.

14 JC Smuts, *Jan Christian Smuts*. Cassell, 1952, p 287.

15 Lord Moran, *Churchill: The Struggle For Survival 1940–1965*, Constable, 1966, p 317.

16 Lord Moran, *Churchill At War 1940–45*. Robinson, 2002, p 61.

17 Andrew Roberts, *Masters and Commanders: How Four Titans Won the War in the West 1941–1945*. Harper Perennial, 2010, p 264.

18 Antony Lentin, *Jan Smuts: Man of Courage and Vision*. Jonathan Ball, 2010, p 37.

19 Ibid., p 39.

20 Lord Alanbrooke, *War Diaries 1939–1945*. University of California Press, 2001, p 336.

21 Arthur Tedder, *With Prejudice: The War Memoirs of the Marshal of the Royal Air Force, Lord Tedder*. Cassell, 1966, p 321.

22 JC Smuts, *Jan Christian Smuts*. Cassell, 1952, p 485.

23 Andrew Roberts, *Masters and Commanders: How Four Titans Won the War in the West 1941–1945*. Harper Perennial, 2010, p 264.

24 Paul H Courtenay, Paper presented at Sixteenth International Churchill Conference, 24 July 1999.

25 Roy Jenkins, *Churchill*. Macmillan, 2001, p 740.

26 Ibid., pp 366–367.

27 *Brief Lives,* Twentieth Century Pen Portraits from The Dictionary of National Biography, ed. Colin Matthew, Oxford University Press, 1997, p 148.

28 Antony Lentin, *Jan Smuts: Man of Courage and Vision*. Jonathan Ball, 2010, p 153.

29 Quoted in *The New York Review of Books*, Vol 54, no 5, 29 March 2007.

30 Lord Moran, *Churchill At War 1940–45*. Robinson, 2002, p 61.

31 JC Smuts, *Jan Christian Smuts*. Cassell, 1952, p 433.

32 Paul H Courtenay, Paper presented at Sixteenth International Churchill Conference, 24 July 1999.

33 Lord Moran, *Churchill At War 1940–45*. Robinson, 2002, p 84.

34 Ibid., p 180.

35 Gregory Garland, The Strange Disappearance of Jan Christian Smuts and What it can Teach Americans, *American Diplomacy*, 21 June 2010, p 3.

36 Ibid., p 13.

37 Ibid., pp 16–17.

38 Ibid., p 12.

39 Ibid.

40 Arthur Herman, *Gandhi and Churchill: The Epic Rivalry that Destroyed an Empire and Forged Our Age*. Hutchinson, 2008, p 601.

41 Ibid.

42 Richard Dowden, Apartheid: Made in Britain, *The Independent*, 18 April 1994.

43 Kenneth Ingham, *Jan Christian Smuts: The Conscience of a South African*. Weidenfeld & Nicolson/Jonathan Ball, 1986, p xi.

44 Ibid., p xii.

45 Lawrence James, *Churchill and Empire: Portrait of an Imperialist*. Phoenix, 2014, p 377.

46 Ibid., p 385.

47 Ibid.

48 Geoffrey Best, *Churchill: A Study in Greatness*, Penguin, 2004, p 335.

49 Ibid.

50 Ashley Jackson, *Churchill*, Quercus, 2011, p 380.

51 Ibid.

Select Bibliography

Alanbrooke, Field Marshal Lord, *War Diaries 1939–1945* (University of California Press, 2001)

Best, Geoffrey, *Churchill: A Study in Greatness* (Penguin, 2004)

Beukes, Piet, *The Holistic Smuts: A Study in Personality* (Human & Rousseau, 1989)

Beukes, Piet, *The Romantic Smuts: Women and Love in his Life* (Human & Rousseau, 1992)

Bolsmann, Eric, *Winston Churchill: The Making of a Hero in the South African War* (Galago, 2008)

Burleigh, Michael, *Small Wars, Far Away Places: The Genesis of the Modern World 1945–65* (Macmillan, 2013)

Cadbury, Deborah, *Princes at War: The British Royal Family's Private Battle in the Second World War* (Bloomsbury, 2015)

Cameron, Trewhella, *Jan Smuts: An Illustrated Biography* (Human & Rousseau, 1994)

Cameron, Trewhella and SB Spies, *An Illustrated History of South Africa* (Southern/Human & Rousseau, 1988)

Cawthorne, Nigel, *Turning the Tide: Decisive Battles of the Second World War* (Arcturus, 2002)

CHAR, The Churchill Archive, Churchill College, Cambridge

Charnley, John, *Churchill: The End of Glory – A Political Biography* (Faber and Faber, 2011)

Churchill, Randolph, *Winston S Churchill: The Official Biography*, Companion Volume I (Heinemann, 1967)

Churchill, Winston S, *His Complete Speeches 1897–1963*, Vol. 6 (Chelsea House Publishers/ RR Bowker, 1974)

Churchill, Winston S, *My Early Life, 1874–1904* (Scribner, 1996)

Churchill, Winston S, *The Great War* (George Newnes, 1935)

Churchill, Winston S, *The Second World War:*

Volume I, The Gathering Storm (Cassell, 1948)

Volume II, Their Finest Hour (Cassell, 1949)

Volume III, The Grand Alliance (Cassell, 1950)

Volume IV, The Hinge of Fate (Cassell, 1951)

Volume V, Closing the Ring (Cassell, 1952)

Volume VI, Triumph and Tragedy (Cassell, 1954)

Churchill, Winston S, *The World Crisis* Volumes 1–6 (Penguin, 2007)

Clarke, Peter, *A Question of Leadership: From Gladstone to Thatcher* (Penguin, 1992)

Clarke, Peter, *Mr Churchill's Profession: Statesman, Orator, Writer* (Bloomsbury, 2013)

Colville, Sir John, *Footprints in Time: Memories* (Michael Russell, 1984)

Colville, Sir John, *The Fringes of Power: Downing Street Diaries*, Vol. 1 and 2 (Sceptre, 1985)

Coughlin, Con, *Churchill's First War: Young Winston and the Fight against the Taliban* (Macmillan, 2013)

Crafford, FS, *Jan Smuts: A Biography* (Howard Timmins, 1945)

Davenport, TRH, *South Africa: A Modern History* (Macmillan, 1977)

D'Este, Carlo, *Warlord: A Life of Winston Churchill at War* (Harper Perennial, 2009)

Dutfield, Michael, *A Marriage of Inconvenience: The Persecution of Seretse and Ruth Khama* (Unwin Hyman, 1990)

Egeland, Leif, *Bridges of Understanding* (Human & Rousseau, 1977)

Enright, Dominique, *The Wicked Wit of Winston Churchill* (Michael O'Mara, 2001)

Fishman, Jack, *My Darling Clementine* (Star, 1974)

Fort, Adrian, *Prof: The Life of Frederick Lindemann* (Jonathan Cape, 2003)

Friedlander, Zelda, *Jan Smuts Remembered* (Howard Timmins, 1970)

Friedman, Bernard, *Smuts: A Reappraisal* (Hugh Keartland, 1975)

Garland, Gregory, The Strange Disappearance of Jan Christian Smuts and What it can Teach Americans, *American Diplomacy*, 21 Junie 2010

Geyser, Ockert, *Jan Smuts and his International Contemporaries* (Covos Day, 2001)

Gilbert, Martin, *Churchill: A Life* (Owl, 1991)

Gilbert, Martin, *Churchill and America* (Free Press, 2005)

Gilbert, Martin, *Finest Hour: Winston S Churchill, 1939–45* (Heinemann, 1983)

Gilbert, Martin, *Never Despair: Winston S Churchill, 1945–65* (Heinemann, 1988)

Gilbert, Martin, *Road To Victory: Winston S Churchill, 1941–1945*, (Heinemann, 1986)

Giliomee, Hermann and Bernard Mbenga, *New History of South Africa* (Tafelberg, 2007)

Gilmour, David, *Curzon: Imperial Statesman* (Farrar, Straus and Giroux, 1994)

Haffner, Sebastian, *Churchill* (Haus Publishing, 2003)

Hancock, WK, *Smuts: The Fields of Force, 1919–1950* (Cambridge University Press, 1968)

Hancock, WK, *Smuts: The Sanguine Years, 1870–1919* (Cambridge University Press, 1962)

Hancock, WK and J van der Poel (eds.), *Selections from the Smuts Papers* (Cambridge University, 1966–73)

Hastings, Max, *Finest Years: Churchill as Warlord 1940–45* (Harper Press, 2009)

Herman, Arthur, *Gandhi and Churchill: The Epic Rivalry that Destroyed an Empire and Forged Our Age* (Hutchinson, 2008)

Holmes, Richard, *In the Footsteps of Churchill: A Study in Character* (Basic Books, 2006)

Ingham, Kenneth, *Jan Christian Smuts: The Conscience of a South African* (Weidenfeld & Nicolson/Jonathan Ball, 1986)

Jackson, Ashley, *Churchill* (Quercus, 2011)

James, Lawrence, *Churchill and Empire: Portrait of an Imperialist* (Phoenix, 2014)

Jenkins, Roy, *Churchill* (Macmillan, 2001)

Johnson, Boris, *The Churchill Factor: How One Man Made History* (Hodder & Stoughton, 2014)

Keegan, John, *Churchill* (Phoenix, 2002)

Keegan, John (ed.), *Churchill's Generals* (Orion, 1991)

L'Ange, Gerald, *Urgent Imperial Service: South African Forces in South West Africa 1914–1915* (Ashanti, 1991)

Langworth, Richard M, *Churchill by Himself: The Definitive Collection of Quotations* (Rosetta Books, 2008)

Leaming, Barbara, *Churchill Defiant: Fighting On 1945–1955* (HarperCollins, 2010)

Lentin, Antony, *Jan Smuts: Man of Courage and Vision* (Jonathan Ball, 2010)

Long, BK, *In Smuts's Camp* (Oxford University Press, 1945)

Lough, David, *No More Champagne: Churchill and His Money* (Head of Zeus, 2015)

Manchester, William, *The Caged Lion: Winston Spencer Churchill 1932–1940* (Cardinal, 1989)

Manchester, William, *The Last Lion: Winston Spencer Churchill – Visions of Glory 1874–1932* (Michael Joseph, 1983)

Manchester, William and Paul Reid, *The Last Lion: Winston Spencer Churchill 1940–1965* (Bantam, 2012)

Matthew, Colin (compiler), *Brief Lives: Twentieth Century Pen Portraits from the Dictionary of National Biography* (Oxford University Press, 2000)

Meintjes, Johannes, *General Louis Botha* (Cassell, 1970)

Meredith, Martin, *Diamonds, Gold and War* (Simon & Schuster, 2007)

Millin, Sarah Gertrude, *General Smuts* (Faber and Faber, 1936)

Moran, Lord, *Churchill At War 1940–45* (Robinson, 2002)

Moran, Lord, *Churchill: The Struggle For Survival 1940–1965* (Constable, 1966)

Murray, Edmund, *Churchill's Bodyguard* (Star, 1988)

Nicolson, Harold, *Diaries and Letters*, vol. II, 1939–1945 (Collins, 1967)

Payne, Robert, *The Life and Death of Mahatma Gandhi* (The Bodley Head, 1969)

Plaut, Martin, *Promise and Despair: The First Struggle for a Non-Racial South Africa* (Jacana, 2016)

Ramsden, John, *Man of the Century: Winston Churchill and His Legend Since 1945* (HarperCollins, 2003)

Rankin, Nicholas, *Churchill's Wizards: The British Genius for Deception 1914–1945* (Faber and Faber, 2009)

Rees, Laurence, *World War Two: Behind Closed Doors – Stalin, the Nazis and the West* (BBC Books, 2008)

Reid, Walter, *Churchill 1940–1945: Under Friendly Fire* (Birlinn, 2012)

Reynolds, David, *In Command of History: Churchill Fighting and Writing the Second World War* (Penguin, 2005)

Rhodes James, Robert, *A Spirit Undaunted: The Political Role of George VI* (Abacus, 1998)

Roberts, Andrew, *Masters and Commanders: How Four Titans Won the War in the West 1941–1945* (Harper Perennial, 2010)

Rose, Norman, *Churchill: An Unruly Life* (Tauris Parke, 2009)

Rose, Norman, *Churchill: The Unruly Giant* (Free Press, 1995)

Smith, Colin, *England's Last War Against France: Fighting Vichy 1940–1942* (Phoenix, 2010)

Smuts, JC, *Jan Christian Smuts* (Cassell, 1952)

Spies, SB and Gail Nattrass, *Jan Smuts: Memories of the Boer War* (Jonathan Ball, 1997)

Steyn, Richard, *Jan Smuts: Unafraid of Greatness* (Jonathan Ball, 2017)

Tedder, Arthur, *With Prejudice: The War Memoirs of the Marshal of the Royal Air Force, Lord Tedder* (Cassell, 1966)

Thompson, Leonard, *A History of South Africa* (Radix/Yale University Press, 1990)

Toye, Richard, *Churchill's Empire: The World That Made Him and the World He Made* (Macmillan, 2010)

Toye, Richard, *Lloyd George and Churchill: Rivals for Greatness* (Macmillan, 2007)

Van der Byl, Piet, *The Shadows Lengthen* (Howard Timmins, 1973)

Welsh, Frank, *A History of South Africa* (HarperCollins, 1998)

Williams, Francis, *A Prime Minister Remembers: The War and Post-War Memoirs of the Rt. Hon. Earl Attlee* (Heinemann, 1961)

Williams, Susan, *Colour Bar: The Triumph of Seretse Khama and his Nation* (Penguin, 2007)

ANTHOLOGIES

Brief Lives: Twentieth Century Pen Portraits from The Dictionary of National Biography, Colin Matthew (ed.) (Oxford University Press, 1997)

The Times, Great Lives: A Century in Obituaries (HarperCollins, 2005)

OTHER SOURCES

The National Archives, Kew

Churchill Archives Centre, Churchill College, Cambridge

The Independent

The International Churchill Society, UK

The Star

Acknowledgements

This book was originally Jonathan Ball's idea, rather than mine. As a life-long admirer of Churchill and Smuts, he believed from his extensive reading of British and South African history that there was enough material for an account of the two men's long and affectionate relationship. It was a book he wished to write himself, but in the end thought better of it and asked me to do the job. We collaborated throughout the writing, however, and I hope I have done him justice.

Few men in history have had their lives examined more minutely and critically than Winston Churchill. Besides his own extensive accounts of the various wars in which he fought himself or was otherwise involved, he has been the subject of more than 1 500 biographies, and the number continues to rise. Is there anything more to be said about him? you may well ask. I believe there is, and this book is the evidence. Many biographies of Churchill downplay or even ignore his friendship with Smuts, possibly because of the odium in which South Africa was held after the latter's death more than six decades ago.

In writing this book, I hasten to acknowledge my enormous debt to Sir Martin Gilbert, biographer supreme, whose research into every aspect of Churchill's life and many books made the task much easier. William Manchester's trilogy, Roy Jenkins's biography, Max Hastings's various books on World War II, and Carlo D'Este's study of Churchill the warrior, were among many other invaluable sources.

Smuts's life has been less extensively researched, but his two-volume official biography by Sir Keith Hancock, the seven-volume Smuts Papers assembled by Hancock and Dr Jean van der Poel, Jannie Smuts's admiring biography of his father, as well as many accounts of the Anglo-Boer War and two world wars are rich sources of information about a truly extraordinary Afrikaner South African.

I should also like to acknowledge the assistance, in Johannesburg, of Ilse Cloete at the South African National (now Ditsong) Museum of Military History and the library staff at the South African Institute of International Affairs, as well as the staff of the Churchill Archives Centre in Cambridge, the National Archives at Kew, and the British Library.

Richard Langworth, of the Churchill Project in the US, was most helpful as was Willem Gravett of the University of Pretoria, who let me have extracts from his doctoral thesis on Smuts. Messrs Paul Courtenay, a senior editor of *Finest Hour* and former chairman of the International Churchill Society (UK), and Fransjohan Pretorius, experts on Churchill and Smuts respectively, were good enough to carefully scrutinise my text.

I am grateful also to Victor, 3rd Lord Killearn, and his son, the Hon Miles Lampson, for the use of two photographs from their private collection, taken in Cairo in 1942.

Jonathan Ball, Derek du Plessis and Alfred le Maitre also read the manuscript and made many helpful suggestions, while Mark Ronan was a most meticulous editor. The staff of Jonathan Ball Publishers, led by Eugene Ashton and Jeremy Boraine, were always a pleasure to work with. On the production side, Ceri Prenter was the soul of efficiency, as were the book's designer, Kevin Shenton, and proof readers, Valda Strauss and Janita Holtzhausen, and Anne-Marie Mischke, my excellent translator into Afrikaans. I thank them all.

I've discovered to my cost that it's almost impossible to write an entirely error-free book, but such mistakes as there are, are my responsibility alone. I'd be pleased to have them pointed out, however, so they may be corrected.

Richard Steyn
Johannesburg
June 2017

Index